THE WORLD'S CLASSICS

575

AMERICAN
CRITICAL ESSAYS
*TWENTIETH
CENTURY*

Oxford University Press, Ely House, London W. 1

GLASGOW   NEW YORK   TORONTO   MELBOURNE   WELLINGTON
CAPE TOWN   SALISBURY   IBADAN   NAIROBI   DAR ES SALAAM   LUSAKA   ADDIS ABABA
BOMBAY   CALCUTTA   MADRAS   KARACHI   LAHORE   DACCA
KUALA LUMPUR   SINGAPORE   HONG KONG   TOKYO

AMERICAN CRITICAL ESSAYS

TWENTIETH CENTURY

SELECTED
WITH AN INTRODUCTION
BY
HAROLD BEAVER

LONDON
OXFORD UNIVERSITY PRESS

This volume of American Critical Essays
(Twentieth Century) *was first published in*
The World's Classics *in* 1959 *and reprinted in*
1961 *and* 1970

S B N 19 250575 0

Selection and Introduction

© *Oxford University Press* 1959

CONTENTS

39496

INTRODUCTION

My aim in gathering these essays together was to show some of the most distinguished critical writers in America of the last thirty years at their most typical and best. This was not easy. There was a host of talent to choose from and often it is as unfair to a critic to present him by a few pages of writing as it is to a poet or novelist. Some critics need space to deploy the amplitude and ingenuity of their arguments. This has necessarily meant the exclusion of a number of writers.

But first it was necessary to decide who *were* the American critics. There has long been a two-way traffic of talent across the Atlantic and now that several decades have passed since the appearance of such epoch-making books as I. A. Richards's *Principles of Literary Criticism*, T. S. Eliot's *The Sacred Wood*, or T. E. Hulme's *Speculations* there is often likely to be more of a common approach between British and American critics of varying school or sensibility than there is a fundamental difference. This is not to deny a difference of tradition or even of language (the opening, polemical, and highly debatable piece by H. L. Mencken should make that clear), but only to assert the strength of common influence. When critics of two nations discuss, dissect, and theorize on the same main body of literature, this alone, after all, must become a dominant, shaping influence on their thoughts.

I have been liberal, therefore, in the interpretation of 'American' in my title, not interpreting the word by place of birth or parentage only, but also by passport and length of residence. I am grateful to Mr. W. H. Auden for allowing me to reprint his introduction to Henry James's *The American Scene* for both he and his subject have been at home on both sides of the Atlantic and there was no one better to welcome the returning expatriate than an American citizen who was himself an Englishman. I am grateful, too, to Professor I. A. Richards, who though British still by nationality has for some twenty years taught and been resident at Harvard University, for his willingness to appear in this volume. He, if anyone, has been a father of modern criticism both in the United States and in Great Britain.

But I wished to give this volume a decidedly American slant. Readers, I felt, might have been disappointed had they found only English and European writers discussed, though such a book would have been as easy and as useful to collect. There are essays here on Shakespeare, on Herrick, and on Flaubert but they are in the minority. Mr. Edmund Wilson I wished to represent in his more cosmopolitan aspect for he has never been hemmed in, as critics so easily are, by his own national literature, but has remained, in Mr. Alfred Kazin's phrase, 'the experimentalist who worked with the whole tradition of literature in his bones'. The main body of the book, however, is devoted to individual American writers and their works. For the general reader a fragmented history of American literature will emerge to which he can add by further reading among the critics presented, often from the very books here quoted. So Mark Twain is discussed by way of his masterpiece, *Huckleberry Finn*, and there are essays on Hawthorne, Melville's *Moby-Dick*, Emily Dickinson, Henry James, Theodore Dreiser, Willa Cather, Sherwood Anderson, Ezra Pound, Robinson Jeffers, T. S. Eliot, Thomas Wolfe, William Faulkner, and Ernest Hemingway. It is in some such order that the reader may prefer to pick his way through this book rather than in that dictated by the seniority of the writers. If he does he may wish to finish with Mr. Richard Chase's 'The American Novel and its Tradition', Mr. Ezra Pound's own famous definitions from *The ABC of Reading*, and Mr. Philip Rahv's provocative division of American creative talent into Palefaces and Redskins, testing its validity by dividing the writers here discussed into either camp and seeing what company they would keep.

This is not a collection primarily intended for the university. Criticism, more and more, has become connected either with academic discipline or the weekly reviews so that in America, it is said, where the tradition of the essay as the English know it has never taken strong hold, the result has been a division of function between the ephemeral review and the exactitude of minute research expressed in a pseudo-scientific jargon which has become standard fare at the universities. Though some pieces reprinted here appeared originally in reviews or as television scripts and though many, if not most, of the critics here represented have at some time found their way into the universities, it is the purpose of this collection to belie such an impression. Mr. T. S. Eliot was surely right when in a lecture delivered at the University of Minnesota he said that 'the critic today may have a somewhat different audience from that of his predecessors', but was he right when he added 'I have the impression that serious criticism now is being written for a different, a more limited though not necessarily smaller public than was that of the nineteenth century'? Mr. Allen Tate in introducing him on that evening of 1956 said that he was introducing their speaker 'to what must surely be the largest audience ever assembled to hear a discourse on literary criticism'.

My purpose, then, is to show critical writing at its

most general, its most unlimited appeal—such writings in fact (to quote again from the same lecture) which 'promote the understanding and enjoyment of literature', which return the reader avid for fresh discoveries of enjoyment to the original authors themselves. I have eschewed such essays which regard a poem or a novel merely as a piece of clockwork to be ingeniously dismantled before the reader's inner eye; at the head of those two pieces which discuss a poem at length I have printed that poem in its entirety. Professor Levin's essay on Hemingway, which originally began as a book review and continued as 'explication de texte', I have allowed to stand for that whole school of university critics who do not lose view of the whole, but by their detailed examination of language and rhetoric achieve that view all the more clearly. Many of the best critics—Mr. Ezra Pound, Mr. W. H. Auden, Mr. Robert Penn Warren, Mr. Yvor Winters, Mr. Horace Gregory, and Mr. Allen Tate, among those represented here—are themselves better known, sometimes only known, for their poetry.

I have mentioned the importance of the universities for the livelihood of many serious critical writers today. It is a problem which, in its widest context, will be found discussed by Mr. Allen Tate in his essay entitled 'The Man of Letters in the Modern World'. In its narrowest context, I must here say a word about 'The New Criticism' which has taken such a hold among American universities as to amount today to an orthodoxy no more new than New College at Oxford. In the quarter of a century that has elapsed since the first volume of American Critical Essays appeared in this series, it is the advent of this movement above all which has most decisively changed the general picture.

The term was, in fact, first used by J. E. Spingarn,

Professor of Comparative Literature at Columbia, for the title of a book published in 1911. But it was revived by Mr. John Crowe Ransome for a book of the same title published in 1941, and since then the phrase has stuck. Speaking generally, it denotes such criticism which concentrates on semantics, metre, imagery, metaphor, and symbol, placing emphasis always on the isolated text (usually a poem) dissociated from biography or historical tradition and background, and applying extra-literary techniques whether from logic, sociology, or psychology to literature. Its immediate forbears, whose views on psychology or organic unity were to be a key influence included T. E. Hulme, Professor I. A. Richards, and Mr. T. S. Eliot. But the ultimate forefather was Coleridge of the *Biographic Literaria*. I need only quote from the first chapter of that work where he speaks of his debts to his headmaster at Christ's Hospital, to catch the modern tone: 'I learnt from him, that Poetry, even that of the loftiest and, seemingly, that of the wildest odes, had a logic of its own, as severe as that of science; and more difficult, because more subtle, more complex, and dependent on more, and more fugitive causes. In the truly great poets, he would say, there is a reason assignable, not only for every word, but for the position of every word. . . .' So complex indeed, so subtle, did the search become that one is sometimes reminded of the remark made by Albert Einstein on returning a Kafka novel to Thomas Mann: 'I couldn't read it; the human mind isn't that complex.'

It is this movement whose beginnings, in the magazine *The Fugitives* published at Vanderbilt University in Nashville for four brief years (1922-5), were already astir at the time the first volume in this series was published, which has increasingly come to occupy the centre of the stage. Since that time criticism has developed in many directions but most critics—certainly most critics represented in this volume—share its legacy and (to quote again from Mr. Eliot's Minnesota lecture, *The Frontiers of Criticism*) 'however widely they differ from each other, all differ in some significant way from the critics of a previous generation'.

In these last thirty years American critics have become increasingly concerned with defining what is distinctively American in American literature. After the First World War, when a new generation of authors began to appear—Ernest Hemingway, William Faulkner, and Robert Frost among many others—American critics, too, felt the challenge of claiming American literature no longer as a trans-Atlantic offshoot but as a literature in its own right, with its own voice, its own traditions, and its own roots in American experience. Melville, who had been virtually unnoticed, was rediscovered; elaborate collected editions of American authors, of which that of the poems of Emily Dickinson is one of the latest, began to appear; and the dominant themes of the American literary consciousness—Puritanism, romance, allegory, the frontier, the discovery of American vernacular—were further and further explored. Curiously an Englishman's book, *Studies in Classic American Literature*, by D. H. Lawrence, was a powerful influence, but most of the work was that of excited self-discovery by Americans themselves. Much of the story is told in this volume.

In concluding, I wish to offer my regret to all those necessarily, but never wilfully, excluded and would like to thank all the writers whose essays follow for their co-operation at every stage of preparing this book. I would also express the hope that this book will reveal to many the wealth of American literature as well as of recent American criticism, quoting from Alfred Kazin's postscript to his interpretation of modern American prose writing, *On Native Grounds*:

'I should even call ours an *age* of American literature, for the key elements in many American books seem to mirror the human situation in our epoch. Our perpetuation of the romantic tradition carries to both Americans and Europeans—in books like *Walden*, *Moby-Dick*, *Leaves of Grass*, *Huckleberry Finn*—a kind of racial memory of the wilderness we have all lost. The truly unexpected, the explosive, the dynamic quality of the undefined, man's awareness of himself moving through an utterly new situation—this is the great fact of life in our time and was prophesied by the Ishmaels, the Walt Whitmans and other world-wanderers of nineteenth century American epic literature.'

H. L. B.

February 1959

ACKNOWLEDGEMENTS

PERMISSION for the use of essays by the following writers was given by those named:

H. L. Mencken	(Alfred A. Knopf Inc. and Routledge & Kegan Paul)
Edmund Wilson, Malcolm Cowley, Allen Tate	(the individual authors)
Ezra Pound	(the author and New Directions)
Van Wyck Brooks	(the author, E. P. Dutton & Co. Inc., and J. M. Dent & Sons)
I. A. Richards	(the author and *Daedalus*, the Journal of the American Academy of Arts and Sciences)
Horace Gregory	(the author and *New World Writing*)
Austin Warren	(the author and The University of the South)
Yvor Winters	(the author and Alan Swallow)
Morton Dauwen Zabel	(the author, the Viking Press and Victor Gollancz)
R. P. Blackmur	(the author, Harcourt, Brace & Co. Inc., and George Allen & Unwin)
Robert Penn Warren	(the author, Random House Inc., and the William Morris Agency)
Lionel Trilling	(the author, Rinehart & Co., and Martin Secker & Warburg)
Cleanth Brooks	(the author, Harcourt, Brace & Co. Inc., and Dennis Dobson)

W. H. Auden   (the author and Charles Scribner's Sons)

Philip Rahv   (the author, New Directions and George Weidenfeld & Nicolson)

Harry Levin   (the author and the Harvard University Press)

Richard Chase   (the author, Doubleday & Co. Inc., and G. Bell & Sons)

Alfred Kazin   (the author and Houghton Mifflin Co.)

Irving Howe   (the author, William Sloane Associates Inc., and Methuen & Co.)

I wish also to thank Jonathan Cape and Harcourt, Brace & Co. Inc. for permission to use a paragraph from the postscript of *On Native Grounds* by Alfred Kazin.

H. L. MENCKEN

1880–1956

THE HALL-MARKS OF AMERICAN

The American Language 1919, revised 1936

THE characters chiefly noted in American English by all who have discussed it are, first, its general uniformity throughout the country; second, its impatient disregard for grammatical, syntactical, and phonological rule and precedent; and third, its large capacity (distinctly greater than that of the English of present-day England) for taking in new words and phrases from outside sources, and for manufacturing them of its own materials.

The first of these characters has struck every observer, native and foreign. In place of the discordant local dialects of all the other major countries, including England, we have a general *Volkssprache* for the whole nation, and if it is conditioned at all it is only by minor differences in pronunciation and vocabulary, and by the linguistic struggles of various groups of new-comers. No other country can show such linguistic solidarity, nor any approach to it—not even Canada, for there a large minority of the population resists speaking English altogether. The Little Russian of the Ukraine is unintelligible to the citizen of Moscow; the northern Italian can scarcely follow a conversation in Sicilian; the Low German from Hamburg is a foreigner in Munich; the Breton flounders in Gascony. Even in the United Kingdom there are wide divergences.[1] 'When we remember',

[1] W. W. Skeat distinguishes nine principal dialects in Scotland, three in Ireland, and thirty in England and Wales. See his *English Dialects From the Eighth Century to the Present Day*, Cambridge, 1911, pp. 107 ff.

says the *New International Encyclopedia*, 'that the dialects of the counties in England have marked differences— so marked, indeed, that it may be doubted whether a Lancashire miner and a Lincolnshire farmer could understand each other—we may well be proud that our vast country has, strictly speaking, only one language.' There are some regional peculiarities in pronunciation and intonation, but when it comes to the words they habitually use and the way they use them all Americans, even the less tutored, follow pretty much the same line. A Boston taxi-driver could go to work in Chicago or San Francisco without running any risk of misunderstanding his new fares. Once he had flattened his *a*'s a bit and picked up a few dozen localisms, he would be, to all linguistic intents and purposes, fully naturalized.

Of the intrinsic differences that separate American from English the chief have their roots in the obvious disparity between the environment and traditions of the American people since the seventeenth century and those of the English. The latter have lived under a relatively stable social order, and it has impressed upon their souls their characteristic respect for what is customary and of good report. Until the World War brought chaos to most of their institutions, their whole lives were regulated, perhaps more than those of any other people save the Spaniards, by a regard for precedent. The Americans, though partly of the same blood, have felt no such restraint, and acquired no such habit of conformity. On the contrary, they have plunged to the other extreme, for the conditions of life in their country have put a high value upon the precisely opposite qualities of curiosity and daring, and so they have acquired that character of restlessness, that impatience of forms, that disdain of the dead hand, which now broadly marks them. From the first, says a literary historian, they have been 'less phlegmatic, less conservative than the English. There were climatic influences, it may be; there was surely a spirit of intensity everywhere that made for short effort.'[1] Thus, in the arts, and thus in business, in politics, in daily intercourse, in habits of mind and speech. The American is not, of course, lacking in a capacity for discipline; he has it highly developed; he submits to leadership readily, and even to tyranny. But, by a curious twist, it is not the leadership that is old and decorous that commonly fetches him, but the leadership that is new and extravagant. He will resist dictation out of the past, but he will follow a new messiah with almost Russian willingness, and into the wildest vagaries of economics, religion, morals, and speech. A new fallacy in politics spreads faster in the United States than anywhere else on earth, and so does a new fashion in hats, or a new revelation of God, or a new means of killing time, or a new shibboleth, or metaphor, or piece of slang. Thus the American, on his linguistic side, likes to make his language as he goes along, and not all the hard work of the schoolmarm can hold the business back. A novelty loses nothing by the fact that it is a novelty; it rather gains something, and particularly if it meets the national fancy for the terse, the vivid, and, above all, the bold and imaginative. The characteristic American habit of reducing complex concepts to the starkest abbreviations was already noticeable in colonial times, and such highly typical Americanisms as O.K., N.G.,[2] and P.D.Q.,[3] have been traced back to the early

---

[1] F. L. Pattee, *A History of American Literature Since 1870*, New York, 1916. See also *The American Novel*, by Carl Van Doren, New York, 1921.

[2] 'No go' or 'no good', Ed.

[3] 'Pretty Damned Quick', Ed.

days of the Republic. Nor are the influences that shaped these tendencies invisible today, for institution-making is yet going on, and so is language-making. In so modest an operation as that which has evolved *bunco* from *buncombe* and *bunk* from *bunco* there is evidence of a phenomenon which the philologian recognizes as belonging to the most lusty stages of speech.

But of more importance than the sheer inventions, if only because much more numerous, are the extensions of the vocabulary, both absolutely and in ready workableness, by the devices of rhetoric. The American, from the beginning, has been the most ardent of recorded rhetoricians. His politics bristles with pungent epithets; his whole history has been bedizened with tall talk; his fundamental institutions rest far more upon brilliant phrases than upon logical ideas. And in small things as in large he exercises continually an incomparable capacity for projecting hidden and often fantastic relationships into arresting parts of speech. Such a term as *rubberneck* is almost a complete treatise on American psychology; it reveals the national habit of mind more clearly than any laboured inquiry could ever reveal it. It has in it precisely the boldness and contempt for ordered forms that are so characteristically American, and it has too the grotesque humour of the country, and the delight in devastating opprobriums, and the acute feeling for the succinct and savoury. The same qualities are in *rough-house*, *water-wagon*, *has-been*, *lame-duck*, *speed-cop*, and a thousand other such racy substantives, and in all the great stock of native verbs and adjectives. There is, indeed, but a shadowy boundary in these new coinages between the various parts of speech. *Corral*, borrowed from the Spanish, immediately becomes a verb and the father of an adjective. *Bust*, carved out of *burst*, erects itself into a noun. *Bum*, coming by way of an earlier *bummer* from the German, becomes noun, adjective, verb, and adverb. Verbs are fashioned out of substantives by the simple process of prefixing the preposition: *to engineer, to stump, to hog, to style, to author.* Others grow out of an intermediate adjective, as *to boom.* Others are made by torturing nouns with harsh affixes, as *to burglarize* and *to itemize,* or by groping for the root, as *to resurrect* and *to jell.* Yet others are changed from intransitive to transitive; a sleeping-car *sleeps* thirty passengers. So with the adjectives. They are made of substantives unchanged: *codfish, jitney.* Or by bold combinations: *down-and-out, up-state, flat-footed.* Or by shading down suffixes to a barbaric simplicity: *scary, classy, tasty.* Or by working over adverbs until they tremble on the brink between adverb and adjective: *right, sure,* and *near* are examples.

All these processes, of course, are also to be observed in the history of the English of England; at the time of its sturdiest growth they were in the most active possible being. They are, indeed, common to all tongues; 'the essence of language', says Dr. Jespersen, 'is activity.' But if you will put the English of today beside the American of today you will see at once how much more forcibly they are in operation in the latter than in the former. The standard southern dialect of English has been arrested in its growth by its purists and grammarians, and burdened with irrational affectations by fashionable pretension. It shows no living change since the reign of Samuel Johnson. Its tendency is to combat all that expansive gusto which made for its pliancy and resilience in the days of Shakespeare.[1] In place of the

---

[1] Rather curiously, the two authorities who were most influential, during the nineteenth century, in keeping it to a rigid pattern were both Americans. They were Lindley Murray (1745–1826) and Joseph E. Worcester (1784–1865). Murray, a Pennsylvanian, went to England after the Revolution, and in

old loose-footedness there is set up a preciosity which, in one direction, takes the form of clumsy artificialities in the spoken language, and in another shows itself in the even clumsier Johnsonese of so much current English writing—the Jargon denounced by Sir Arthur Quiller-Couch in his Cambridge lectures. This 'infirmity of speech' Quiller-Couch finds 'in parliamentary debates and in the newspapers; . . . it has become the medium through which Boards of Government, County Councils, Syndicates, Committees, Commercial Firms, express the processes as well as the conclusions of their thought, and so voice the reason of their being'. Distinct from journalese, the two yet overlap, 'and have a knack of assimilating each other's vices'.[1]

American, despite the gallant efforts of the pedagogues, has so far escaped any such suffocating formalization. We, too, of course, have our occasional practi-

1795 published his *Grammar of the English Language*. It had an extraordinary sale in England, and was accepted as the court of last resort in usage down to quite recent times. Worcester's *Universal and Critical Dictionary of the English Language*, 1846, divided the honours of authority in England with B. H. Smart's *Dictionary*, published during the same year. It was extensively pirated. Thus, says Thomas R. Lounsbury (*The Standard of Pronunciation in English*, New York, 1904, p. 220), 'the Londoner frequently got his pure London pronunciation from a citizen of this country who was never outside of New England for more than a few months of his life'. Worcester was also accepted at Harvard and at the University of Virginia, but elsewhere in the United States Webster prevailed.

[1] See, the chapter, 'Interlude on Jargon', in Quiller-Couch's *On the Art of Writing*; New York, 1916. Appropriately enough, large parts of the learned critic's book are written in the very Jargon he attacks. See also Chap. vi of *Growth and Structure of the English Language*, by O. Jespersen, 3rd ed., rev., Leipzig, 1919, especially pp. 143 ff. See also 'Official English', in *English*, Mar. 1919, p. 7; Apr., p. 45, and Aug., p. 135, and 'The Decay of Syntax', in the London *Times Literary Supplement*, 8 May 1919, p. 1.

tioners of the authentic English jargon, but in the main our faults lie in precisely the opposite direction. That is to say, we incline toward a directness of statement which, at its greatest, lacks restraint and urbanity altogether, and toward a hospitality which often admits novelties for the mere sake of their novelty, and is quite uncritical of the difference between a genuine improvement in succinctness and clarity, and mere extravagant raciness. 'The tendency', says one English observer, 'is . . . to consider the speech of any man, as any man himself, as good as any other.'[1] The Americans, adds a Scots professor, 'are determined to hack their way through the language, as their ancestors through forests, regardless of the valuable growths that may be sacrificed in blazing the trail'.[2] But this Scot dismisses the English neologisms of the day, when ranged beside the American stock, as 'dwiny, feeble stuff'; 'it is to America', he admits, 'that we must chiefly look in future for the replenishment and freshening of our language.' I quote one more Briton, this time an Englishman steeped in the public school tradition:

The English of the United States is not merely different from ours; it has a restless inventiveness which may well be founded in a sense of racial discomfort, a lack of full accord between the temperament of the people and the constitution of their speech. The English are uncommunicative; the Americans are not. In its coolness and quiet withdrawal, in its prevailing sobriety, our language reflects the cautious economies and leisurely assurance of the average speaker. We say so little that we do not need to enliven our vocabulary and underline our sentences, or cry 'Wolf!' when we wish to be heard. The more stimula-

[1] Alexander Francis, *Americans: An Impression*, New York, 1900.
[2] *Breaking Priscian's Head*, by J. Y. T. Greig, London, 1929.

ting climate of the United States has produced a more eager, a more expansive, a more decisive people. The Americans apprehend their world in sharper outlines and aspire after a more salient rendering of it.[1]

This revolt against conventional bonds and restraints is most noticeable, of course, on the lower levels of American speech; in the regions above there still linger some vestiges of eighteenth-century tightness. But even in those upper regions there are rebels a-plenty, and some of them are of such authority that it is impossible to dismiss them. I glance through the speeches of the late Dr. Woodrow Wilson, surely a conscientious purist and Anglomaniac if we have ever had one, and find, in a few moments, half a dozen locutions that an Englishman in like position would certainly hesitate to use, among them *we must get a move on*,[2] *to hog*,[3] *to gum-shoe*,[4] *onery* in place of *ordinary*,[5] and *that is going some*.[6] I turn to the letters of that most passionate of Anglomaniacs, Walter Hines Page, and find *to eat out of my hand*, *to lick to a frazzle*, *to cut no figure*, *to go gunning for*, *nothin' doin'*, *for keeps*, and so on. I proceed to Dr. John Dewey, probably the country's most respectable metaphysician, and find him using *dope* for *opium*.[7] In recent years certain English magnificoes have shown signs of going the same route, but whenever they yield the corrective bastinado is laid on, and nine times out of ten they are

---

[1] *Pomona, or The Future of English*, by Basil de Sélincourt, London, 1929.

[2] Speech before the Chamber of Commerce Convention, Washington, 19 Feb. 1916.

[3] Speech at a working-man's dinner, New York, 4 Sept., 1912.

[4] *Wit and Wisdom of Woodrow Wilson*, comp. by Richard Linthicum, New York, 1916, p. 54.

[5] Speech at Ridgewood, N.J., 22 Apr. 1910.

[6] *Wit and Wisdom . . .* , p. 56.

[7] *New Republic*, 24 Dec. 1919, p. 116, col. 1.

accused, and rightly, of succumbing to American influence.

Let American confront a novel problem alongside English, and immediately its superior imaginativeness and resourcefulness become obvious. *Movie* is better than *cinema*; and the English begin to admit the fact by adopting the word; it is not only better American, it is better English. *Bill-board* is better than *hoarding*. *Office-holder* is more honest, more picturesque, more thoroughly Anglo-Saxon than *public servant*. *Stem-winder* somehow has more life in it, more fancy and vividness, than the literal *keyless watch*. Turn to the terminology of *railroading* (itself, by the way, an Americanism): its creation fell upon the two peoples equally, but they tackled the job independently. The English, seeking a figure to denominate the wedge-shaped fender in front of a locomotive, called it a *plough*; the Americans, characteristically, gave it the far more pungent name of *cow-catcher*. So with the casting which guides the wheels from one rail to another. The English called it a *crossing-plate*; the Americans, more responsive to the suggestion in its shape, called it a *frog*. American is full of what Bret Harte called the 'saber-cuts of Saxon'; it meets Montaigne's ideal of 'a succulent and nervous speech, short and compact, not as much delicated and combed out as vehement and brusque, rather arbitrary than monotonous, not pedantic but soldierly, as Suetonius called Cæsar's Latin'. One pictures the common materials of English dumped into a pot, exotic flavourings added, and the bubblings assiduously and expectantly skimmed. What is old and respected is already in decay the moment it comes into contact with what is new and vivid. 'When we Americans are through with the English language', says Mr. Dooley, 'it will look as if it had been run over by a musical comedy.'

All this boldness of conceit, of course, makes for vulgarity. Unrestrained by any critical sense—and the critical sense of the pedagogues counts for little, for they cry wolf too often—it flowers in such barbaric inventions as *tasty*, *alright*, *go-getter*, *he-man*, *goaheadativeness*, *tony*, *goof*, *semi-occasional*, and *to doxologize*. But vulgarity, after all, means no more than a yielding to natural impulses in the face of conventional inhibitions, and that yielding to natural impulses is at the heart of all healthy language-making. The history of English, like the history of American and of every other living tongue, is a history of vulgarisms that, by their accurate meeting of real needs, have forced their way into sound usage, and even into the lifeless catalogues of the grammarians. The purist performs a useful office in enforcing a certain logical regularity upon the process, and in our own case the omnipresent example of the greater conservatism of the English restrains, to some extent, our native tendency to go too fast, but the process itself is as inexorable in its workings as the precession of the equinoxes, and if we yield to it more eagerly than the English, it is only a proof, perhaps, that the future of what was once the Anglo-Saxon tongue lies on this side of the water. Standard English now has the brakes on, but American continues to leap in the dark, and the prodigality of its movement is all the indication that is needed of its intrinsic health, its capacity to meet the ever-changing needs of a restless and emotional people, inordinately mongrel, and disdainful of tradition. Language, says A. H. Sayce,

is not artificial product, contained in books and dictionaries and governed by the strict rules of impersonal grammarians. It is the living expression of the mind and spirit of a people, ever changing and shifting, whose sole standard of correctness is custom and the common usage of the community. . . . The first lesson to be learned is that there is no intrinsic right or wrong in the use of language, no fixed rules such as are the delight of the teacher of Latin prose. What is right now will be wrong hereafter; what language rejected yesterday she accepts today.[1]

EZRA POUND

1885–

WHAT IS LITERATURE,
WHAT IS LANGUAGE, ETC.??

The ABC of Reading, 1934

LITERATURE is language charged with meaning.

'Great literature is simply language charged with meaning to the utmost possible degree' (E. P. in *How to Read*).

But language?

Spoken or written?

---

[1] *Introduction to the Science of Language*, 4th ed., London, 1900, vol. ii, pp. 33–34. All this, of course, had been said long before Sayce. 'Language', said Quintilian in his *Institutiones Oratoriae*, i (c. 95), 'is like money, which becomes current when it receives the public stamp.' 'Custom', said Ben Jonson in his *Grammar* (1640), 'is the most certain mistress of language.' 'Language', said George Campbell in *The Philosophy of Rhetoric*, ii (1776), 'is purely a species of fashion, in which by the general, but tacit, consent of the people of a particular state or country, certain sounds come to be appropriated to certain things as their signs.' 'Established custom', said Hugh Blair in his *Lectures on Rhetoric and Belles Lettres* (1783), 'is the standard to which we must at last resort for determining every controverted point in language.' To which Noah Webster added in his *Dissertations on the English Language* (1789): 'The general practice of a nation is the rule of propriety.'

Spoken language is noise divided up into a system of grunts, hisses, &c., they call it 'articulate' speech.

'Articulate' means that it is zoned, and that a number of people are agreed on the categories.

That is to say, we have a more or less approximate agreement about the different noises represented by

a, b, c, d, &c.

Written language can consist (as in Europe, &c.) of signs representing these various noises.

There is a more or less approximate agreement that groups of these noises or signs shall more or less correspond with some object, action or condition.

cat, motion, pink.

The other kind of language starts by being a picture of the cat, or of something moving, or being, or of a group of things which occur under certain circumstances, or which participate a common quality.

APPROACH

It doesn't, in our contemporary world, so much matter where you begin the examination of a subject, so long as you keep on until you get round again to your starting-point. As it were, you start on a sphere, or a cube; you must keep on until you have seen it from all sides. Or if you think of your subject as a stool or table, you must keep on until it has three legs and will stand up, or four legs and won't tip over too easily.

WHAT is the USE OF LANGUAGE? WHY STUDY LITERATURE?

Language was obviously created, and is, obviously, USED for communication.

'Literature is news that STAYS news.'

These things are matters of degree. Your communication can be more or less exact. The INTEREST in a statement can be more or less durable.

I cannot, for example, wear out my interest in the 'Ta Hio' of Confucius, or in the Homeric poems.

It is very difficult to read the same detective story twice. Or let us say, only a very good 'tec' will stand re-reading, after a very long interval, and because one has paid so little attention to it, that one has almost completely forgotten it.

The above are natural phenomena, they serve as measuring-rods, or instruments. For no two people are these 'measures' identical.

The critic who doesn't make a personal statement, *in re* measurements he himself has made, is merely an unreliable critic. He is not a measurer but a repeater of other men's results.

KRINO, TO PICK OUT FOR ONESELF, TO CHOOSE.

That's what the word means.

No one would be foolish enough to ask me to pick out a horse or even an automobile for him.

Pisanello painted horses so that one remembers the painting, and the Duke of Milan sent him to Bologna to BUY horses.

Why a similar kind of 'horse sense' can't be applied in the study of literature is, and has always been, beyond my comprehension.

Pisanello had to LOOK at the horses.

You would think that anyone wanting to know about poetry would do one of two things or both. I.E., LOOK AT it or listen to it. He might even think about it?

And if he wanted advice he would go to someone who KNEW something about it.

If you wanted to know something about an automobile, would you go to a man who had made one and driven it, or to a man who had merely heard about it? And of two men who had made automobiles, would you go to one who had made a good one, or one who had made a botch?

Would you look at the actual car or only at the specifications?

In the case of poetry, there is, or seems to be, a good deal to be looked at. And there seem to be very few authentic specifications available.

Dante says: 'A canzone is a composition of words set to music.'

I don't know any better point to start from.

Coleridge or De Quincey said that the quality of a 'great poet is everywhere present, and nowhere visible as a distinct excitement', or something of that sort.

This would be a more dangerous *starting*-point. It is probably true.

Dante's statement is the better place to begin because it starts the reader or hearer from what he actually sees or hears, instead of distracting his mind from that actuality to something which can only be approximately deduced or conjectured FROM the actuality, and for which the *evidence* can be nothing save the particular and limited extent of the actuality.

I

Literature does not exist in a vacuum. Writers as such have a definite social function exactly proportioned to their ability AS WRITERS. This is their main use. All other uses are relative, and temporary, and can be estimated only in relation to the views of a particular estimator.

Partisans of particular ideas may value writers who agree with them more than writers who do not, they may, and often do, value bad writers of their own party or religion more than good writers of another party or church.

But there is one basis susceptible of estimation and independent of all questions of viewpoint.

Good writers are those who keep the language efficient. That is to say, keep it accurate, keep it clear. It doesn't matter whether the good writer wants to be useful, or whether the bad writer wants to do harm.

Language is the main means of human communication. If an animal's nervous system does not transmit sensations and stimulae, the animal atrophies.

If a nation's literature declines, the nation atrophies and decays.

Your legislator can't legislate for the public good, your commander can't command, your populace (if you be a democratic country) can't instruct its 'representatives', save by language.

The fogged language of swindling classes serves only a temporary purpose.

A limited amount of communication *in re* special subjects, passes via mathematical formulas, via the plastic arts, via diagrams, via purely musical forms, but no one proposes substituting these for the common speech, nor does anyone suggest that it would be either possible or advisable.

UBICUNQUE LINGUA ROMANA, IBI ROMA

Greece and Rome civilized BY LANGUAGE. Your language is in the care of your writers.

['Insults o'er dull and speechless tribes']

but this language is not merely for records of great

things done. Horace and Shakespeare can proclaim its monumental and mnemonic value, but that doesn't exhaust the matter.

Rome rose with the idiom of Caesar, Ovid, and Tacitus, she declined in a welter of rhetoric, the diplomat's 'language to conceal thought', and so forth.

The man of understanding can no more sit quiet and resigned while his country lets its literature decay, and lets good writing meet with contempt, than a good doctor could sit quiet and contented while some ignorant child was infecting itself with tuberculosis under the impression that it was merely eating jam tarts.

It is very difficult to make people understand the *impersonal* indignation that a decay of writing can cause men who understand what it implies, and the end whereto it leads. It is almost impossible to express any degree of such indignation without being called 'embittered', or something of that sort.

Nevertheless the 'statesman cannot govern, the scientist cannot participate his discoveries, men cannot agree on wise action without language', and all their deeds and conditions are affected by the defects or virtues of idiom.

A people that grows accustomed to sloppy writing is a people in process of losing grip on its empire and on itself. And this looseness and blowsiness is not anything as simple and scandalous as abrupt and disordered syntax.

It concerns the relation of expression to meaning. Abrupt and disordered syntax can be at times very honest, and an elaborately constructed sentence can be at times merely an elaborate camouflage.

II

The sum of human wisdom is not contained in any one language, and no single language is CAPABLE of expressing all forms and degrees of human comprehension.

This is a very unpalatable and bitter doctrine. But I cannot omit it.

People occasionally develop almost a fanaticism in combating the ideas 'fixed' in a single language. These are generally speaking 'the prejudices of the nation' (any nation).

Different climates and different bloods have different needs, different spontaneities, different reluctances, different ratios between different groups of impulse and unwillingness, different constructions of throat, and all these leave trace in the language, and leave it more ready and more unready for certain communications and registrations.

THE READER'S AMBITION may be mediocre, and the ambitions of no two readers will be identical. The teacher can only aim his instruction at those who most *want* to learn, but he can at any rate start them with an 'appetizer', he can at least hand them a printed list of the things to be learned in literature, or in a given section thereof.

The first bog of inertia may be simple ignorance of the extent of the subject, or a simple unwillingness to move away from one area of semi-ignorance. The greatest barrier is probably set up by teachers who know a little more than the public, who want to exploit their fractional knowledge, and who are thoroughly opposed to making the least effort to learn anything more.

III

'Great literature is simply language charged with meaning to the utmost possible degree.'

Dichten = condensare.

I begin with poetry because it is the most concentrated form of verbal expression. Basil Bunting.

fumbling about with a German–Italian dictionary, found that this idea of poetry as concentration is as old almost as the German language. *Dichten* is the German verb corresponding to the noun *Dichtung* meaning poetry, and the lexicographer has rendered it by the Italian verb meaning 'to condense'.

The charging of language is done in three principal ways: You receive the language as your race has left it, the words have meanings which have 'grown into the race's skin'; the Germans say 'wie in den Schnabel gewachsen', as it grows in his beak. And the good writer chooses his words for their 'meaning', but that meaning is not a set cut-off thing like the move of knight or pawn on a chess-board. It comes up with roots, with associations, with how and where the word is familiarly used, or where it has been used brilliantly or memorably.

You can hardly say 'incarnadine' without one or more of your auditors thinking of a particular line of verse.

Numerals and words referring to human inventions have hard, cut-off meanings. That is, meanings which are more obtrusive than a word's 'associations'.

Bicycle now has a cut-off meaning.

But tandem, or 'bicycle built for two', will probably throw the image on a past decade upon the reader's mental screen.

There is no end to the number of qualities which some people can associate with a given word or kind of word, and most of these vary with the individual.

You have to go almost exclusively to Dante's criticism to find a set of OBJECTIVE categories for words. Dante called words 'buttered' and 'shaggy' because of the different NOISES they make. Or *pexa et hirsuta*, combed and hairy.

He also divided them by their different associations. NEVERTHELESS you still charge words with meaning mainly in three ways, called phanopoeia, melopoeia, logopoeia. You use a word to throw a visual image on to the reader's imagination, or you charge it by sound, or you use groups of words to do this.

Thirdly, you take the greater risk of using the word in some special relation to 'usage', that is, to the kind of context in which the reader expects, or is accustomed, to find it.

This is the last means to develop; it can only be used by the sophisticated.

(If you want really to understand what I am talking about, you will have to read, ultimately, Propertius and Jules Laforgue.)

IF YOU WERE STUDYING CHEMISTRY you would be told that there are a certain number of elements, a certain number of more usual chemicals, chemicals most in use, or easiest to find. And for the sake of clarity in your experiments, you would probably be given these substances 'pure' or as pure as you could conveniently get them.

IF YOU WERE A CONTEMPORARY book-keeper you would probably use the loose-leaf system, by which business houses separate archives from facts that are in use, or that are likely to be frequently needed for reference.

Similar conveniences are possible in the study of literature.

Any amateur of painting knows that modern galleries lay great stress on 'good hanging', that is, of putting important pictures where they can be well seen, and where the eye will not be confused, or the feet wearied by searching for the masterpiece on a vast expanse of wall cumbered with rubbish.

At this point I can't very well avoid printing a set of categories that considerably antedate my own 'How to Read'.

IV

When you start searching for 'pure elements' in literature you will find that literature has been created by the following classes of persons:

1. Inventors. Men who found a new process, or whose extant work gives us the first known example of a process.

2. The masters. Men who combined a number of such processes, and who used them as well as or better than the inventors.

3. The diluters. Men who came after the first two kinds of writer, and couldn't do the job quite as well.

4. Good writers without salient qualities. Men who are fortunate enough to be born when the literature of a given country is in good working order, or when some particular branch of writing is 'healthy'. For example, men who wrote sonnets in Dante's time, men who wrote short lyrics in Shakespeare's time or for several decades thereafter, or who wrote French novels and stories after Flaubert had shown them how.

5. Writers of *belles lettres*. That is, men who didn't really invent anything, but who specialized in some particular part of writing, who couldn't be considered as 'great men' or as authors who were trying to give a complete presentation of life, or of their epoch.

6. The starters of crazes.

Until the reader knows the first two categories he will never be able 'to see the wood for the trees'. He may know what he 'likes'. He may be a 'compleat book-lover', with a large library of beautifully printed books, bound in the most luxurious bindings, but he will never be able to sort out what he knows or to estimate the value of one book in relation to others, and he will be more confused and even less able to make up his mind about a book where a new author is 'breaking with convention' than to form an opinion about a book eighty or a hundred years old.

He will never understand why a specialist is annoyed with him for trotting out a second- or third-hand opinion about the merits of his favourite bad writer.

Until you have made your own survey and your own closer inspection you might at least beware and avoid accepting opinions:

1. From men who haven't themselves produced notable work (*vide* p. 14).

2. From men who have not themselves taken the risk of printing the results of their own personal inspection and survey, even if they are seriously making one.

VAN WYCK BROOKS

1886–1963

THEODORE DREISER

The Confident Years 1885–1915, 1955

THE wandering journalist Theodore Dreiser had drifted from city to city—Chicago, St. Louis, Toledo, Cleveland, Pittsburgh—before he settled in New York in 1895 as a free-lance writer and editor of magazines. He turned out 'life stories of successful men' about Philip Armour, Marshall Field, and other financial magnates and popular artists, haunting the lobbies of the great hotels that appeared in so many of his novels later, allured by the luxurious crowds of well-dressed people. He saw himself in Lucien de Rubempré, Balzac's young provincial, the journalist who longed to be a novelist when he went to Paris, where he was dazzled by the beautiful women and struck by the contrasts of poverty and wealth that appealed with even greater force to Dreiser. For at the moment when Dreiser delighted in the power of the strong he was more intensely drawn to the unfortunate and beaten. It pleased him to see the 'grasping' Woolworth build his glittering tower while at the same time his sympathy went out to the poor; and it was the strength of his compassion, with the depth of his feeling for life itself, that made this blundering writer unique in his time.

Dreiser had published in 1900 a novel, *Sister Carrie*, which Frank Norris, the publisher's reader, acclaimed as a 'wonder' although it was virtually stillborn and withdrawn from circulation on the ground that it was too sordid or pornographic. This event was all but disastrous for Dreiser; it drove him into neurasthenia; for nearly three years he was confused and lost, drifting for a while to Philadelphia, the setting of his later *The Financier*, sweeping out carpenter-shops, working on a railroad. Re-established in the end, he became a conspicuous editor before *Sister Carrie*, reissued in 1907, was taken up by college students who saw in Dreiser an American author of the calibre of the great new Europeans. But his second novel was not published until 1911. Dreiser was crushed for a while, in fact; and yet how could he have been surprised by the failure of *Sister Carrie* to achieve recognition? He knew the *Century*, *Scribner's*, *Harper's*, which had astounded him at first by their atmosphere of unruffled peace and charm in which there was never a hint of the cruel, the vulgar, or the base that every journalist saw as the substance of life. In the city news-room where Dreiser was at home the mask was always off and life was handled without gloves in a rough-and-ready fashion, whereas this magazine world of the Pages and Cables was all compact of illusions, as it seemed to him. At any rate, lawyers and doctors were always virtuous in this world and marriage was never marred by erratic behaviour. Dreiser, who had no such tales to tell, concluded that one could not transplant in a novel the facts that filled the news columns of the daily press; and indeed the romantic prudery of the time was more marked in America than in France or England, though not as much as Americans sometimes thought. For Zola's English publisher had been imprisoned for two years, as Flaubert was prosecuted, like Baudelaire, for pornographic writing. There was no consistency in American prudery and it was not to be forgotten that Havelock Ellis's *Studies in the Psychology of Sex* was published in America when it was prohibited in England. The fate of *Sister Carrie* was symptomatic, none the less, and the eventual triumph of this vigorous novel broke the taboo for others of its kind.

If what one desired was the 'real life' that every novelist professed to give, one found it in *Sister Carrie*, and even with a vengeance, as one found it later in *Jennie Gerhardt*, a story that was better still and equally abounding in the reality of flesh, blood, and heart. For one felt in both the 'uncritical upwelling of grief for the weak and the helpless' that Dreiser imputed to the heroine of his first novel, the pity with which he himself had regarded his German-American parents and the sisters who appeared in disguise in both these books. He was to describe them again in *Dawn* and *A Book about Myself*, obsessed as he was with the tragedy that surrounded his childhood, while he dwelt on other humble souls like old Rogaum and his Theresa and the daughter whom he felt obliged to lock out at night. His own father, the morose bereft old man, his mother, with her wondering dreamy mind, who kept a poor workingmen's boarding-house and washed for a living, his brother, the 'train butcher' who was sent to jail— 'popcorn, candy, all the latest magazines'—constantly figured in his novels and recollections. His sisters had run away to the city where one was deserted with a stillborn child and the other eloped with an embezzler who was already married. Dreiser's throat tightened and his heart ached over their miseries, he confessed, for they were affectionate, wistful, gentle creatures, only soft, yielding, sensuous, nebulous, fatally attractive to men and beset, as he was, with thoughts of romance and pleasure. Dreiser had seen too much of the sadder sides of life to accept conventional American standards in fiction, and, besides, one felt in his reports the authoritative note of Whitman's phrase, 'I was the man, I suffered, I was there'. He shared the dreams and hopes of his wayward sisters. Had he not himself at sixteen felt all the excitement of Carrie Meeber as she left Columbia City for Chicago, with her small trunk and satchel of imitation alligator-skin and her sister's address written on a scrap of paper? For Dreiser too that early journey had been 'intense and wonderful' as it was for the bright little timid, pretty Carrie, warm with the illusions of ignorance and youth and the marvel of the lights, the mystery and the gleam and glow of the approaching city. The glamour of the great world had filled his own imagination when, as a boy, he had asked himself, sitting on the porch, or lying on the grass, or under a tree, where and when and how he was to go and find it, even as the beauty of the girls addled his wits like moon-madness or the odour and witchery of the flowers, as he said, in springtime.

It was the note of actuality that won the day for *Sister Carrie*, for all the banalities and stylistic defects of the novel—the sense it conveyed of the breathing presence of this 'lone figure in a tossing sea' who 'had no excellent home principles fixed upon her'. One shared the desire that filled her heart amid all the bustle and shine of the shops, her longing for so many objects that were new and pretty, hungry as she was for life and love, yet too overwhelmed with wonder to be greedy. She was as passive as a child in the hands of the men who were kind to her. Jennie Gerhardt was still more appealing, though scarcely more living than Carrie, because of the tragic depth of her affection and devotion to the poor German parents who were so like Dreiser's, to the child whom her first lover left, to the man who abandoned her and claimed her again at the end. Whether for pathos or tragedy there were surely few American novels that matched these two of Dreiser's, which had much in common, not least in their feeling for what the author called the 'dark flower of passion that glorifies and terrifies the world'. What pictures these books gave moreover of the chaos of much of American life, the ambitions and interests of the men who swarmed in the hotels, the commercial travellers whom one saw 'flashing a roll of greenbacks', the proprietors of 'polished resorts' and 'swell saloons'. On his first visit to New York, observing the tramps on park benches, Dreiser, in the grey chill December weather, had imagined the story of Hurstwood sinking to the slums as he read about Carrie's rise in the headlines in the papers. Both these novels brimmed over with a sense of the wonder, the colour and the beauty of life, and its cruelty, rank favouritism, uncertainty, indifference, and sorrow.

All this triumphed in Dreiser's work over the journalistic style, flat-footed, unleavened at best, inept, elephantine, the occasional bad grammar, the grotesque misuse of words, the touches that recalled *No Mother to Guide Her*. James Huneker said he had sweated blood correcting

the manuscript of *Jennie Gerhardt*, for the author had
no 'ear for prose' or 'eye for form,' and, absorbed as
Dreiser had been by Balzac, whom he 'ate, slept,
dreamed and lived' for months, he had also read the
novels of Laura Jean Libbey. As a boy, in a 'family story
paper', he had read about beautiful working-girls who
were seized by evil men and carried off, and a trace of
the influence of these tales appeared in *Sister Carrie*, as a
vestige of Horatio Alger was to linger in *The Titan*. His
banalities were painful now and then, but they possessed
at other times the charm that invested some of the
banalities of Whitman, who shared his affection for what
Howells called the 'fond foolish face' of life, the common
scene, the naiveties of artless people. Flat or absurd as
these may have been, his affection made them lovable.
He was able to communicate some of the pleasure with
which he heard two girls remark that they were 'down
town for a soda', and he liked to hear men greet one
another as 'Cap' or 'Doc' on a country road or perhaps
at a 'Chicago lunch' or 'dairy kitchen'. It was this delight in the banal that made *A Hoosier*[1] *Holiday*, the story
of his return to Indiana, so human and so winning, for
life, as he saw it anywhere, in the simplest lines of the
commonest streets, possessed for Dreiser an infectious
and a tireless attraction. He could never understand the
complaint of Americans that their country was not
worth travelling in, because of its lack of patina and
historical depth, when it had such new and varied roads,
such bridges, dams, and sea-walls, such forest silences,
streams, and grassy slopes. A blue sky, cattle on the hills,
green woods and yellow grain-fields excited his eyes
and stirred his imagination, and so did the rich smoky
atmosphere enshrouding mills and factories that sug-

[1] Nickname for a resident or native of Indiana; so, a frontiers-
man, a countryman. Ed.

gested to him the settings of tragic novels. He was even pleased by the sight of a grocer arranging his goods on a village street and, devoid as the brisk towns might be of history or of art, the general spectacle of their life touched and moved him. While Dreiser was drawn to the uncommon too, to forceful and singular men like Thoreau, to whom he later devoted a sympathetic essay, he never lost his feeling for the near and the common, and, undoubtedly lacking an ear for prose, as Huneker was only the first to say, he had a wonderful ear for the idiom of the people.

Dreiser, in short, was often at one with the folksy Western writers from whom in other respects he diverged so far. Thus he was drawn to James Whitcomb Riley 'with a whole heart' and 'loving thoughts', as he read Eugene Field with avidity in Chicago. He had tried to imitate, in fact, Field's whimsical comments on life when his own favourite pastime, as he later remembered, was to 'view the activities of others' as he walked the streets, and there was a touch of a kind of humour in his newspaper stories of sport that allied him to George Ade and perhaps Ring Lardner. At a time when his ambition was above all to write plays and he was the theatre critic on a St. Louis paper, he planned a comic opera, *Jeremiah I*, on a theme that was precisely in the vein of Ade, the Hoosier. He dreamed of rivalling his brother Paul as an author of operas like *The Isle of Champagne*, as a rich and famous librettist of tin-pan alley. There was much again in *A Traveller at Forty*, recounting his impressions on a tour of Europe, that might have been the work of any of the Hoosier writers, so amiable, tolerant, and kindly was the tone of the book, so unlike the note of the Dreiser of literary legend. He was enchanted as they too might have been by the charm of English country life, by the architecture of Amiens cathedral, by the lustre of Florence, and they would have felt the same thrill of response to St. Francis at Assisi and found themselves in deep accord with him. The zest and curiosity that his travelling companion observed in Dreiser were those of any sensitive Mid-western tourist, and the special Dreiserian touch appeared only in his notes on the London slums, which he haunted as Jack London and Flynt had haunted them before him. There in the East End he felt again that the poor were somehow artistically great, as Jean François Millet must have felt when he painted his peasants. The genial air that pervaded this book seemed to suggest that the author had more than a little in common with his fellow-Hoosiers.

What led him so far away from them was a family experience that was unlike theirs and a depth of perception and feeling that accompanied this difference, a temperament that soon made reporting too shallow an occupation for him, tortured as he was by a sense of the tragedy of living. As a reporter in St. Louis he was obsessed with the 'lightning of chance' that was always striking blindly, leaving in its wake, good fortune for some, for others destruction and death—an obsession that led him to say later, 'I acknowledge the Furies. I believe in them. I have heard the disastrous beating of their wings.' He was tormented by the contradictions of the life that he observed, the failures on one hand, on the other the unmerited successes, and he was so struck by the cruelty of life, haphazard and casual as it seemed, that he felt he was obliged to explore the mystery of it. Life was so niggardly to many, to others so lavish. He was puzzled over the rights and wrongs of everything he saw, over the relation, for instance, between morals and success, and his restlessness in the presence of problems that he could not solve had led him to feel dissatisfied with the journalistic life. He felt that he could no longer remain on the surface reporting events, that somehow he must interpret his observations, and by the time he arrived in New York he had virtually withdrawn from newspaper life and begun to seek for some other means of expression.

All this removed Dreiser from the cheerful domain of the other Hoosier writers whose minds played over the exterior of the life they knew and whose childhood experience was so different from that of an offspring of poor German peasants in a Western world which they had never made. The others might have been barefoot boys—Riley, the country lawyer's son, or Ade, the son of a storekeeper in an Indiana village—but they had grown up, like the prosperous Booth Tarkington, in an older American atmosphere in which they knew their bearings and felt at home. Their first memories might have been like Dreiser's, who crept about the floor observing the holes in his mother's worn-out shoes, and they might have lived in fear of hunger and cold, but the fatalism that hovered over the Catholic-Mennonite Dreisers was remote from the usual Hoosier frame of mind. The world of the Tarkingtons, Ades, and Rileys was mettlesome, brisk and up-and-coming, while Dreiser's heavy plodding German mind struck to the end the note of the household of his childhood. It was precisely the note of the peasant whom Mencken found in later years consulting an old woman who was telling his fortune in tea-leaves, the quality that his sisters had in common with Gertrude Stein's poor German girls in the book, *Three Lives*, that was published in 1909. For how much in common both Sister Carrie and Jennie Gerhardt had with 'Poor Anna who had no power to say No' and Lena who was 'patient, gentle, sweet and German' and who died—and 'nobody knew just how it

happened.' They passively acquiesced in fate like the
mother of the Dreisers who accepted help for her family
from the mistress of a brothel in which her son Paul
lived when he visited the town—the brothel in which
Dreiser as a young boy had his first glimpse of luxurious
living when he went there to see this one brother who
had risen in the world.

Now, without doubt, Dreiser's point of view, his
philosophic outlook, the nature of his interests, his
sympathies and obsessions and ambitions, all these were
shaped by the circumstances in which his early life was
passed in the 'nebulous, emotional, traditionless' Dreiser
household. For so he characterized in *Dawn* the family
life of the poor weaver and miller and the mother who
was 'without moral bias or social training'. A profoundly
emotional man himself, his mind was governed to the
end by the image of this mother, whom he adored, and
the image of the father, the religious fanatic who reviled
his wife for accepting the aid of the devil when he
totally failed himself to support the household. To
Dreiser, naturally loving the mother whose devotion
saved the family, whatever the father stood for was
inevitably hateful, for would not any child have felt that
a father must be wrong who upbraided and vilified his
wife under these conditions? Only by desperate devices
could she keep her children alive at all—she also accepted
the help of her daughter's seducer—and what child
would not have confusedly gathered that, if she was
breaking the moral law, the law deserved the abuse
rather than the mother? Had she not made their home
'as sweet as dreams'? For Dreiser his mother was doing
right—how else could he have seen her?—while he was
compelled to listen to the tirades of his father, so that
naturally he thought of morals as negative and false; and
the case was further complicated by the fact that Paul,

who lived in the brothel, was not only the most prosperous but the kindest and most loyal of the children. What then could morals have meant to this little boy? He could not blame his mother and therefore he saw her as irresponsible—to have held that she was responsible would have been to blame her—and from this it was only a step to the notion that no one was ever responsible and that human beings were wholly the victims of fate. They were totally unable to control the conditions of their lives. The Darwinism, or Spencerism, that Dreiser encountered as he grew up, a philosophy that was common talk among young reporters, was a theoretical explanation of what he had observed, that life was a blind struggle in which the weak were helpless. Society, as Dreiser came to see it, was a counterpart of nature, a chaos of inscrutable forces, a 'chemic drift', in which wealth and poverty were inevitable facts and a man was an atom in the whirl to be blamed for nothing he did or failed to do. This was not quite what Lafcadio Hearn had found in Herbert Spencer, still less what John Fiske had found in an earlier decade. But everyone finds in philosophy what he looks for and Dreiser found the mirror of the jungle he had known.

Dreiser, with his brooding mind, a lifelong student in his way and a reader of philosophy, as he said, 'from Democritus to Einstein', made much of these mechanistic views in *Hey, Rub-a-Dub-Dub* and elsewhere, while at other times he departed freely from them. Life, as he remarked in *A Traveller at Forty*, is an 'expression of contraries' and his own inconsistencies were striking, for, fatalistic as he was, he acted as if he believed in free will, as if men most certainly could control their fate. Although he was opposed to what he called the 'cocksureness' of reformers—which puts one 'out of harmony with the great underlying life forces'—he bristled as an

editor with plans of reform, and, too aloof and too confused to join the circle of the muckrakers, he investi-
gated strikes in mines and aided the workers. As a
young man he had wondered whether something could
not be done to diminish the inequalities of life, a feeling
that drew him into socialism and communism later—
'incorrigible individualist' that he said he was; and all his
activities as a pamphleteer, in his book on Russia, in
Tragic America, were based on the assumption that man
has a fighting will. Whatever his philosophy was,
meanwhile, he was deeply drawn to the victims of life,
to the miseries of 'Nigger Jeff', the Negro who was
lynched, to the old German farmer who lost his Phoebe
and to 'Old Ragpicker' who had forgotten his name and
lived by grubbing in ash-cans for refuse and bottles. He
was obsessed with the ironies of fate, how men died of
cold in the bread-line, for instance, while they were
waiting for bundles of cast-off clothes, how a Negro
riding the rails was swept into a blizzard on his way
north at a moment when he was trying to better his
condition. In *The Girl in the Coffin*, one of his plays,
the mill-girl died of a pregnancy that was caused by the
labour-leader who had just won the strike. While these
ironies also touched the rich, like the millionaire brewer
who died of joy because he was elected snare-drummer
of a Shriners' lodge, most of them concerned for Dreiser
the people who were not potential Napoleons but poor
little Spitoveskys and John Paradisos.

But, filled as Dreiser always was with a genuine compassion for the woes of the weak and a sense of the
'blundering inept cruelty of life', he was equally drawn
to the forceful, to powerful men, and when he repeated
in *Hey, Rub-a-Dub-Dub* that 'the race is to the swift
and the battle to the strong' he expressed a reality that
he did not entirely regret. If Dreiser was to be remem-

bered later as the best painter in American fiction of the great type of the capitalist in the age of exploitation— the Cowperwood of *The Financier*, *The Titan*, and *The Stoic*—it was partly because he sympathized with it through another line of feeling that also had its origin in the conditions of his childhood. Who could forget, in *An American Tragedy*, the craving of the young bell-boy Clyde for the luxury, wealth, beauty, and show that he observed in the hotel, his envy of the rich well-dressed people whom his eyes followed in the lobby, starved as he was for want of any pleasure. When Clyde longed to escape from the squalor of his childhood in a family that was looked down upon and lived from hand to mouth in half a dozen towns, when he dreamed of the high world in his uncle's Lycurgus and pined for money and fine clothes, was he not the image of the Dreiser of *A Book about Myself*? Clyde's sister also ran away and returned with an illegitimate child, and Dreiser, the cash-boy in a dry-goods store, the newsboy, the driver of a laundry wagon, had shared Clyde's hunger for a beauty he connected with wealth. Was it not Dreiser who grieved in youth over his sense of inferiority in the presence of the other smartly dressed reporters, whose lives he had envied because they were passed among what he called 'great people', because they were received as equals by the powerful and famous? It took him years to overcome the feeling of poverty and defeat that had mentally coloured his own childhood, and his eyes were fixed, as he recalled, on 'bankers, millionaires, artists, executives, leaders, the real rulers of the world'. No one more than he desired 'material and social supremacy', and was it not this that drew him to Balzac's brooding ambitious beginners, whom he discovered in the months he spent in Pittsburgh? Dissatisfied with reporting there, he read for days in the public library and found himself enthralled by Balzac's heroes, the eager awkward Raphael of the *Peau de Chagrin* and that other seeker of success, Lucien de Rubempré. He saw himself in Raphael, dreaming of women and grieving over his poverty and unrecognized greatness, and it was Balzac who crystallized his wish to be a novelist, 'life-hungry and love-hungry' as he was and ready for this clue. He thought of the reporter in St. Louis who had urged him to 'remember Zola and Balzac'—Zola with his art of presenting the drab and the gross, Balzac with his feeling for the sensual and the pageantry of life. He began to see Balzac's Paris in Pittsburgh, with its rivers and bridges and powerful men, and, during those days when he was ostensibly doing 'police and city hall', he dreamed of becoming another, an American, Balzac. He even planned to present in a novel one of the great financial barons about whom he gathered data while he was in Pittsburgh—notes about the houses and clubs of the Fricks and Carnegies—to which he was to return in time when he fixed his attention on Yerkes and went to Philadelphia to study him in the home of his youth. His visions were all of a kind of novel such as Balzac or Tolstoy had written that was quite unlike the traditional American novel, that fruit of an Anglo-Saxon mind which was schooled in Thackeray, Dickens, and Lamb, who had agreed to call spades by other names.

Thus Dreiser sympathized in his way with the 'swift' and the 'strong', the victors of life, in the sense of sharing their dreams and aspirations, almost as much as he sympathized with the weak, the victims, and if the novels he wrote about them were scarcely less close to the bone it was because he had lived their life as well. For had he not for a while experienced, as a highly-paid editor in New York, the kind of success and power for which they lived, an experience he recorded in his novel

The 'Genius' in which Eugene Witla—again himself—exulted in the authority he achieved among practical men. Had not Dreiser, like Eugene the artist, rejoiced in the 'dizzy eminence' that made his life for a while 'one triumph after another,' that made him, 'among his large company of assistants, a sort of Oriental potentate' while he 'gravitated to the wealthy, the beautiful, the strong and able'? Dreiser, at the peak of his material success, had branched out, almost like Mark Twain, into money-making plans and enterprises—real estate, apple orchards, a series of cheap books, and why, for that matter, did he postpone the composition of *Jennie Gerhardt* when he had recovered from his breakdown and was able to write? Why did he push it aside unfinished, repaying sums advanced by publishers, if it was not because he enjoyed this success, because this feeling of an 'upward progress'—Eugene's sense of 'making good'—had for Dreiser a rather special meaning? 'Luxury is a dream of delight . . . to those who have come out of poverty', he remarked, referring to the artist who was the hero of *The 'Genius'*. When he was at the height of this phase of his life and Mencken, who wrote for his magazine, sent him the book he had written on the philosophy of Nietzsche, Dreiser told Mencken that Nietzsche and he were 'hale fellows well met'—if Mencken's interpretation of this philosophy was true. Was he not having his own taste of the will to power that Nietzsche extolled, the kind of success that he had always dreamed of, the success he admired when he praised Chicago, a few years later, as the city 'where the weak must go down and the strong remain'? It was notable that when he resumed his writing, after giving up his editorship, he ceased for some years to be interested in the helpless and the passive—once he had finished the novel *Jennie Gerhardt*—and turned to writing about forceful men, the 'rebellious Lucifers' whom he understood far better because of his own struggles and victorious efforts. He was all for 'untrammelled individualism' when he was writing *The Financier*, he called communism a 'lunatic theory' then, and, admiring the 'average American' who loves 'power . . . far more earnestly than he loves mere living', he believed that the law of the jungle was the only law. If, as he said in *A Traveller at Forty*, he liked labour-leaders, it was partly because they too were 'big raw men' who were also 'eager for gain, for self-glorification', and he was happy that the wretched workers had acquired the sense to appoint these fellows who 'show their teeth and call great bitter strikes'.

So Theodore Dreiser, who followed life with a hearty zest wherever it led and who had delighted in the throb and sting of Chicago, understood the robber barons who ruled the great world of finance in which he, like Eugene, had 'vaguely hoped to shine'. He had shared their feeling for stocks and bonds, for brownstone palaces with fountains and courts, for private collections of the artists who were in vogue at the moment, for the power that appealed to their anarchistic temperament and their sometimes chronic promiscuity in the matter of sex. For Cowperwood was not unique among captains of finance in his need for what Henry Adams called 'sex as force', for what Dreiser called 'varietism', the perpetual presence of the new and young, 'like the odour of roses and dew, the colour of bright waters'. He was possessed at all times by the charm of eighteen-year-old girls and the mystery of their personalities, especially those of the newer order who overrode every social rule and were bent on upsetting conventions for the fun of the thing. In Cowperwood, whose motto was 'I satisfy myself', Dreiser presented far better than anyone else the type of the buccaneer of American finance, and he went far to destroy the myth of the millionaire as hero by showing what he actually was and actually did. It was idle to say with Frank Harris that Cowperwood was not typical because American financiers were not sent to prison and because Eastern financiers did not go West —that Cowperwood's original, Yerkes, was a special case—for no one conveyed as well as Dreiser the pulsation of energy in this type or the cold sharp stratospheric air of the high world of finance. No one else had begun to suggest the dynamic note of such a man, the vigour with which, defeated in Philadelphia, in Chicago, he could seek, at sixty, in London, new worlds to conquer, or the tangled webs he wove or the ruin that he spread as he raged like a force of nature through city after city.

It was Dreiser's own masculine love of life, the strength of his desire that enabled him to re-create this American type, as it enabled him to traverse—'wide-eyed, with an open heart'—a range of experience still greater than his own Eugene's. He never lost the sense of wonder, the ingenuousness, the candour that is, after all, with novelists, so essential and so rare, the wonder that characterized Balzac and Tolstoy and invested for him with a kind of magic the spectacles and the charms of everyday existence. It gave him the perpetual feeling of a 'guest at a feast', and he for whom in early life the newspaper-office was a 'wonderland' found wonderlands on all sides in after life, in smoky groups of factory buildings, in theatre-going crowds at night, in shop-girls brushing their hair by open windows. Eugene, his impressionist painter, expressed one facet of Dreiser's mind as clearly as his financier expressed another, showing how much he had in common with the painters who called themselves the 'Eight' and who shared his delighted response to the American scene. In his account of the work of Eugene he had Everett Shinn in mind, he said, though more often it suggested John Sloan, Glackens, or Luks and their canvasses of sandwich-men, bums on benches, fire-engines with streaming smoke and lighted restaurants seen through a driving rain. Some of Dreiser's prose vignettes in *The Colour of a Great City* paralleled the pushcart-men of the 'ash-can' school, their bread-lines, beaches, morgues, and slaughter-houses, their tugs on the river hauling barges, their dingy box-cars, red, yellow, and blue, and their Bowery missions and flop-houses enveloped in a fog. They sometimes suggested Edward Hopper or Stieglitz's early photographs of battered old street-cars with teams of unkempt horses struggling through swirling winds and flying snow, and they were full of the zest with which Dreiser discovered the secret and thrilling in a thousand corners of the city. Dreiser in this resembled O. Henry and the Howells who had explored New York and described it in *A Hazard of New Fortunes*, and Dreiser resembled Howells too in the great variety of his American settings, farms, villages, small towns, and cities in the East as in the West. Like Howells he was deeply at home in America, rebellious as he also was, and no one ever showed more respect for the probity of its corporate life than this writer who was supposed to have libelled it so often. With what authenticity and scrupulous care he de-scribed, in *An American Tragedy*, the integrity of the judge and the court and the governor of the state who tried so hard to find reasons for pardoning Clyde; and how many other American novelists have created a Protestant minister who was vital, saintly, and intense? The historian Parkman called clergymen 'vermin'—a short and simple word for them—and Melville estab-lished in his Mr. Falsgrave, the clergyman in *Pierre*, a convention that American novelists continued to follow. Booth Tarkington's Mr. Kinosling in *Penrod* was scarcely less odious than Elmer Gantry; and what was one to say of Theron Ware? It was left for the supposedly godless Dreiser to portray in his Duncan McMillan the Protestant minister as he ought to be.

For Dreiser was a deeply religious man, bewildered as he was no doubt and as superstitious as any other peasant, a believer in omens and magic symbols for whom a heavy black-bearded man suddenly appearing on a train was a sign of good luck. But he was a lover of goodness too who wrote several stories like *Another Samaritan*, *A Doer of the Word*, and *A True Patriarch* in the collection *Twelve Men*. With his tragic sense of the mystery of life, he was drawn to religion more and more and especially to Elias Hicks's teachings, which had something in common with the original faith of his Mennonite mother, who had lived as a child in Pennsylvania, the land of the Quakers. Before his death Dreiser had steeped himself in the writings of the early Friends, in John Woolman's journal and Bartram's *Travels*, and had come to feel their spiritual beauty somewhat in the manner of Esther Barnes when she returned, in *The Bulwark*, to make peace with her father. So also, in *The Stoic*, the other novel that Dreiser was finishing at the moment of his death, Berenice, Cowperwood's mistress, who had studied Yoga, became a nurse and built a hospital in order to express her new-found belief in 'something beyond human passion' and its selfish wishes. This was Dreiser's own final note when, joining the Communist party, he also received communion in a Protestant church, on the Good Friday of the year in which he died, attempting thus to reconcile the contradictions in a mind that felt life more deeply perhaps than any other in his time.

I. A. RICHARDS

1893–

THE SENSE OF POETRY: SHAKESPEARE'S 'THE PHOENIX AND THE TURTLE'[1]

Daedalus, lxxxvii, Summer 1958

Is it not fitting that the greatest English poet should have written the most mysterious poem in English? 'The Phoenix and the Turtle' is so strange a poem—even so unlike anything else in Shakespeare, as to have caused doubts that he wrote it. And yet, no one else seems in the least likely as author.

One of the odd things about the poem is that it has engendered curiosity and praise only in relatively recent times. Emerson was among the first: 'To unassisted readers', he says, 'it would appear to be a lament on the death of a poet, and of his poetic mistress.' 'This poem,' he adds, 'if published for the first time, and without a known author's name, would find no general reception. Only the poets would save it.'

Since then many notable efforts have been made to assist 'unassisted readers' without taking us perhaps very much farther than Emerson himself went: 'a lament on the death of a poet'—or is it the poetic endeavour?—'and his poetic mistress'—or could it be *that* whereto the poetic endeavour devotes itself: poetry?

Let us see. Let us read the poem through twice, once

---

[1] Based on a talk in a series given during the winter 1957–8 over WGBH-TV in Boston, and distributed nationally by the Educational Television and Radio Center.

for detail and structure and pondering, and then again
for life and motion.

THE PHOENIX AND THE TURTLE

Let the bird of lowdest lay,
On the sole *Arabian* tree,
Herauld sad and trumpet be:
To whose sound chaste wings obay.

But thou shriking harbinger,
Foule precurrer of the fiend,
Augour of the feuers end,
To this troupe come thou not neere.

From this Session interdict
Euery foule of tyrant wing,
Saue the Eagle feath'red King,
Keepe the obsequie so strict.

Let the Priest in Surples white,
That defunctive Musicke can,
Be the death-deuining Swan,
Lest the *Requiem* lacke his right.

And thou treble dated Crow,
That thy sable gender mak'st,
With the breath thou giu'st and tak'st,
'Mongst our mourners shalt thou go.

Here the Antheme doth commence,
Loue and Constancie is dead,
Phoenix and the *Turtle* fled,
In a mutuall flame from hence.

So they loued as loue in twaine,
Had the essence but in one,
Two distincts, Diuision none,
Number there in loue was slaine.

Hearts remote, yet not asunder;
Distance and no space was seene,
Twixt this *Turtle* and his *Queene*;
But in them it were a wonder.

So betweene them loue did shine,
That the *Turtle* saw his right,
Flaming in the *Phoenix* sight;
Either was the others mine.

Propertie was thus appalled,
That the selfe was not the same:
Single Natures double name,
Neither two nor one was called.

Reason in it selfe confounded,
Saw Diuision grow together,
To themselves yet either neither,
Simple were so well compounded.

That it cried, how true a twaine,
Seemeth this concordant one,
Loue hath Reason, Reason none,
If what parts, can so remaine.

Whereupon it made this *Threne*
To the *Phoenix* and the *Doue*,
Co-supremes and starres of Loue,
As *Chorus* to their Tragique Scene.

THRENOS

Beautie, Truth, and Raritie,
Grace in all simplicitie,
Here enclosde, in cinders lie.

Death is now the *Phoenix* nest,
And the *Turtles* loyall brest,
To eternitie doth rest,

Leauing no posteritie,
Twas not their infirmitie,
It was married Chastitie.

Truth may seeme, but cannot be,
Beautie bragge, but tis not she,
Truth and Beautie buried be.

To this vrne let those repaire,
That are either true or faire,
For these dead Birds, sigh a prayer.

The Phoenix here is a unique bird, singular indeed—
there can be but the one Phoenix. And the Turtle Dove
is so devoted a lover of his Queen—so entirely hers, as
she is his—that, like an Indian suttee, he is consumed,
burnt up on the pyre, in the flames of her regeneration.

Let the bird of lowdest lay,
On the sole *Arabian* tree,
Herauld sad and trumpet be:
To whose sound chaste wings obay.

Who is speaking? Who is this 'bird of lowdest lay'
who summons this company of birds and has this
authority over 'chaste wings'? (You will note, near the
end, a very strong use indeed of the word 'Chastitie'.)

I like best the suggestion that the reborn Phoenix
herself is here summoning the birds to the celebration of
her own (and the Turtle's) obsequies. If so, this Phoenix,
this Queen, is perched on her own throne. In *The
Tempest* (III. iii. 22–24) Sebastian cries:

Now I will believe that . . . in Arabia
There is one tree, the phoenix' throne; one phoenix
At this hour reigning there.
[On the sole *Arabian* tree]

If so, she herself is *Herauld sad and trumpet*; and the

sadness is for the Turtle—lost in the fiery rite required for the Phoenix' rebirth.

Various birds are excluded: the ill-omened, the screech-owl, say, because this is a beginning anew, another cycle of the Phoenix' life.

> But thou shriking harbinger,
> Foule precurrer of the fiend,
> Augour of the feuers end,
> To this troupe come thou not neere.

Birds of prey are to be kept out too—except the symbol of authority, the Kingly Eagle, which can overawe violence as Henry VII put an end to the Wars of the Roses. Nothing arbitrary or unjust has a place here:

> From this Session interdict
> Euery foule of tyrant wing,
> Saue the Eagle feath'red King,
> Keepe the obsequie so strict.

Obsequie is a deep word here: a following after and a due compliance. These birds are to take part in a commemorative procession chanting the anthem, a song with the power of a spell.

> Let the Priest in Surples white,
> That defunctive Musicke can,
> Be the death-deuining Swan,
> Lest the *Requiem* lacke his right.

Defunctive Musicke: music which has to do with death; the Swan knows how to sing its swan song before its death and knows beforehand when it is to die.

Lacke his right: lack a rightness his participation can give. Some dictionaries say *right* is just Shakespeare's misspelling of *rite* (ritual). More modern critics will call it a pun. It is better perhaps to reflect and recognize how closely interwoven the meanings of the two words can be. A rite may be the observance it is right to give, to accord.

This choral service contains an anthem, a song of praise and gladness; a requiem, a solemn dirge for the repose of the dead; and a *threne* or *threnos*, a lamentation or dirge of honour. Note, too, a curious thing about the structure of the poem: the mourning birds, when assembled and ordered, chant an anthem in which Reason (something being described, talked about, conjured up, released, in the anthem) after going through a strange change, cries out suddenly and then composes the threne, sung at the close, and this threne, so composed

> To the *Phoenix* and the *Doue*,
> Co-supremes and starres of Loue,
> As *Chorus* to their Tragique Scene

ends with directions for a pilgrimage and a prayer.

This singular involvement—each part of the poem being included in and produced by, put into a mouth created in the part before it—has a lot to do with the power and spring of this most concentered and compacted poem.

The next bird, the last of the birds, the only one to be mentioned after the Swan-Priest, may have an importance suited to this special position. The *treble dated* Crow lives, so the legend says, three times, any number of times, longer than man. A 'lived happily ever after' flavour hangs about him. Moreover, he engenders his offspring by breathing: a very ethereal mode of propagation, the mode by which poems and poetic ideas inter-inanimate and beget their successors. He is as black as ink, dressed in proper funeral attire, and yet is directed, somewhat as though he did not belong and could not expect to be invited, to join the mourners. Perhaps, being a carrion crow, he is a kind of contaminated character. Here he is:

> And thou treble dated Crow,
> That thy sable gender mak'st,
> With the breath thou giu'st and tak'st,
> 'Mongst our mourners shalt thou go.
>
> Here the Antheme doth commence,
> Loue and Constancie is dead,
> *Phoenix* and the *Turtle* fled,
> In a mutuall flame from hence.

Loue and Constancie: the attraction to beauty and the attachment in truth.

Notice *is dead*: the two are so much one that even from the first mention the verb used is singular: 'is' dead, not 'are' dead. This confounds grammar, as Reason, itself, is going to be confounded in what follows.

> So they loued as loue in twaine,
> Had the essence but in one,
> Two distincts, Diuision none,
> Number there in loue was slaine.

They loved as do two people who love one another, and yet they were not two but one, and one is not a number. For this duality the same questions arise as in the Doctrine of the Trinity.

> Hearts remote, yet not asunder;
> Distance and no space was seene,
> Twixt this *Turtle* and his *Queene*;
> But in them it were a wonder.

But in them it were a wonder: in any others than 'this concordant one' all this would be 'a wonder'; not so here.

> So betweene them loue did shine,
> That the *Turtle* saw his right,

> Flaming in the *Phoenix* sight;
> Either was the others mine.

The Phoenix' eyes are traditionally of fire; they flame like the sun. But, more than that, the Turtle sees *his right* flaming in them.

His right: all he can ask or be entitled to; all that is due and just; all that he truly is, his true being.

Let me quote a few lines here from *The Birds Parliament* by Attar, the twelfth-century Persian saint and mystic, also about the Phoenix, which in Attar's poem is the leader in the soul's return to God. The poem is translated by Edward Fitzgerald, who translated Omar Khayyám.

> Once more they ventured from the Dust to raise
> Their eyes up to the Throne, into the Blaze;
> And in the Centre of the Glory there
> Beheld the Figure of THEMSELVES, as 'twere
> Transfigured—looking to Themselves, beheld
> The Figure on the Throne enmiracled,
> Until their Eyes themselves and that between
> Did hesitate which SEER was, which SEEN.

Or as in Shelley's lines from his 'Hymn of Apollo':

> I am the Eye with which the universe
> Beholds itself and knows itself divine.

Either was the others mine: diamond mine, ruby mine, yes, perhaps; but, more important, each entirely possessed and was possessed by the other.

> Propertie was thus appalled,
> That the selfe was not the same:
> Single Natures double name,
> Neither two nor one was called.
>
> Reason in it selfe confounded,
> Saw Diuision grow together,
> To themselves yet either neither,
> Simple were so well compounded.

> That it cried, how true a twaine,
> Seemeth this concordant one,
> Loue hath Reason, Reason none,
> If what parts, can so remaine.

Any other poem, I sometimes think, would have made Reason cry

> How true a one
> Seemeth this concordant twain.

But the poem goes the further step, makes *Reason in it selfe confounded* speak in character and show itself to be confounded. Very Shakespearian, this dramatic actuality!

> Whereupon it made this *Threne*
> To the *Phoenix* and the *Doue,*
> Co-supremes and starres of Loue,
> As *Chorus* to their Tragique Scene.

Note that Reason is the singer:

THRENOS

> Beautie, Truth, and Raritie,
> Grace in all simplicitie,
> Here enclosde, in cinders lie.

> Death is now the *Phoenix* nest,
> And the *Turtles* loyall brest,
> To eternitie doth rest,

To the Phoenix, death is now a nest, a symbol of rebirth, but to

> the *Turtles* loyall brest,

it is a place of final repose.

> Leauing no posteritie,
> Twas not their infirmitie,
> It was married Chastitie.

What these

> Co-supremes and starres of Loue

have been concerned with has not been offspring.
Besides, there can be but the one Phoenix, although in
this poem, we may imagine, the sacrifice, the devotion
of a Dove is needed for each new regeneration or
reincarnation.

> The intellect of man is forced to choose
> Perfection of the life or of the work,

wrote W. B. Yeats. Must poets give up their lives so
that poetry may be renewed?

> Truth may seeme, but cannot be,
> Beautie bragge, but tis not she,
> Truth and Beautie buried be.

As a poem may be something beyond anyone's
reading or apprehension of it?

> To this vrne let those repaire,
> That are either true or faire,
> For these dead Birds, sigh a prayer.

This prayer is wordless; it is sighed only, not spoken.
What it might have said is what the whole poem has
been conveying, an endeavour to apprehend a mystery.
And it is no good asking what this mystery is apart from
this endeavour itself.

We may say if we like that this mystery is the mystery
of being, which is forever dying into cinders and arising
to flame and die anew; and always, perhaps, demanding
a sacrifice of constancy for the sake of that to which it is
loyal and true. But no remarks on this poem can be
more than snapshots of something someone has thought
he saw in it: helpful maybe to some but merely curiosi-
ties of opinion to others.

There are two remarks I would like, however, to make before inviting the reader to read the poem again straight through.

Beautie, Truth, and Raritie.

The truth celebrated in the poem is chiefly loyalty, faithfulness, and constancy, which, as with Troilus, the true knight, the true lover, is truth spelled *Troth*. At first sight troth may not seem to have very much to do with the ways in which a statement in a science may be true (or false), or evidence offered in a law court may be true (or false), or philosophical or critical or historical or literary views may be true (or false). And yet, for all of these, if we search and imagine faithfully enough, we will find that the statement or opinion, whatever it is, hangs in the midst of and is dependent upon a vast network of loyalties toward everything that may be relevant. Its truth is a matter of inter-inanimations and co-operations among loyalties, among troths.

And very significant parallels to all this hold for beauty.

This poem, one may well think, is not about any such high and remote abstractions but about two people; two people, who may be thought to have been 'the very personifications, the very embodiments', as we lightly say, of beauty and truth, though they are spoken of in the poem as two birds. That is how the poem feels, no doubt about it. But, as certainly, there is a religious quality in its movement, a feeling in it as though we were being related through it to something far beyond any individuals. This Phoenix and this Turtle have a mythic scale to them, as though through them we were to become participants in something ultimate. All this, however, is so handled that it seems as easy and as natural and as necessary as breathing.

Let us read the poem again with a wider and more relaxed attention. Was it Mr. Eliot who remarked: 'There is such a thing as page fright as well as stage fright'? The very greatness of a poem can stupefy the reader.

> To this vrne let those repaire. . . .

No one who repairs to this urn will think there can be any end to wondering about it.

EDMUND WILSON

1895–

THE POLITICS OF FLAUBERT

The Triple Thinkers, revised edition 1948

GUSTAVE FLAUBERT has figured for decades as the great glorifier and practitioner of literary art at the expense of human affairs both public and personal. We have heard about his asceticism, his nihilism, his consecration to the search for *le mot juste*. His admirers have tended to praise him on the same assumption on which his critics have found him empty and sterile: the assumption that he had no moral or social interests. At most, *Madame Bovary* has been taken as a parable of the romantic temperament.

Really Flaubert owed his superiority to those of his contemporaries—Gautier, for example, who professed the same literary creed—to the seriousness of his concern with the large questions of human destiny. It was a period when the interest in history was intense; and Flaubert, in his intellectual tastes as well as in his personal relations, was almost as close to the historians Michelet, Renan, and Taine, and to the biographical critic Sainte-Beuve, as to Gautier and Baudelaire. In the case of Taine and Sainte-Beuve, he came to deplore their preoccupation in their criticism with the social aspects of literature at the expense of all its other values; but he himself seems always to see humanity in social terms and historical perspective. His point of view may be gauged pretty accurately from his comments in one of his letters on Taine's *History of English Literature*:

There is something else in art beside the milieu in which it is practised and the physiological antecedents of the worker. On this system you can explain the series, the group, but never the individuality, the special fact which makes him this person and not another. This method results inevitably in leaving *talent* out of consideration. The masterpiece has no longer any significance except as an historical document. It is the old critical method of La Harpe exactly turned around. People used to believe that literature was an altogether personal thing and that books fell out of the sky like meteors. Today they deny that the will and the absolute have any reality at all. The truth, I believe, lies between the two extremes.

But it was also a period in France—Flaubert's lifetime, 1820–81—of alternating republics and monarchies, of bogus emperors and defeated revolutions, when political ideas were in much confusion. The French historians of the Enlightenment tradition, which was the tradition of the Revolution, were steadily becoming less hopeful; and a considerable group of the novelists and poets held political and social issues in contempt and staked their careers on art as an end in itself: their conception of their relation to society was expressed in their damnation of the bourgeois, who gave his tone to all the world, and their art was a defiance of him. The Goncourts in their journal have put the attitude on record:

Lying phrases, resounding words, hot air—that's just about all we get from the political men of our time. Revolutions are a simple *déménagement* followed by the moving-back of the same ambitions, corruptions and villainies into the apartment which they have just been moved out of—and all involving great breakage and expense. No political morals whatever. When I look about me for a disinterested opinion, I can't find a single one. People take risks and compromise themselves on the chance of getting future jobs. . . . You are reduced, in the long run, to disillusion, to a disgust with all beliefs, a tolerance of any power at all, an indifference to political passion, which I find in all my literary friends, and in Flaubert as in myself. You come to see that you must not die for any cause, that you must live with any government that exists, no matter how antipathetic it may be to you—you must believe in nothing but art and profess only literature. All the rest is a lie and a booby-trap.

In the field of art, at least, it was possible, by heroic effort, to prevent the depreciation of values.

This attitude, as the Goncourts say, Flaubert fully shared. 'Today', he wrote Louise Colet in 1853, 'I even believe that a thinker (and what is an artist if he is not a triple thinker?) should have neither religion nor fatherland nor even any social conviction. It seems to me that absolute doubt is now indicated so unmistakably that it would almost amount to an absurdity to take the trouble to formulate it.' And: 'The citizens who work themselves up for or against the Empire or the Republic', he wrote George Sand in 1869, 'seem to be just about as useful as the ones who used to argue about efficacious grace and efficient grace.' Nothing exasperated him more—and we may sympathize with him today—than the idea that the soul is to be saved by the profession of correct political opinions.

Yet Flaubert is an idealist on a grandiose scale. 'The idea' which turns up in his letters of the fifties—'genius like a powerful horse drags humanity at her tail along the roads of the idea', in spite of all that human stupidity can do to rein her in—is evidently, under its guise of art, none other than that Hegelian 'Idea' which served Marx and so many others under a variety of different guises. There are great forces in humanity, Flaubert feels, which the present is somehow suppressing but which may some day be gloriously set free. 'The soul is asleep today, drunk with the words she has listened to, but she will experience a wild awakening, in which she will give herself up to the ecstasies of liberation, for there will be nothing more to constrain her, neither government nor religion, not a formula; the republicans of all shades of opinion seem to me the most ferocious pedagogues, with their dreams of organizations, of legislations, of a society constructed like a convent.'

When he reasons about society—which he never does except in his letters—his conceptions seem incoherent. But Flaubert, who believed that the artist should be triply ('to the nth degree') a thinker and who had certainly one of the great minds of his time, was the kind of imaginative writer who works directly in concrete images and does not deal at all in ideas. His informal expressions of his general opinions are as unsystematized and impromptu as his books are well built and precise. But it is worth while to quote a few from his letters, because, though he never came anywhere near to expounding a social philosophy—when George Sand accused him of not having one, he admitted it—they do indicate the instincts and emotions which are the prime movers in the world of his art.

Flaubert is opposed to the socialists because he regards them as materialistic and because he dislikes their authoritarianism, which he says derives straight from the tradition of the Church. Yet they have 'denied *pain*, have blasphemed three-quarters of modern poetry, the blood of Christ, which quickens in us'. And:

O socialists, there is your ulcer: the ideal is lacking to you; and that very matter which you pursue slips through your fingers like a wave; the adoration of humanity for itself and by itself (which brings us to the doctrine of the useful in Art, to the theories of public safety and reason of state, to all the injustices and all the intolerances, to the immolation of the right, to the levelling of the Beautiful), that cult of the belly, I say, breeds wind.

One thing he makes clear by reiteration through the various periods of his life: his disapproval of the ideal of equality. What is wanted, he keeps insisting, is 'justice'; and behind this demand for justice is evidently Flaubert's resentment, arising from his own experience, against the false reputations, the undeserved rewards, and the stupid repressions of the Second Empire. And he was sceptical of popular education and opposed to universal suffrage.

Yet among the men of his time whom Flaubert admired most were democrats, humanitarians, and reformers. 'You are certainly the French author', he wrote Michelet, 'whom I have read and reread most'; and he said of Victor Hugo that Hugo was the living man 'in whose skin' he would be happiest to be. George Sand was one of his closest friends: *Un Cœur simple* was written for her—apparently in answer to her admonition that art was 'not merely criticism and satire' and to show her that he, too, had a heart.

When we come to Flaubert's books themselves, we find a much plainer picture of things.

It is not true, as is sometimes supposed, that he disclaimed any moral intention. He deliberately refrained in his novels from commenting on the action in his own character: 'the artist ought not to appear in his work any more than God in nature.' But, like God, he rules his universe through law; and the reader, from what he hears and sees, must infer the moral system.

What *are* we supposed to infer from Flaubert's work? His general historical point of view is, I believe, pretty well known. He held that 'the three great evolutions of humanity' had been 'paganisme, christianisme, muflisme [muckerism]', and that Europe was in the third of these phases. Paganism he depicted in *Salammbô* and in the short story *Hérodias*. The Carthaginians of *Salammbô* had been savage and benighted barbarians: they had worshipped serpents, crucified lions, sacrificed their children to Moloch, and trampled armies to death with herds of elephants; but they had slaughtered, lusted, and agonized superbly. Christianity is represented by the two legends of saints, *La Tentation de Saint Antoine* and *La Légende de Saint Julien l'Hospitalier*. The Christian combats his lusts, he expiates human cruelty; but this attitude, too, is heroic: Saint Anthony, who inhabits the desert, Saint Julien, who lies down with the leper, have pushed to their furthest limits the virtues of abnegation and humility. But when we come to the *muflisme* of the nineteenth century—in *Madame Bovary* and *L'Éducation sentimentale*—all is meanness, mediocrity and timidity.

The villain here is, of course, the bourgeois; and it is true that these two novels of Flaubert ridicule and damn the contemporary world, taking down its pretensions by comparing it with Carthage and the Thebaid. But in these pictures of modern life there is a complexity of human values and an analysis of social processes which does not appear in the books that deal with older civilizations; and this social analysis of Flaubert's has, it seems to me, been too much disregarded—with the result that *L'Éducation sentimentale*, one of his most remarkable books, has been rather underestimated.

In *Madame Bovary*, Flaubert is engaged in criticizing that very longing for the exotic and the faraway which played such a large part in his own life and which led him to write *Salammbô* and *Saint Antoine*. What cuts Flaubert off from the other romantics and makes him primarily a social critic is his grim realization of the futility of dreaming about the splendours of the Orient and the brave old days of the past as an antidote to bourgeois society. Emma Bovary, the wife of a small country doctor, is always seeing herself in some other setting, imagining herself someone else. She will not face her situation as it is, and the result is that she is eventually undone by the realities she has been trying to ignore. The upshot of all Emma's yearnings for a larger and more glamorous life is that her poor little daughter, left an orphan by Emma's suicide and the death of her father, is sent to work in a cotton mill.

The socialist of Flaubert's time might perfectly have approved of this: while the romantic individualist deludes himself with unrealizable fantasies, in the attempt to evade bourgeois society, and only succeeds in destroying himself, he lets humanity fall a victim to the industrial-commercial processes, which, unimpeded by his dreaming, go on with their deadly work.

Flaubert had more in common with, and had perhaps been influenced more by, the socialist thought of his time than he would ever have allowed himself to confess. In his novels, it is never the nobility—indistinguishable for mediocrity from the bourgeoisie—but the peasants and working people whom he habitually

uses as touchstones to show up the pretensions of the
bourgeois. One of the most memorable scenes in
Madame Bovary is the agricultural exhibition at which
the pompous local dignitaries award a medal to an old
farm servant for forty-five years of service on the same
farm. Flaubert has told us about the bourgeois at length,
made us listen to a long speech by a town councillor on
the flourishing state of France; and now he describes the
peasant—scared by the flags and drums and by the
gentlemen in black coats, and not understanding what is
wanted of her. Her long and bony hands, with which
she has worked all her life in stable dust, lye, and greasy
wool, still seem dirty, although she has just washed them,
and they hang at her sides half open, as if to present a
testimony of toil. There is no tenderness or sadness in
her face: it has a rigidity almost monastic. And her long
association with animals has given her something of their
placidity and dumbness. 'So she stood up before those
florid bourgeois, that half-century of servitude.' And
the heroine of *Un Cœur simple*, a servant who devotes
her whole life to the service of a provincial family and
gets not one ray of love in return, has the same sort of
dignity and pathos.

It is, however, in *L'Éducation sentimentale* that Flaubert's account of society comes closest to socialist theory.
Indeed, his presentation here of the Revolution of 1848
parallels in so striking a manner Marx's analysis of the
same events in *The Eighteenth Brumaire of Louis Napoleon*
that it is worth while to focus together the diverse
figures of Flaubert and Marx in order to recognize how
two of the most searching minds of the century, pursuing courses so apparently divergent, arrived at almost
identical interpretations of the happenings of their
own time.

When we do this, we become aware that Marx and

Flaubert started from very similar assumptions and that they were actuated by moral aims almost equally uncompromising. Both implacably hated the bourgeois, and both were resolved at any cost of worldly success to keep outside the bourgeois system. And Karl Marx, like Flaubert, shared to some degree the romantic bias in favour of the past. The author of *Das Kapital* can hardly, of course, be said to have had a very high opinion of any period of human history; but in comparison with the capitalist nineteenth century, he did betray a certain tenderness for Greece and Rome and the Middle Ages. He pointed out that the slavery of the ancient world had at least purchased the 'full development' of the masters, and that a certain Antipater of Thessalonica had joyfully acclaimed the invention of the water wheel for grinding corn because it would set free the female slaves who had formerly had to do this work, whereas the bourgeois economists had seen in machinery only a means for making the workers work faster and longer in order 'to transform a few vulgar and half-educated upstarts into "eminent cotton spinners," "extensive sausage makers" and "influential blacking dealers."' And he had also a soft spot for the feudal system before the nobility had revolted against the Crown and while the rights of all classes, high and low, were still guaranteed by the king. Furthermore, the feudal lords, he insisted, had spent their money lavishly when they had it, whereas it was of the essence of capitalism that the capitalist saved his money and invested it, only to save and reinvest the profits.

Karl Marx's judgement on his age was the *Communist Manifesto*. Let us examine the implications of Flaubert's political novel. The hero of *L'Éducation sentimentale*, Frédéric Moreau, is a sensitive and intelligent young man equipped with a moderate income; but he has no stability of purpose and is capable of no emotional integrity. He becomes aimlessly, will-lessly, involved in love affairs with different types of women and he is unable to make anything out of any of them: they simply get in each other's way till in the end he is left with nothing. Frédéric is most in love from the very beginning of the story with the virtuous oval-faced wife of a sort of glorified drummer, who is engaged in more or less shady business enterprises; but, what with his timidity and her virtue, he never gets anywhere with her—even though she loves him in return—and leaves her in the hands of the drummer. Flaubert makes it plain to us, however, that Frédéric and the vulgar husband at bottom represent the same thing: Frédéric is only the more refined as well as the more incompetent side of the middle-class mediocrity of which the dubious promoter represents the more flashy and active aspect. And so in the case of the other characters, the journalists and the artists, the members of the various political factions, the remnants of the old nobility, Frédéric finds the same shoddiness and lack of principle which are gradually revealed in himself—the same qualities which render so odious to him the banker M. Dambreuse, the type of the rich and powerful class. M. Dambreuse is always ready to trim his sails to any political party, monarchist or republican, which seems to have a chance of success. 'Most of the men who were there', Flaubert writes of the guests at the Dambreuse house, 'had served at least four governments; and they would have sold France or the human race in order to guarantee their fortune, to spare themselves an anxiety or a difficulty, or even from simple baseness, instinctive adoration of force.' 'Je me moque des affaires!' cries Frédéric when the guests at M. Dambreuse's are complaining that criticism of the government hurts business;

but he cannot give up going to the house, because he
always hopes to profit by Dambreuse's investments and
influence.

The only really sympathetic characters in *L'Éducation
sentimentale* are, again, the representatives of the people.
Rosanette, Frédéric's mistress, is the daughter of poor
workers in the silk mills, who sold her at fifteen as mistress to an old bourgeois. Her liaison with Frédéric is a
symbol of the disastrously unenduring union between
the proletariat and the bourgeoisie, of which Karl Marx
had written in *The Eighteenth Brumaire*. After the suppression of the workers' insurrection during the June days
of '48, Rosanette gives birth to a weakly child, which dies
at the same time that Frédéric is already arranging a love
affair with the dull wife of the banker. Frédéric believes
that Mme Dambreuse will be able to advance his interests. And bourgeois socialism gets a very Marxist
treatment—save in one respect, which we shall note in a
moment—in the character of Sénécal, who is eternally
making himself unpleasant about communism and the
welfare of the masses, for which he is ready to fight to the
last barricade. When, later, Sénécal gets a job as fore-
man in a pottery factory, he at once becomes a harsh
little tyrant; and as soon as it begins to appear, after the
putting-down of the June riots, that the reaction is sure
to triumph, he decides, like certain radicals turned
fascists, that the strong centralization of the government
is already a kind of communism and that authority is in
itself a great thing.

You have, on the other hand, the clerk Dussardier, a
strapping and obtuse fellow, who is one of the few
honest characters in the book. When we first see him, he
has just knocked down a policeman in a political brawl
on the street. Later, when the National Guard, of which
Dussardier is a member, turns against the proletariat in

the interests of law and order, Dussardier fells one of the insurgents from the top of a barricade and gets at the same time a bullet in the leg, thereby becoming a great hero of the bourgeois. But the poor fellow himself is unhappy. The boy that he had knocked down had wrapped the tricolor around him and shouted to the National Guard: 'Are you going to fire on your brothers?' Dussardier is not at all sure that he ought not to have been on the other side. His last appearance is at the climax of the story, constitutes, indeed, the climax: he turns up in a proletarian street riot, which the cavalry and the police are putting down. Dussardier refuses to move, crying 'Vive la République!'; and Frédéric comes along just in time to see one of the policemen kill him. Then he recognizes this policeman: it is the socialist, Sénécal.

L'Éducation sentimentale, unpopular when it first appeared, is likely, if we read it in youth, to prove baffling and even repellent. The title may have given the impression that we are going to get a love story, but the love affairs turn out invariably to be tepid or incomplete, and one finds oneself depressed or annoyed. Is it a satire? The characters are too close to life, and a little too well rounded, for satire. Yet they are not quite vitalized enough, not quite responsive enough, to seem the people of a straight novel. But we find that it sticks in our crop. If it is true, as Bernard Shaw has said, that *Das Kapital* makes us see the nineteenth century 'as if it were a cloud passing down the wind, changing its shape and fading as it goes', so that we are afterwards never able to forget that 'capitalism, with its wage slavery, is only a passing phase of social development, following primitive communism, chattel slavery and feudal serfdom into the past'—so Flaubert's novel plants deep in our mind an idea which we never quite get rid of: the suspicion that our middle-class society of manufacturers, businessmen, and bankers, of people who live on or deal in investments, so far from being redeemed by its culture, has ended by cheapening and invalidating all the departments of culture, political, scientific, artistic and religious, as well as corrupting and weakening the ordinary human relations: love, friendship, and loyalty to cause—till the whole civilization seems to dwindle.

But fully to appreciate the book, one must have had time to see something of life and to have acquired a certain interest in social and political dramas as distinct from personal ones. If one rereads it in middle age, one finds that the author's tone no longer seems quite so acrid, that one is listening to a muted symphony of which the varied instrumentation and the pattern, the marked rhythms and the melancholy sonorities, had been hardly perceptible before. There are no hero, no villain, to arouse us, no clowns to entertain us, no scenes to wring our hearts. Yet the effect is deeply moving. It is the tragedy of nobody in particular, but of the poor human race itself reduced to such ineptitude, such cowardice, such commonness, such weak irresolution— arriving, with so many fine notions in its head, so many noble words on its lips, at a failure which is all the more miserable because those who have failed in their roles have even forgotten what roles they were cast for. We come to understand the statement of Mr. Ford Madox Ford that he has found it is not too much to read the book fourteen times. Though L'Éducation sentimentale is less attractive on the surface and less exciting as a story than Madame Bovary, it is certainly the book of Flaubert's which is most ambitiously planned and into which he has tried to put most. And once we have got the clue to the immense and complex drama which unrolls itself behind the half-screen of the detached and monotonous style, we find it as absorbing and satisfying as a great play or a great piece of music.

The one conspicuous respect in which Flaubert's point of view on the events of 1848 *diverges* from that of Marx has been thrown into special relief by the events of our own time. For Marx, the evolution of the socialist into a proletarian-persecuting policeman would have been blamed on the bourgeois in Sénécal; for Flaubert, it is a development of socialism implicit in socialist beginnings. He distrusted, as I have shown above, the authoritarian aims of the socialists. It is Flaubert's conception that Sénécal, given his bourgeois hypocrisy, is still carrying out a socialist principle—or rather, that his behaviour as a policeman and his yearnings toward socialist control are both derived from his impulse toward despotism.

We may not be prepared to conclude that the evolution of Sénécal represents the whole destiny of socialism, but we must recognize that Flaubert had here brought to attention a danger of which Marx was not aware. We have had the opportunity to see how even a socialism which has come to power as the result of a proletarian revolution can breed a political police of almost unprecedented ruthlessness—how the example of Marx himself, with his emphasis on dictatorial control rather than on democratic processes, has contributed to produce this disaster. Flaubert, who believed that the artist should rid himself of social convictions, has gauged the tendencies of a political doctrine as the greatest of doctrinaires could not; and here the attitude he proposed has been justified.

The war of 1870 was a terrible shock to Flaubert: the nervous disorders of his later years have been attributed to it. He had the Prussians in his house at Croisset and had to bury his manuscripts. When he made a trip to Paris after the Commune, he came back to the country deeply shaken. 'This would never have happened', he said when he saw the wreck of the Tuileries, 'if they had only understood *L'Éducation sentimentale*.' What Flaubert meant, no doubt, was that if the French had seen the falsity of their politics, they would never have fought about them so fiercely. 'Oh, how tired I am', he wrote George Sand, 'of the ignoble worker, the inept bourgeois, the stupid peasant and the odious ecclesiastic.'

But in his letters of this period, which are more violent than ever, we see him taking a new direction. The effect of the Commune on Flaubert, as on so many of the other French intellectuals, was to bring out in him the class-conscious bourgeois. Basically bourgeois his life had always been, with his mother and his little income. He had, like Frédéric Moreau himself, been 'cowardly in his youth', he wrote George Sand. 'I was *afraid* of life.' And, even moving amongst what he regarded as the grandeurs of the ancient world, he remains a moderate Frenchman of the middle nineteenth century, who seems to cultivate excess, systematically and with a certain self-consciousness, in the hope of horrifying other Frenchmen. Marcel Proust has pointed out that Flaubert's imagery, even in books which do not deal with the bourgeois, tends to be rather banal. It was the enduring tradition of French classicism which had saved him from the prevailing shoddiness: by discipline and objectivity, by heroic application to the mastery of form, he had kept the enemy at a distance. But now when a working-class government had held Paris for two months and a half and had wrecked monuments and shot bourgeois hostages, Flaubert found himself as fierce against the Communards as any respectable 'grocer'. 'My opinion is', he wrote George Sand, 'that the whole Commune ought to have been sent to the galleys, that those sanguinary idiots ought to have been made to clean up the ruins of Paris, with chains around their necks like convicts. That would have wounded *humanity*, though. They treat the mad dogs with tenderness, but not the people whom they have bitten.' He raises his old cry for 'justice'. Universal suffrage, that 'disgrace to the human spirit', must first of all be done away with; but among the elements of civilization which must be given their due importance he now includes 'race and even money' along with 'intelligence' and 'education'.

For the rest, certain political ideas emerge—though, as usual, in a state of confusion.

The mass, the majority, are always idiotic. I haven't got many convictions, but that one I hold very strongly. Yet the mass must be respected, no matter how inept it is, because it contains the germs of an incalculable fecundity. Give it liberty, but not power. I don't believe in class distinctions any more than you do. The castes belong to the domain of archeology. But I do believe that the poor hate the rich and that the rich are afraid of the poor. That will go on forever. It is quite useless to preach the gospel of love to either. The most urgent need is to educate the rich, who are, after all, the strongest.

. . . . .

The only reasonable thing to do—I always come back to that—is a government of mandarins, provided that the mandarins know something and even that they know a great deal. The people is an eternal minor, and it will always (in the hierarchy of social elements) occupy the bottom place, because it is unlimited number, mass. It gets us nowhere to have large numbers of peasants learn to read and no longer listen to their priest; but it is infinitely important that there should be a great many men like Renan and Littré who can live and be listened to. Our salvation now is in a *legitimate aristocracy*, by which I mean a majority which will be made up of something other than numerals.

Renan himself and Taine were having recourse to similar ideas of the salvation of society through an 'élite'. In Flaubert's case, it never seems to have occurred to him that his hierarchy of mandarins and his project for educating the rich were identical with the notions of Saint-Simon, which he had rejected with scorn years before on the ground that they were too authoritarian. The Commune has stimulated in Flaubert a demand for his own kind of despotism.

He had already written in 1869:

It's no longer a question of imagining the best form of government possible, because they are all alike, but of making sure that science prevails. That is the most urgent problem. Everything else will inevitably follow. The purely intellectual type of man has done more for the human race than all the Saint Vincent de Pauls in the world! And politics will remain idiotic forever so long as it does not derive from science. The government of a country ought to be a department of the Institute, and the least important of all.

'Politics', he reiterated in 1871, 'must become a positive science, as war has already become'; and, 'The French Revolution must cease to be a dogma and become part of the domain of science, like all the rest of human affairs'. Marx and Engels were not reasoning otherwise; but they believed, as Flaubert could not do, in a coming-of-age of the proletariat which would make possible the application of social science. To Flaubert the proletariat made a certain pathetic appeal, but it seemed to him much too stupid to act effectively in its own behalf; the Commune threw him into such a panic that he reviled the Communards as criminals and brutes. At one moment he writes to George Sand: 'The International may end by winning out, but not in the way that it hopes, not in the way that people are afraid of'; and then, two days later, 'the International will collapse, because it is on the wrong path. No ideas, nothing but envy!'

Finally, he wrote her in 1875:

The words 'religion' or 'Catholicism,' on the one hand, 'progress,' 'fraternity,' 'democracy,' on the other, no longer answer the spiritual needs of the day. The dogma of equality—a new thing—which the radicals have been crying up, has been proved false by the experiments of physiology and by history. I do not at the present time see any way of setting up a new principle, any more than of still respecting the old ones. So I search unsuccessfully for the central idea from which all the rest ought to depend.

In the meantime, his work becomes more misanthropic. 'Never, my dear old chap,' he had written Ernest Feydeau, 'have I felt so colossal a disgust for mankind. I'd like to drown the human race under my vomit.' His political comedy, *Le Candidat*, produced in 1874, is the only one of his works which does not include a single character for whom one can feel any sympathy. The rich parvenu who is running for deputy not only degrades himself by every form of truckling and trimming in order to win the election, but sacrifices his daughter's happiness and allows himself to be cuckolded by his wife. The audiences would not have it; the actor who played the candidate came off the stage in tears. And, reading the play today, one cannot but agree with the public. It has some amusing and mordant passages, but one's gorge rises against it.

Flaubert then embarked on *Bouvard et Pécuchet*, which occupied him—with only one period of relief, when he indulged his suppressed kindliness and idealism in the relatively human *Trois Contes*—for most of the rest of his life. Here two copyists retire from their profession and set out to cultivate the arts and sciences. They make a mess of them all. The book contains an even more withering version of the events of 1848, in which the actors and their political attitudes are reduced to the scale of performing fleas. (There is one bitter scene, however, which has a terrible human force: that in which, the revolution having failed and the reaction having entrusted to the clergy the supervision of public education, the village priest visits the village school-master, a freethinker who has been on the revolutionary side, and compels him, by threatening to dismiss him from the job which he needs to support his children, to consent to betray his principles by teaching catechism and sacred history.) When Bouvard and Pécuchet find at last that everything has 'cracked in their hands', they go back to copying again. Flaubert did not live to finish the book; but he had already compiled some of the materials which he had intended to use in the second part: a collection of ridiculous statements and idiotic sentiments that Bouvard and Pécuchet were to find in the works they should copy.

This last uncompleted novel has somewhat mystified those critics who have taken it for an attack on the bourgeois like *L'Éducation sentimentale*—though there would not have been much point in Flaubert's simply doing the same thing again in a smaller and drier way. But M. René Dumesnil, one of the principal authorities on Flaubert, believes that *Bouvard et Pécuchet* was to have had a larger application. The anthology of 'idées reçues' was to have been not merely a credo of the bourgeois: it was to have included, also, many lapses by distinguished men of the past as well as the present, of writers, in certain cases, whom Flaubert immensely admired, and some passages, even, from Flaubert himself (in the first part of the book, it is obvious that the author is caricaturing his own ideas along with those of everybody else). Bouvard and Pécuchet, having realized the stupidity of their neighbours and discovered their own limitations, were to be left with a profound impression of the general imbecility and ignorance. They were themselves to assemble this monument to the inanity of the human mind.

If this be true—and the papers left by Flaubert seem to make his intention clear—he had lifted the blame from a social class and for the first time written a work of the type of *Gulliver's Travels*: a satire on the human race. The bourgeois has ceased to preach to the bourgeois: as the first big cracks begin to show in the structure of the nineteenth century, he shifts his complaint to the incompetence of humanity, for he is unable to believe in, or even to conceive, any non-bourgeois way out.

HORACE GREGORY

1898–

POET WITHOUT CRITICS: A NOTE ON ROBINSON JEFFERS

New World Writing, April 1955

I

A T the moment there are good reasons for rereading the poetry of Robinson Jeffers. First of all, the poet himself is a singular figure in American letters and he occupies the rare position in this country of being a 'poet' in the European sense of the word. He insists upon holding to a world view as well as his own handful of currently unpopular opinions. He has become a master of a style without nervous reference to recent fashions in literary criticism. 'I can tell lies in prose', he once wrote, which means that his primary concern is with the statement of a few essential poetic truths. Today it is obvious that he is willing to leave a final judgement of what he has written to the decision of posterity.

To reread him is to step aside from the classroom discussions and shop-talk of poetry that flood the rear sections of literary quarterlies where his name is seldom mentioned at all. He is well removed from the kind of company where poetry is 'taught' so as to be understood, where critics and reviewers are known to be instructors of literature in colleges and universities. But he is also at some distance from the time when his Californian narratives in verse, 'Roan Stallion' and 'Tamar', swept through the furnished rooms and studios of Greenwich Village with the force of an unpredicted hurricane. That was thirty years ago. Today as Jeffers is reread there is no danger of being smothered by the heavily breathing presence of a deep-throated, bare-thighed-and-breasted Jeffers–D. H. Lawrence cult, which had read Freud not wisely but with artless ardour and spent vacations in New Mexico.

Writers like Lawrence and Jeffers, who are worshipped by cults, frequently inspire the more violent forms of academic snobbery. Neither came from the 'right' prep school, college, or university; neither Oxford nor Cambridge could claim Lawrence, nor could the Ivy League universities and colleges in the United States gather their share of glory from Jeffers's reputation. Both Lawrence and Jeffers have outlived their cults; and Lawrence, safely dead and of British origin, no longer irritates the thin, tightly stretched surfaces of academic temper in the United States. This phenomenon, which is not without its trace of envy, partly explains the neglect, in quarterly reviews, of Jeffers's later writings. It can be said that in recent years Jeffers has been a poet without critics, but this does not mean that his name is forgotten, his books unread, or his plays in verse neglected on the stage. A few years ago his *Medea* had a respectable run on Broadway, and last summer an off-Broadway theatre in New York found audience for his new play, *The Cretan Woman*.

The initial advantage of rereading Jeffers's poetry now is that it can be approached without the formulas of critical fashions ringing in one's ears. Since 1925 he has published more than fifteen books of verse—a quantity of poetry which resembles the production of his ancestors, the romantic poets of nineteenth-century Britain. Rereading his poems, one finds them falling into three divisions: the South-western narratives with their richness of California sea-sky-and-landscape; the shorter poems which are largely conversation pieces—for Jeffers is not a lyric poet—and a fine group of elegies, his 'Descent to the Dead', the result of a visit in 1929 to the British Isles; and the semidramatic poems inspired by Greek themes and overlaid with Nietzschean and twentieth-century philosophies.

II

It is best to begin when and where Jeffers's earlier reputation began: the time was 1925 and the place was New York; and credit for the publication of *Roan Stallion, Tamar, and Other Poems* should be given to James Rorty, a writer, who met Jeffers during a stay in California and with selfless enthusiasm persuaded New York friends to read 'Tamar', to write about it, to make the presence of Jeffers known to New York publishers. Although Jeffers never shared the excitements and diversions of literary circles on the Atlantic Coast, the moment was prepared to receive his semi-Biblical, semi-Sophoclean American South-western narratives. Discussions of Steinach operations for restoring sexual vitality were in the air, and so were quotations from Krafft-Ebing, Freud, and Jung; D. H. Lawrence's *The Rainbow* was in print as well as Sherwood Anderson's *Dark Laughter*. If a post World War I urban generation had not discovered sex, it had learned to talk loudly and almost endlessly about it. Nothing was easier than to apply cocktail party conversations to Jeffers's 'Tamar' and 'Roan Stallion', which at first reading—and particularly to those who lived in cities—held the same attractions as an invitation to a nudist colony on the Pacific Coast.

Yet it was not without self-critical discernment that Jeffers gave first place to 'Tamar' when he prepared his *Selected Poetry* in 1937. For whatever reasons his public had accepted it twelve years earlier, at a time when he had passed the age of thirty-five, the poem has all the merits of a style that he had made his own. As early as 1912 he had paid for the printing of a first book, *Flagons and Apples*; in 1916 a second book, *Californians*, had been published by Macmillan; and neither, aside from the praise of a small group of friends, had received encouragement. His friendships, which included the long-sustained devotion of his wife, Una Call, also embraced the goodwill of George Sterling, who had known Ambrose Bierce, Joaquin Miller, and Jack London, and who was one of the few to see promise in Jeffers's early books of poems. Like Jeffers, who had been born in Pittsburgh in 1887, Sterling, a native of New York State, had become a converted Californian. Sterling's own verse had been inspired by the pages of

The Savoy and *The Yellow Book* as well as by readings
in Oscar Wilde and Ernest Dowson. 'Poetry . . .', he
said, 'must . . . cherish all the past embodiments of
visionary beauty, such as the beings of classical mythology.' Sterling's last work was a pamphlet written in
praise of Jeffers shortly before his suicide in 1926. No
doubt Jeffers had been made aware of the presence of
evil through his wide readings, but it was through the
loyal patronage of Sterling that he became an heir of
'Bitter' Bierce. To the general reader, however, Jeffers's
first two books offered little more than glimpses of a
belated debt to Dante Gabriel Rossetti in *Flagons and
Apples*, and a Wordsworthian manner, which included
hints of pantheism, in *Californians*.

Before Jeffers met his wife and Sterling, he had had an
unusual education. He was the precocious son of a
teacher of theology at Western Theological Seminary
in Pittsburgh. His father taught him Greek, Latin, and
Hebrew; and when the boy was five and six, took him
on trips to Europe. For three years, between the ages of
twelve and fifteen, his father sent him to boarding
schools in Switzerland and Germany; and at fifteen
Jeffers entered the University of Western Pennsylvania.
The next four years were spent at Occidental College
and the Universities of Zurich and Southern California,
and these years included studies in medicine and forestry.
All this would be of no importance if it did not throw
light on the individual ranges of Jeffers's poetry, his
familiarity with Greek and Roman and Biblical themes,
with German philosophy, with medical terms and
semi-scientific details, and—since he read French with
facility—his possible knowledge of the writings of Sade.
Certainly his education[1] provided reasons for an affinity

_____
[1] Jeffers's education was of a kind familiar to well-to-do
European gentry of the nineteenth century, but considerably

with Sterling, whose idea of poetry embraced, however vaguely, 'beings of classical mythology'. At the very least, Jeffers is a writer whose early years had prepared him for more than a regional view of the world and its affairs.

A second reading of 'Tamar' reveals it as a Biblical story in Californian undress. Characters in Jeffers's South-western narratives, from 'Tamar' to 'The Loving Shepherdess', from 'Give Your Heart to the Hawks' to 'Hungerfield,' are often lightly clothed and are subject to the wind, sun, and rain of Californian climate. Chapter 13 of the second book of Samuel is one source of Jeffers's parable,[1] which contains the story of Amnon's love for his sister Tamar. Other associations taken from the two books of Samuel permeate the poem, for the sons of Samuel 'walked not in his ways, but turned aside after lucre and took bribes, and perverted judgment', a statement which is appropriate to Jeffers's view of America and Western civilization. As a parable the poem acquires the force of a Calvinist sermon spoken from an American pulpit, yet it also carries within it echoes of Nietzsche's speech of Silenus, 'What is best of all is beyond your reach forever: not to be born, not to *be*, to be *nothing*', and behind these words Sophocles' remark, 'Not to be born is best for man.' In Tamar's words the echoes are clearly heard: 'O God, I wish /I too

less so to young Americans of the same period. Exceptions in the United States were Henry James's early travels with his father, and the continued educations after college of Longfellow, Trumbull Stickney, George Cabot Lodge, and Henry Adams. Jeffers's development as a narrative poet also follows the precedent of many major nineteenth-century poets; Jeffers and his writings are 'in the tradition'.

[1] For biographical information concerning Jeffers, as well as the fact that one of the sources of 'Tamar' may be found in the second book of Samuel, I am indebted to Lawrence Clark Powell's *Robinson Jeffers: The Man and His Work*.

had been born too soon and died with the eyes un-opened. . . .' Jeffers also puts into the mouth of Tamar a remark which has its origins in the doctrines of Sade 'we must keep sin pure / Or it will poison us, the grain of goodness in a sin is poison. / Old man, you have no conception / Of the freedom of purity.' And as Tamar speaks she has given herself over to unchecked forces of evil. In Sade's novel *Justine*, his heroine is tortured because she fails to purge her taint of goodness; as the poem nears its end, the whipping of Tamar by her brother is the last love scene between them.

This is not to say that Jeffers by voicing echoes of Sade's doctrines had advanced them as examples for Californians to follow; it is rather that he has given the forces of evil a well-established voice of authority, but in doing so he has succeeded with such vehemence that he might be misunderstood by a careless reader. Even at this risk, he has also succeeded in giving the unleashed forces of hell refreshed reality. In his poem, the house of David, Tamar's father—and Tamar is the daughter of King David in the second book of Samuel—is destroyed by fire which in its first association creates a literal image of hell and, in its second, of the funeral pyres of the Romans.

So far I have mentioned only the principal elements of 'Tamar', its Californian setting, one of the sources of its story, and a few of the concepts which are made relevant to the retelling of the story—but these do not complete the list of associations that the poem brings to mind, for 'Tamar', beneath the surface of a swiftly moving plot, has a richness of detail which rivals the complex fabric of Elizabethan dramatic verse. In the Biblical story the seduction of Tamar by Amnon is scarcely more than an invitation to come to bed; in Jeffers's version the seduction scene has an Ovidian ring;

a hidden stream, a pool tempts brother and sister; naked, they enter it and one recalls Ovid's stories of Narcissus and Echo, Hermaphroditus and Salmacis, and by association there is a particularly Roman touch, a glimpse of Phoebus' chariot wheel, from a window of David's house overlooking the Pacific:

> It was twilight in the
> room, the shiny side of the wheel
> Dipping toward Asia; and the year dipping toward win-
> ter en-
> crimsoned the grave spokes of sundown. . . .

It is this kind of richness that places 'Tamar' among the major accomplishments in twentieth-century poetry. And what of the ghosts that haunt the house of David in Tamar? They are very like the images of guilt that invade the darkened walls of Macbeth's castle. An idiot sets fire to David's house, and one thinks of the line '. . . a tale told by an idiot, full of sound and fury'. In this instance, an idiot hastens the end of sound and fury.

How deliberate Jeffers was in making a highly individual combination of California locale, Biblical and Graeco-Roman themes, Elizabethan richness of detail, plus Nietzschean ethics and Calvinist denouements,

---

¹ In Jeffers's short poem, 'Self-Criticism in February', there are the following lines which describe the nature of his ghosts, his romanticism, his unchurched belief in God:

It is certain you have loved the beauty of storm disproportionately.
But the present time is not pastoral, but founded
On violence, pointed for more massive violence: perhaps it is
Perversity but need that perceives the storm-beauty.   [not
Well, bite on this: your poems are too full of ghosts and demons,
And people like phantoms—how often life's are—
.   .   .   .   .   .
        you have never mistaken
Demon nor passion nor idealism for the real God.
Then what is most disliked in those verses
Remains most true.

it is impossible to say. The great probability is that, having a deeply felt desire to warn the world of the dangers of its involvements in world wars, Jeffers brought all the resources, conscious or hidden, of his imagination into play. To Jeffers, World War I was a warning of weaknesses inherent in a civilization that permitted mass murders and a situation that approached total war. War, by example, creates a precedent for violent action; and in 'Tamar' that conclusion is shown by the desire of Tamar's brother to leave his father's house to go to war, not merely to escape the consequences of evil at home, but to plunge himself into mass scenes of destruction. Private violence and public warfare are mutually influential—and the essential sin was not to walk in the ways of Samuel.

Whatever else may be said of Jeffers's beliefs and opinions as they appear with marked consistency throughout the various poems he has written, he has gone to war in the cause of peace; and it should also be said that Jeffers's emotional fervour, his honesty, and his lack of personal vanity strongly resemble the evangelical passion of his Protestant heritage: his image of Christ is always divine. His poem to America, his 'Shine, Perishing Republic', has that fervour, its eloquence, its nobility, its protest against earthly tyrants:

And boys, be in nothing so moderate as in love of man, a
    clever servant, insufferable master.
There is in the trap that catches noblest spirits, that caught
    —they say—God, when he walked on earth.

But before one reconsiders the merits of Jeffers's best writings, one should spare breath for certain of their failures, for Jeffers is a poet of large flaws and no weaknesses—and the flaws are often easier to see than his larger merits. In the great army of characters that his

poems present to us, one has yet to discover a wholly
admirable or completely rounded human being—the
nearest approach, and her virtue is one of courage, is the
heroine of 'Give Your Heart to the Hawks', a woman
who attempts to save her husband from suicide and
fails. An impatient reader of Jeffers, overwhelmed, yet
half attracted, and then repelled by the scenes of overt
Lesbianism in 'The Women at Point Sur' and by the
sight of a mother offering herself, half naked, to her
son in 'Such Counsels you Gave to Me', would conclude
that the poet kept bad company and was himself
'immoral'. The same reader would also find difficulties
in fully accepting Jeffers's beautiful pastoral, 'The Loving
Shepherdess', which may have been written with a
memory of the Elizabethan John Fletcher's *The Faithful
Shepherdess* in mind.[1] The witless little shepherdess,
dressed in the fewest of rags, is open to all men, young
and old; and it is as though she had obeyed Sade's
instructions to little girls. Whenever in Jeffers's poetry
one finds a possible echo of Sade's doctrines, the mind,
if not the blood, runs cooler. Even Robespierre and
Bonaparte, worldly men enough at the sight of blood,
and who welcomed Sade as a forthright critic of elder
institutions, were shocked and grew chilled when they
read Sade's manifestoes in the cause of sexual freedom;
they were not prudes, but they concluded that Sade's
remarks were too much of a good thing. And truly
enough Sade implied too much deliberation in the
pursuits of his particular happiness; his logic created a

[1] This supposition is not so fantastic as it may seem: John
Fletcher's lyrical *The Faithful Shepherdess* was far too static in
its movement to be a successful play; it is, however, an excellent
poem. Its plot closely resembles Jeffers's poem with this
difference: Fletcher's shepherdess is deceived into being promiscuous through magic worked by a sullen shepherd and she
is at last rescued and absolved by a river god.

law for sexual lawlessness that all institutions, ancient or modern, have been forced to reject. Jeffers's desire to deal solely with elemental passions tends to mislead the reader into the colder regions of hell which are a paradox of romantic agony: the reader is repelled.[1]

Another reader, equally impatient, finds something ridiculous in Jeffers's scenes of sexual violence; since no comic relief is given to the reader in Jeffers's Californian narratives, the reader is forced to supply that missing element in the progress of the story—and sex viewed from a point outside the scene itself always has a touch of the ridiculous in it; if it did not there would be no moments of relaxation in the stories that used to be told in smoking cars. It is almost gratuitous to say that Jeffers's characters lack humour, which is a flaw that Jeffers shares with Wordsworth; and in the progress of his more violent scenes of action, a need is felt for a drunken porter to cross the stage as in *Macbeth*. This does not mean, however, that Jeffers lacks ability to write of drunkenness; few scenes in contemporary fiction can equal the vividness of the drunken party which is prelude to the story of 'Give Your Heart to the Hawks'; in poetry, and in its own grim fashion, its veracity equals the mild, half-melancholy scene of E. A. Robinson's 'Mr. Flood's Party'. (Robinson, by the way, is one of the few elder American poets for whom Jeffers has expressed firm admiration.) 'Such Counsels You Gave to Me' must be counted as one of Jeffers's more conspicuous failures: the bare bones of the 'Oedipus

---

[1] In a footnote to the pamphlet called 'Frenchmen! A further effort is needed if you would be republicans!' in his *La Philosophie dans le Boudoir* (1795), Sade wrote: 'The first stirring of desire that a girl feels is the moment that Nature means her to prostitute herself, and with no other consideration in mind, she should obey Nature's voice; she outrages Her laws if she resists them.'

complex' shine too brightly through it. As the story opens one knows only too well that the weak son is fated to poison his red-faced, hard-drinking father; since 1900 this situation has been the stock property of countless novels and plays: a sinister yet charming hero-villain disposes of a father who is overweight or a rich aunt who spikes her tea with whiskey. But in Jeffers's case these flaws are not those of a small-minded writer or a minor poet.

III

Jeffers's merits as a poet are less well known than the flaws which I have just enumerated. From 'Roan Stallion' and 'Tamar' onward, Jeffers's technical contribution to twentieth-century poetry has been the mastery of alternate ten and five stress lines in narrative verse; in some of his shorter poems and in passages of some of his dramatic sequences, he employs a five and three stress variation of his narrative line. In this particular art no living poet has equalled him, and no other poet in America, from Philip Freneau to E. A. Robinson, has developed a narrative style of greater force, brilliance, and variety than his. While reading one of Jeffers's poems one never falls asleep; although there are times when his moral fervour is overweighted and has results which seem far from his stated intentions, he has never committed the greatest of all literary crimes—dullness. Among his shorter poems, his conversation pieces have contained prophecies which at the moment of publication seemed wrongheaded, probably mad, or wilfully truculent. Time has proved Jeffers right more frequently than his adverse readers had thought possible; although the poem is too long for quotation here, the thoughtful reader cannot fail to be impressed by his 'Woodrow Wilson (February, 1924)' today. Wilson, the nearly

tragic American hero, has been and still is the most
difficult of all public figures to write about, yet Jeffers
has succeeded in doing so. The poem's last lines, words
spoken as if from Wilson's lips, indicate, however
briefly, the nature of Wilson's failure:

'This is my last
Worst pain, the bitter enlightenment that buys peace.'

Jeffers's opinions (which are less political than coloured
by his hatred of war, his adaptation of Nietzschean
ethics, and nonchurchgoing Christianity) occasioned his
publishers, in a recent book of his poems, *The Double
Axe*, to disclaim responsibility for them. Jeffers had
strange things to say of World War II and its aftermath,
which he had predicted long before they arrived; he was
much too familiar with the scene to be tactful; in another
ten years he will probably be found less far from the
truth than the majority of his contemporaries. There has
been considerable misunderstanding of Jeffers's portrait
of Hitler which he included in *Be Angry at the Sun* in
1941; his Hitler was a figure not unlike Macbeth, a
Macbeth who had also become the hero of a Wagnerian
opera; his doom was accurately foretold; yet at the time
Jeffers's poem appeared, many thought that Jeffers had
praised Hitler, or at least had made him seem too powerful. There is less doubt today that Jeffers's portrait needs
no retouching to give it greater veracity.

Of the shorter poems, his volume *Descent to the Dead*
is among his masterpieces; it includes his lines on
'Shakespeare's Grave', 'In the Hill at New Grange',
'Ghosts in England', 'Iona: The Graves of the Kings'—
all memorable poems. It is impossible for an anthologist
to make a neat selection of Jeffers's poems and then
bind them shrewdly between the poems written by his
contemporaries. It so happens that Jeffers has never

written an 'anthology poem';[1] he is best represented by
his *Selected Poetry* which shows the range of his narratives tempered by his elegies, self-critical comments, and
occasional observations; many of them may be read as
footnotes to his longer poems. Selections of his shorter
poems by anthologists distort the essential qualities of
his poetry.

A few quotations from Jeffers's shorter poems do
show, however, how he has shocked people of rigidly
fixed political opinions; from 'Blind Horses' one may
take the lines:

Lenin has served the revolution,
Stalin presently begins to betray it. Why? For the sake of
    power, the Party's power, the state's
Power, armed power, Stalin's power, Caesarean power.

And these were printed in 1937 when many people
throughout Europe and some in the United States
thought differently or would have feared to make their
opinions known at all. And from 'Thebaid' the observation:

How many turn back toward dreams and magic, how
    many children
Run home to Mother Church, Father State.

This is a statement which, like other elements in
Jeffers's poetry, many may find easy to read but difficult to take; and yet it defines with Jeffers's insight and

---

[1] The perfect 'anthology poem' is a showpiece of which
Poe's 'The Raven' and Tennyson's 'May Queen' and 'Crossing
the Bar' were valiant examples; many minor poets seem to
write for anthologies alone; and indeed, some poets like A. E.
Housman are at their best when a small selection of their
poems are reprinted in anthologies. With more wit and,
incidentally, more truth than tact, Laura Riding and Robert
Graves reviewed the practice of editing anthologies in their
book, *A Pamphlet Against Anthologies.*

discernment a symptom of the times through which
he has lived. Of the same temper are these lines from
'Ave Caesar':

We are easy to manage, a gregarious people,
Full of sentiment, clever at mechanics, and we love our
    luxuries.

Something of the force of Jeffers's sense of the past
may be glimpsed at in these lines from 'Ghosts in
England':

                                    There was also a
    ghost of a king, his cheeks hollow as the brows
Of an old horse, was paddling his hands in the reeds of
    Dozmare
Pool, in the shallow, in the rainy twilight,
Feeling for the hilt of a ruinous and rusted sword. But
    they said
'Be patient a little, you king of shadows,
But only wait, they will waste like snow.' Then Arthur left
    hunting for the lost sword, he grinned and stood up
Gaunt as a wolf; but soon resumed the old labour, shaking the
    reeds with his hands.

It is scarcely necessary to add that this image of King
Arthur searching for Excalibur and his early moment of
glory has the character of major verse. And the style in
which it is written also reveals Jeffers's interlinear art of
writing verse.

IV

Jeffers's success in reviving Greek themes through
Nietzschean and even Wagnerian interpretation has also
been a source of annoyance to those who hope to read
their classics in 'pure' translations. The 'pure' translation
of Graeco-Roman classics does not and cannot exist in
English; and it is a truism that absolute translations of

poetry from one language into another cannot be made. The best that can be hoped for is that the translator has a more than literal understanding of the poetry he translates and that he has the genius to convert his original sources into poetry in English. Jeffers's re-creations of ancient stories, particularly the plays of Euripides into English dramatic verse, have never pretended to be more than adaptations of situations, scenes, and characters. Actually, his performances are as far removed from their original sources as Shakespeare's adaptations from Plutarch's *Lives* in *Julius Caesar* and *Antony and Cleopatra*, as far as Jeffers's 'Tamar' is from the second book of Samuel in the Old Testament. In his own way he has applied to ancient writings Ezra Pound's rule, 'make it new'. Like W. B. Yeats, Jeffers was not 'a born dramatist'; as Yeats was essentially a lyric poet, so Jeffers has been a distinguished writer of contemplative and narrative verse. As Yeats's adaptation of *Oedipus at Colonus* reflects Irish seascape in a Dublin accent, so Jeffers's adaptations from the Greek are never far from the climate of the California Pacific coast.

If Jeffers, even more than Yeats, is not a professional dramatist and is far removed from those who can be called 'men of the theatre', there are times when his poetry reaches high levels of dramatic power. This has long been evident in his variation of the Orestes cycle in 'The Tower Beyond Tragedy'; and its concluding statement of how Orestes 'climbed the tower beyond time, consciously, and cast humanity, entered the earlier fountain' (walked then, as Nietzsche would say, beyond good and evil) places the poem among the major accomplishments of our time. The same power enters his poem 'At the Fall of an Age', with its story of the death of Helen on the island of Rhodes where she was worshipped as a tree-goddess, twenty years after the fall of

Troy. The two speeches of Achilles' Myrmidons, risen
from the dead, have all the accents of living yet timeless
verse; the second speech runs as follows:

Is there any stir in the house?
Listen: or a cry?
Farm-boys with spears, you sparrows
Playing hawk, be silent.
Splendid was life
In the time of the heroes, the sun went helmeted, the
  moon was maiden,
When glory gathered on Troy, the picketed horses
Neighed in the morning, and long live ships
Ran on the wave like eagle-shadows on the slopes of
  mountains.
Then men were equal to things, the earth was beautiful,
  the crests of heroes
Waved as tall as the trees.
Now all is decayed, all corrupted, all gone down.
Men move like mice under the shadows of trees,
And the shadows of the tall dead.
The brightness of fire is dulled,
The heroes are gone.
In naked shame Agamemnon
Died of a woman.
The sun is crusted and the moon tarnished,
And Achilles has chosen peace.
Tell me, you island spearmen, you plowboy warriors,
Has anyone cried out in the dark door?
Not yet. The earth darkens.

There is nothing in poetry written during the
twentieth century that is quite like this speech; few poets
have written as well and the authority of the speech is
unmistakable. Jean Cocteau once wrote that a true
poet writes to be believed, not praised, and in these lines
Jeffers's art of persuading the reader is unquestionable.
Nor is he less convincing in the writing of Aphrodite's

speech in his recent play, *The Cretan Woman*, a play inspired by and not a translation of Euripides:

. . . So I have come down to this place,
And will work my will. I am not the least clever of the powers
  of heaven. . .
               I am the goddess
  the Greeks call Aphrodite; and the Romans will call me
  Venus; the Goddess of Love. I make the orchard-trees
Flower, and bear their sweet fruit. I make the joyful birds
  to mate in the branches. I make the man
Lean to the woman. I make the huge blue tides of the ocean
  follow the moon; I make the multitude
Of the stars in the sky to love each other, and love the earth.
  Without my saving power
They would fly apart into the horror of night. And even the
  atoms of things, the hot whirling atoms,
Would split apart: the whole world would burst apart into
  smoking dust, chaos and darkness; all life
Would gasp and perish. But love supports and preserves them:
  my saving power.

  This is my altar,
Where men worship me. Sometimes I grant the prayers of
  those that worship me: but those who reject me
I will certainly punish.

The quality of this speech equals the speeches in the plays of the Greek dramatists, but it is also singularly modern poetry; the quality of its language is direct and unstrained—no irrelevant effort at meaning is forced into it: the poetic nature of the speech is *there*, and for its purpose cannot be said in any other way; it is evidence enough of the genius of the man who wrote it. *The Cretan Woman* is a far more successful play to read than Jeffers's *Medea*; for his *Medea* opens with a flood of emotional speeches that cannot be sustained throughout the first act, therefore the play is top-heavy, and his readers as well as his audiences are likely to be exhausted long before the final curtain falls. Jeffers's version of Euripides' *Hippolytus* reserves its strength for the last scene and agony of Theseus; and at this conclusion, one believes that Jeffers has lost none of the mastery that he acquired thirty years ago, rather he has set himself the further task of transforming his narrative genius into writing verse for the stage, or perhaps television.

Robinson Jeffers's accomplishments and the modesty of his private life, now saddened by the recent death of his wife, should serve as an example to the present as well as the next generation of writers. Within the last thirty years he has made no compromise with the changing fashions of the day. For some readers Jeffers's attitude, which is not unlike the positions held by William Faulkner and W. B. Yeats, has always seemed too aristocratic. Even now I can hear someone saying, 'Jeffers loves nothing but rocks and stones; I love mankind.' But those who love abstract mankind too feverishly deny the rights of individual distinction and all the choices between men of good and bad, and by implication they also deny the right of the artist to be himself. Jeffers has re-established the position of the poet as one of singular dignity and courage. He is neither voiceless nor without his readers; and he is not without wisdom in seeming to await the verdict of posterity.

MALCOLM COWLEY

1898–

THOMAS WOLFE: THE PROFESSIONAL DEFORMATION

The Atlantic Monthly, December 1957

DURING his early days in New York, Wolfe used to write in bound ledgers opened on top of the icebox, so that he stood at his work like a factory hand. Later he wrote at a table, using ordinary sheets of manuscript paper, but more of them than anyone else with good eyesight, for ninety of his pencilled words filled a sheet. He wrote at top speed, never hesitating for a word, as though he were taking dictation. The moment a sheet was finished, he would push it aside without stopping to read it over or even to number it. In the course of filling thousands of sheets with millions of words, he developed a wart on the middle finger of his right hand 'almost as large and hard', he said in a letter, 'but not as valuable, as a gambler's diamond'.

He was not so much an author of books as a member of that much less familiar species, the writing man, *homo scribens*. His life was spent in conjugating a single verb in various tenses—*scribam, scripsi, scriptum est*—with the result that his working habits and problems are even more interesting to study than the works themselves. Indeed, they reveal the works in a rather unexpected light and help to explain why their real virtues were achieved at an inevitable cost to the writing man and his readers.

The first of his problems was how to maintain a steady flow of words from the vast reservoir of his conscious memories to the moving tip of his pencil. Before the flow could be established he would go through weeks or months of self-torture, walking the streets of Brooklyn at night, fleeing to Europe, staying drunk for days on end. Once the flow started, it might continue for months, during which his pencil sprayed out words like water from a hose. 'You forget to eat, to shave, to put on a clean shirt when you have one', says Wolfe's autobiographical hero George Webber in *You Can't Go Home Again*. 'You almost forget to sleep, and when you do try to you can't—because the avalanche has started and it keeps going night and day. . . You can't stop yourself—and even if you could you'd be afraid to because there'd be all that hell to go through getting started up again.'

Revision formed part of his system too, but not the usual sort of revision that consists in making inter-linear changes, then having the draft retyped. 'When he was dissatisfied with a scene or character', says his friend Edward C. Aswell, who had watched him working, '. . . he would put it aside, and rewrite it some different way from start to finish.' In other words, he had to start the flow over again and continue until he had reached the end of an episode. He would remember new details and incidents the second time, so that his rewritten manuscripts were longer—often several times longer—than the first drafts. After being copied by a typist, they were tied in a bundle and put away in the big pine packing box that stood in the middle of his parlour. Then, in the same frenzy of production, he might go to work on another episode, often one re-membered from a different period of his life.

His friends wondered how it was that he could reach into the packing box and, after a little fumbling, produce the desired episode, even if it had been written

months or years before. I think the answer must be that
he had his own filing system, chronological by subject-
matter. If the episode belonged to his boyhood, it would
go below the episodes relating to his studies at Harvard,
which in turn went below his years of teaching at
Washington Square College and his love affair with
Aileen Bernstein, which went below his struggles to
write a second novel. All were parts of 'the book' into
which he planned to transcribe all his life, his world and
time, in a continuous flow of memories. His ambition,
announced by George Webber, was 'To use myself to
the top of my bent. To use everything I have. To milk
the udder dry, squeeze out the last drop, until there is
nothing left.'

Unfortunately the book of his life was too big to
be published or even to be written. His memories would
have to be divided into separate books, or novels, and
each of these would have to be something more than a
chronological series of events; it would also have to
possess its own structure and controlling theme. That
was the problem of changing flow into form, which
always puzzled him and for which he found a solution
only in his first novel, as if without trying.

Look Homeward, Angel had a natural unity because,
as Wolfe said in a letter to Mrs. Margaret Roberts, his
English teacher in Asheville, it was 'the story of a
powerful creative element'—that is, Eugene Gant, or
the author as a boy—'trying to work its way toward an
essential isolation; a creative solitude; a secret life—its
fierce struggles to wall this part of its life away from birth,
first against the public and savage glare of an unbalanced,
nervous, brawling family group, later against school,
society, all the barbarous invasions of the world'. As always it was a book of memories, but they were shaped
and controlled by a theme close to the author's heart,

the familiar theme of the young artist in a hostile environment. It had a natural beginning, which was the artist's birth, and a natural end, which was his escape from the environment.

But what could he do after writing *Look Homeward, Angel*? 'I've got too much material', George Webber tells his friend Randy Shepperton. 'It keeps backing up on me . . . until sometimes I wonder what in the name of God I'm going to do with it—how I'm going to find a frame for it, a channel, a way to make it flow. . . Sometimes it actually occurs to me that a man may be able to write no more because he gets drowned in his own secretions.' Then after a pause George says, 'I'm looking for a way. I think it may be something like what people vaguely mean when they speak of fiction. A kind of legend, perhaps.'

In 1930, the year after the publication of *Look Homeward, Angel*, Wolfe was looking for a legend into which he could fit everything he had felt and seen after leaving Asheville. Since he was in Europe at the time, and since his strongest emotion, outside of the passionate desire to write another book, was longing for the home he had lost—irretrievably, so he thought, for Asheville people had threatened to lynch him if he came back—he fixed upon the Antaeus legend of the giant born from the marriage of earth and water. He gave the legend a special turn, however, to fit his circumstances. In a letter to Maxwell Perkins, his editor at Scribner's, he explained that the argument of the new book would be:

. . . of the Lybyan giant, the brother of Polyphemus, the one-eyed, and the son of Gaea and Poseidon, whom he hath never seen, and through his father, the grandson of Cronos and Rhea, whom he remembereth. He contendeth with all who seek to pass him by, he searcheth alway for

his father, he crieth out: 'Art thou my father? Is it thou?'
and he wrestleth with that man, and he riseth up from each
fall with strength redoubled, for his strength cometh up
out of the earth, which is his mother. Then cometh
against him Heracles, who contendeth with him, who
discovereth the secret of his strength, who lifteth him
from the earth whence his might ariseth, and subdueth
him. But from afar now, in his agony, he heareth the
sound of his father's foot: he will be saved for his father
cometh!

Of course the giant born of earth was Eugene Gant
again, or Wolfe in person. His brother Polyphemus was
intended to stand for the sterility that hates life; probably
he was to be represented by Francis Starwick, the homo-
sexual dramatist who appears in *Of Time and the River*.
Gaea or Earth was to be introduced in the same novel
as Mrs. Esther Jack, but the manuscript chapters about
her were omitted from the published book and filed
away; later they would figure in *The Web and the Rock*.
Heracles the antagonist was to be the city of New York.
As for the father, Wolfe's plan was that he should never
be seen. But in a final chapter called 'Pacific End'—
later Wolfe thought of it as a final complete book,
though he never got round to writing it—Antaeus was
to hear 'the thunder of horses on a beach (Poseidon and
his horses); the moon dives out of clouds; he sees a print
of a foot that can belong only to his father, since it is like
his own; the sea surges across the beach and erases the
print; he cries out "Father" and from the sea far out, and
faint upon the wind, a great voice answers "My Son!"'

It was a magnificent conception, if slightly over-
blown; the trouble was that Wolfe was psychologically
unable to carry it through. Like Eugene Gant he was
gripped by an obsessive desire to say everything, with
the result that 'all ordered plans, designs, coherent

projects for the work he had set out to do . . . were burned up in a quenchless passion, like a handful of dry straw'. Soon the Antaeus legend got mixed with others, and the hero—without ceasing to be Thomas Wolfe— was called upon to play the successive parts of Orestes, Faustus the student, Telemachus, Jason, and Faustus in love. The more he worked on the book, the farther he seemed from its 'Pacific End'. By the beginning of the fourth year after the publication of *Look Homeward, Angel*, he had written a million new words, on his own estimate, and the great conception was not so much burned up as buried like Herculaneum under a flow of lava. It was Perkins who saved him, by suggest- ing how he might make a novel out of one segment of the material, saving the rest for other books. Even then almost half the segment had to be pared away before *Of Time and the River* was published in 912 pages.

The plan he evolved for a third novel was less Wagnerian. As he described the book in a letter to Aswell, who had become his editor after Wolfe left Scribner's, 'It is about one man's discovery of life and the world, and in this sense it is a book of apprenticeship.' The hero's name would be changed from Eugene Gant to George Webber, and his height would shrink from six feet five to five feet nine; Wolfe was looking for a protagonist whose angle of vision didn't quite duplicate the author's, so that his world could be treated more objectively. Webber would be the eternal innocent on his painful way to knowledge—another Candide or Wilhelm Meister—and the lessons he learned in a suc- cession of adventures would be summed up in the title, *You Can't Go Home Again*.

It was a conception better suited to Wolfe's writing habits than that of his second novel had been, for it was loose enough so that one episode after another could be fitted into the scheme. But already, as he worked on it, the episodes had proliferated and some of them had grown almost to the length of separate books. His immense store of memories was imposing its pattern on the narrative, or its lack of pattern. The bandy-legged figure of George Webber was being presented less and less objectively until it became indistinguishable from the author's figure; George seemed to grow taller as one looked at him. By the spring of 1938 Wolfe had once again written more than a million words, which he turned over to Aswell before leaving for the West. Most of the words—too many of them—were published in three volumes after his death. No one can say how Wolfe himself would have finished the novel, or group of novels, or in how much time, or how and whether, if he had lived, he could have brought himself to relinquish all that private wealth of words.

But although he was incapable of solving the larger problem of form, he did solve a lesser problem in a way that is often overlooked. Wolfe's unit of construction was the episode, not the scene or chapter or novel. He always had trouble connecting the episodes, many of which were complete and strikingly effective in themselves. Two of the best are 'The Web of Earth' and 'A Portrait of Bascom Hawke', both of which were printed in *Scribner's Magazine*, although the 'Portrait' was afterward taken apart and fitted into *Of Time and the River*. Other fine episodes are the long passage about the death of Old Gant, written for inclusion in the same novel while Wolfe and Perkins were revising it; the account of the students in Professor Hatcher's (or Baker's) famous course in the drama; the disintegration of Francis Starwick; the story of Nebraska Crane (partly in *The Web and the Rock* and partly in *You Can't Go Home Again*); and the visit to Nazi Germany called 'I Have a Thing to

Tell You'. If these had been published separately, from the text of the original manuscripts—as *The Story of a Novel* was published—Wolfe might have gained a different reputation, not as an epic poet in prose, but as the author of short novels and portraits, little masterpieces of sympathy and penetration. But with his mania for bigness, one can't be sure that he would have enjoyed that other kind of fame.

Most of Wolfe's faults as a writer were closely and fraternally connected with his virtues; both resulted from his method of composition. Take for example the fault most frequently and justifiably urged against him: that he was unable to criticize his own work, that he couldn't distinguish what was good in it from what was absurd or pretentious, and that he wouldn't take criticism from others. Wolfe acknowledged the fault even when he was a very young man; at twenty-two he said in a letter to George Pierce Baker, 'I admit the virtue of being able to stand criticism. Unfortunately it is a virtue I do not happen to possess.' It wasn't that he was lacking either in humility or in critical talent. One couldn't talk with him about books for ten minutes without finding that he was perceptive and discriminating about other people's work, if he had read it. He didn't apply that sort of discrimination to his own work not through inability to do so, as he sometimes said, but chiefly as a matter of policy.

In a sense he chose to be only half of an author. The usual author is two persons or personalities working in partnership. One of them says the words to himself, then writes them down; the other listens to the words, or reads them, and then silently exclaims, 'This is good, this is what you wanted to say, but *this*! Can't you say it again and say it better?' A result of the dialogue between the writer and the reader within is that the usual manuscript moves ahead spasmodically—a sentence or two, a pause while another sentence is phrased and rejected and rephrased, then a rapidly written paragraph, then another pause while reader and writer argue silently (or even aloud) about what has been said, then the sound of a page crumpled and dropped into the waste-basket, then a day's interval, perhaps, then another page that goes better . . .

With time always pressing him, Wolfe couldn't afford to stumble ahead by a process of inner dialectic. There had to be that uninterrupted flow of memories from mind to paper; if he once questioned the value of the memories or changed the words that came to him, the flow halted for the day or night or perhaps for weeks. The solution he found instinctively, but later supported with arguments, was to suppress the critical side of his nature, or at least to keep it silent until an episode was finished; then if the inner critic objected to what he had written, he would do it over from the beginning, again without allowing the critic to interrupt. It was an effective system for producing words—very often accurate and truly inspired words—but it involved a great deal of wasted effort for the writer and wasted time for the reader of his published work.

Another fault urged against him is his use of formulas, including stock phrases, paired nouns or verbs where only one is needed ('grief and anguish', 'sneered at and derided'), as well as the inevitable and therefore useless epithet. Here again the fault results from his system of writing and is closely connected with virtues that it helped him to achieve. Wolfe composed his novels, or rather the episodes that went into his novels, much as ancient bards, standing before a company of warriors, composed their epic poems. Like them, if for different reasons, he had to maintain an unbroken flow of words, with the result that there had to be moments when his pencil moved automatically while his mind was preparing the next powerful effect.

I couldn't help thinking of Wolfe when reading a passage in Moses Finley's illuminating book, *The World of Odysseus*:

The repeated formula [Finley says] is indispensable in heroic poetry. The bard composes directly before his audience; he does not recite memorized lines. In 1934, at the request of Professor Milman Parry, a sixty-year-old Serbian bard who could neither read nor write recited for him a poem of the length of the *Odyssey*, making it up as he went along, yet retaining metre and form and building a complicated narrative. The performance took two weeks, with a week in between, the bard chanting for two hours each morning and two more in the afternoon. Such a feat makes enormous demands in concentration on both the bard and his audience. That it can be done at all is attributable to the fact that the poet, a professional with long years of apprenticeship behind him, has at his disposal the necessary raw materials: masses of incidents and masses of formulas, the accumulation of generations of minstrels who came before him.

Wolfe was perhaps the only American author of this century who could have duplicated the feat of the Serbian bard. That was because he had the same sort of equipment: partly an enormous store of characters and incidents (drawn from his own experience, not from the traditions of the race), and partly a supply of epithets, metaphors, and synonyms (remembered from his early reading) that could be applied to any human situation. His writing was a sort of chant, like the declamation of a Homeric bard.

Poetry of a traditional sort can be written faster than

prose, and Wolfe kept falling into traditional poetry.
His books, especially *Of Time and the River*, are full of
lines in Elizabethan blank verse:

> Were not their howls far broken by the wind?

> huge limbs that stiffly creak in the remote
> demented howlings of the burly wind,

> and something creaking in the wind at night.

Page after page falls into an iambic pattern, usually a
mixture of pentameters and hexameters. Other passages
—in fact there is a whole book of them called *A Stone, A
Leaf, A Door*, selected from Wolfe's writing by John
S. Barnes—are a rather simple kind of cadenced verse:

> Naked and alone we came into exile.
> In her dark womb
> We did not know our mother's face.

Often there are internal rhymes and half-rhymes:
'October is the season for *returning*: the bowels of youth
are *yearning* with lost love. Their mouths are *dry* and
bitter with *desire*: their hearts are *torn* with the *thorns* of
spring.' Again there are phrases almost meaningless in
themselves, but used as musical themes that are stated
and restated with variations, sometimes through a whole
novel. 'A stone, a leaf, a door' is one of the phrases;
others are 'O lost' and 'naked and alone', in *Look Homeward, Angel*, and 'of wandering forever and the earth
again', repeated perhaps a hundred times in *Of Time and
the River*. All these patterns or devices—cadence, metre,
rhyme, assonance, refrains—are those into which the
language naturally falls when one is trying to speak or
write it passionately and torrentially. They are not the
marks of good prose—on the contrary—and yet in
Wolfe's case, as in that of a few other natural writers,
they are the means of achieving some admirable effects,

including an epic movement with its surge and thunder. They also help Wolfe to strike and maintain a *tone*, one that gives his work a unity lacking in its structure, a declamatory tone that he needs for his effort to dignify a new race of heroes and demigods, to suffuse a new countryside with legend, and to bring new subjects into the charmed circle of those considered worthy to be treated in epic poems.

His persistent immaturity—still another fault that is often urged against him—was not so much a weakness of character as it was a feature of his literary policy. He had to play the part of an innocent in the great world. He had to have illusions, then lose them painfully, then replace them with others, because that repeated process was the story he wanted to tell. He had to be naïve about his emotions in order to feel them more intensely and in order to convey the impression—as he does in his best work—that something as commonplace as boarding a train or writing a book is being experienced not only for the first time in the author's life but for the first time in history. If he had learned from the experience of others, he would have destroyed that sense of uniqueness. If he had said to himself with the wisdom of middle age, 'There must be a catch somewhere', in his exultation, or, 'You'll feel better about it tomorrow', in his bottomless despair, he would have blunted the edge of both feelings and made them less usable as memories.

God said in the proverb, 'Take what you want and pay for it.' That might have been the motto and moral of Wolfe's collected works and of his private life as well. Determined as he was to find words for every experience, he denied himself many of the richest experiences because they might have interfered with his writing, or simply because he had no time for them. He never had a real home after he was seven years old; he never owned so much as a square foot of the earth he loved (even his grave is in a family plot); he never planted a tree or a garden, never married, never fathered a child. Much as he loved good company, he spent most of his time alone in dingy lodgings or roaming the streets at night. He played no games, took part in no sports, displayed no social accomplishments. Indeed, he had few amusements: eating and drinking were the first two, and afterward came travel, making love, and conversation, in about that order of importance. He didn't enjoy music, or much enjoy art (except the paintings of Breughel and Cranach); he stopped going to the theatre after his quarrel with Mrs. Bernstein; and though he liked to talk about books, I suspect that he did comparatively little reading after he left Harvard. His real avocation was the physical act of writing; his one preoccupation was preparing for the act. He said in a letter to Mrs. Roberts, written a few months before his death:

. . . there is no rest, once the worm gets in and begins to feed upon the heart—there can never after that be rest, forgetfulness, or quiet sleep again. . . After this happens, a man becomes a prisoner; there are times when he almost breaks free, but there is one link in the chain that always holds; there are times when he almost forgets, when he is with his friends, when he is reading a great book or poem, when he is at the theatre, or on a ship, or with a girl—but there is one tiny cell that still keeps working; even when he is asleep, one lamp that will not go out . . .

As far as I am concerned, there is no life without work —at least, looking back over my own, everything I can remember of any value is somehow tied up with work.

The price Wolfe paid in his life was not the price of his debauches, which were intense while they lasted, like all his other activities—once he landed in jail and another time in a German hospital with a broken head, richly deserved—but which were occasional or intermittent. He paid more for his one great virtue than for all his vices. He paid for his hours of steady writing, for his sleepless nights, for his efforts to remember and interpret everything that happened, to find a key to it all, to give form to his memories. The price was partly in terms of health, for he was drawing sight drafts against his constitution without stopping to ask whether there was still a credit balance. But there was also a price in mental health that most of his critics have been too considerate to mention, even long after his death. His alternating moods of exuberance and despair became more extreme; expecially the periods of despair were longer and deeper. Many physicians would say that in his last years he was a victim of manic-depressive psychosis.

He also developed paranoid symptoms, as manic-depressives often do. There were ideas of reference and delusions of persecution and grandeur. At times he thought the whole literary world was leagued in a conspiracy to keep him from working. 'As for that powerful and magnificent talent I had two years ago', he wrote to Perkins in January 1937, '—in the name of God is that to be lost entirely, destroyed under the repeated assaults and criminalities of this blackmail society under which we live? *Now* I know what happens to the artist in America.' His farewell letter to Perkins was a magnificent piece of sustained eloquence—130 of his manuscript pages—but in places it was a crazy man's letter. One fine sentence is often quoted: 'And I shall wreak out my vision of this life, this way, this world and this America, to the top of my bent, to the height of my ability, but with an unswerving devotion, integrity and purity of purpose that shall not be menaced, altered or weakened by any one.' But the following sentences, which reveal his state of mind, are usually slurred over:

I will go to jail because of this book if I have to. I will lose my friends because of it, if I will have to. I will be libeled, slandered, blackmailed, threatened, menaced, sneered at, derided and assailed by every parasite, every ape, every blackmailer, every scandalmonger, every little Saturday Reviewer of the venomous and corrupt respectabilities. I will be exiled from my country because of it, if I have to. . . But no matter what happens I am going to write this book.

That is impressive as eloquence, but not as a statement of the facts. Wolfe was planning to write a book that might have hurt a few persons, notably Mrs. Bernstein and some of the staff at Scribner's, but not so much as some of his neighbours in Asheville had been hurt by *Look Homeward, Angel*. Nobody was trying to keep him from writing it. For the author it would involve absolutely no danger of prison, blackmail, ostracism, or exile. 'I am a righteous man', he said in the letter, with an undertone of menace, 'and few people know it because there are few righteous people in the world.' There are many with delusions of righteousness, which they use as an excuse for being unjust to others. Wolfe was becoming one of them, as he must have realized in part of his mind—the Dr. Jekyll part, as he sometimes called it. At this point, as at some others, he was losing touch with reality.

It had better be made clear that his fits of despair were not the 'down' phase of a manic-depressive cycle. There was no loss of appetite or vigour, no moping in silence; on the contrary there were quarrels, broken furniture, and a torrent of spoken and written words. The fits did not recur at regular intervals and they were not induced by mere pretexts; on the contrary they had understandable causes, usually connected with his work. As Wolfe said to Alfred S. Dashiell of *Scribner's Magazine* in one of his many letters of apology:

> The effort of writing or creating something seems to start up a strange and bewildering conflict in the man who does it, and this conflict at times almost takes on physical proportions so that he feels he is struggling not only with his own work but also with the whole world around him, and he is so beset with demons, nightmares, delusions and bewilderments that he lashes out at everyone and everything, not only people he dislikes and mistrusts, but sorrowfully enough, even against the people that he knows in his heart are his friends.
>
> I cannot tell you how completely and deeply conscious I have been of this thing and how much bloody anguish I have sweat and suffered when I have exorcised these monstrous phantoms and seen clearly into what kind of folly and madness they have led me.

It had all started so boyishly and admirably with his gift for feeling joys and sorrows more deeply than others. He chose to cultivate the gift because it helped him in his writing, and gradually it had transformed his character. At first he was proud, if in a rather sheepish fashion, of sometimes losing control of himself. He wrote to his sister Mabel in May 1929: 'Don't be afraid of going crazy—I've been there several times and it's not at all bad.' It was indeed an almost normal state for a romantic artist forcing himself, provoking himself, beyond the natural limit of his emotions. Soon he began to feel the sort of dismay he expressed in the letter to Dashiell, but it was becoming too late to change his professional habits. There were always occasions in the literary life for those fits of manic exultation and, increasingly, of despair—the sense of loss on publishing a book, the insults of a few reviewers (notably Bernard

DeVoto), the strain of getting started again, the fatigue that followed months of steady writing, the disappointment when Perkins felt that his latest work wasn't quite his best, the injustice of a suit against him for libel—and all these hurts became more painful as he brooded over them in solitude or drank to forget them, until at last he couldn't help interpreting them as signs that his talent was threatened by a vast conspiracy. His psychosis, if we call it that, was not organic or toxic, nor was it functional in the usual sense of being an illness due to unsolved emotional conflicts. Like the oversized wart on the middle finger of his right hand, it was a scar he had earned in combat, a professional deformation.

AUSTIN WARREN

1899–

EMILY DICKINSON

Sewanee Review, Autumn 1957

I

THOMAS JOHNSON has produced what has long been desired—a carefully edited and annotated *complete* text of Emily Dickinson's poems.[1]

It fills three large volumes. The format seems, and is, incongruous with the nature of Emily's poems, so characteristically and richly short—and, as Johnson remarks, always in revision shortened, not lengthened.

This is not the edition in which to enjoy Emily. I

[1] *The Poems of Emily Dickinson. Including variant readings critically compared with all known manuscripts.* Edited by Thomas H. Johnson, The Belknap Press of Harvard University Press, 1955, 3 vols.

recall the pleasure of reading her in the slender grey volumes of the 1890's. For pleasure, as for edification, Emily should not be read in big tomes, or much of her at a time. Johnson prints 1775 poems. I felt the immediate need to reduce them to 300 or less. Many of her poems are exercises, or autobiographical notes, or letters in verse, or occasional verses. There are poems which are coy or cute; others which are romantically melodramatic.

But the business of the scholar is to publish all the 'literary remains', to establish a correct text, to elucidate obscure words or references—whenever possible, by the citation of apposite passages from his writer's other poems or prose (in Emily's case, there are her own brilliant letters); to make possible the study of a poet's development by fixing, with what precision may be possible, the dates of composition.

These tasks of an editor Johnson has carefully and satisfactorily fulfilled. To do them, it was necessary to have access to Emily Dickinson's original manuscripts—her pencilled jottings, her work-sheets and the little stitched books of 'packets' into which at intervals she collected her final or semi-final versions. These 'packet' versions provide—when, as for the vast majority of the poems, they are available—the authoritative text, that of the author's most considered judgement.

In the past, Emily Dickinson suffered from two sets of editors. Mrs. Todd could decipher Emily's handwriting; but she and Colonel Higginson, the minor poet and man of letters who became Emily's half-reluctant mentor, felt the need to amend so far as they could Emily's deviations from normal educated usage—her provincial words, her use of the subjunctive in subordinate clauses, her 'inaccurate' rhymes. Emily's niece, Mme Bianchi, less skilled at the handwriting, latterly difficult, was given to exploiting her aunt's strangeness. It used to be thought that Mme Bianchi, who so shrewdly 'discovered' further poems at marketable season, perhaps constructed some of the weaker ones; but this conjecture is tacitly refuted by a study of the originals.

In 'Notes on the Present Text', Johnson exhibits his fidelity to Emily's spelling (some of it, like 'Febuary', is notation of rural New England speech habits), her capitalization, and her punctuation. The latter are capricious. She inclines to capitalize nouns (after the fashion of Carlyle and the German language); her capitalization of adjectives cannot be reduced to principle. The dash is almost her exclusive mark of punctuation, exceeding much the latitude allowed to nineteenth-century women. It sometimes stands for the comma, sometimes indicates the pause of anticipation or suspense, sometimes might be described as equivalent to the phrasing marks of music. But categories do not suffice. Take no. 344, for example:

> 'Twas the old—road—through pain—
> That unfrequented—one—
> With many a turn—and thorn—
> That stops—at Heaven—
>
> This—was the Town—she passed—
> There—where she—rested—last—
> Then—stepped more fast—
> The little tracks—close prest——

The dashes before 'through pain', 'and thorn', 'at Heaven', and 'last' mark the pauses of suspense and anticipation. Those separating off 'That unfrequented one', an appositive, might, in current use, be commas or dashes. Those at the ends of lines 5 and 6 stand for commas or dashes. But what of the dashes separating 'old' and 'road', or 'unfrequented' and 'one', or 'This' and 'was', 'There' and 'where'? These seem designed to phrase: in the first two instances, indicating stress on both the adjective and the noun, in the last two, giving the stress of italics to 'This' and 'There'; probably the enclosure of 'rested' is also to ensure its being stressed. The dash in the eighth line seems intended to emphasize the seeming contradiction between 'little' and 'close prest'.

I analyse this specimen to show both the oddity of Emily's pointing and also the difficulty of repunctuating it in any fashion which does not constitute an interpretation. Johnson says, 'Quite properly such "punctuation" can be omitted in later editions, and the spelling and capitalization regularized, as surely she would have expected had the poems been published in her lifetime.' Editions for general reading should undoubtedly 'regularize'; but how to treat Emily's punctuation is the difficult point. Apart from her periods, the overall effect of the dashes is either to reproduce pauses in her own reading of the poems or to render the clauses and phrases a fluidity of transition lost by a rigid system. The best method I can propose is to omit—after the fashion of some contemporary poetry—all punctuation, or all save that of the period: a method which would not, in any case I can summon up, obscure the comprehension of her poetry.

The poems, through to no. 1648, are now presented in a chronological arrangement—the dating based partly on allusions to contemporary events, partly on the dates of letters in which they were enclosed, partly on the changes in Emily's handwriting (on which an 'expert' contributes a special essay), partly on the order of the 'packets' in which the final versions were placed, from the earliest packet, assembled in 1858, to the latest in 1872.

The packet poems constitute two-thirds of her poetry.

Nos. 1649–1775 Johnson does not attempt to date. These poems, for which no autograph copies exist, are printed from transcripts, chiefly those made by Emily's sister-in-law. Though properly put together, at the end of Vol. III, their authenticity can scarcely be doubted. They include a few of Emily Dickinson's snake poems and 'Elysium is as far as to / The very nearest Room.'

Long ago I worked out my own chart of Emily's poetic development, setting off as 'early' the conventional and sentimental pieces, and using as my tests for the mature poems the increasing substitution for rhyme of assonance and consonance and the increasing freshness and precision of language. I postulated a consistency of method: expected the poems systematically to grow more Dickinsonian. Having achieved her manner, her best style, she could not, I supposed, have turned back to styles not so definitely hers.

This theory was too neat. Emily did, to the end, 'look back'. Unlike Mozart and Beethoven and Hopkins and James, she had no 'late manner' so integrally held that she could not, in conscience, deviate therefrom.

This inconsistency was certainly helped by her ambiguous character of being a poet yet not a publishing poet. She never sharply differentiated between poetry and occasional verse and prose. The prose of her letters is so metonymic and metaphoric and cryptic as to be always the prose of a poet and thus to admit the intercalation of verse written as prose.

In 1860 Emily wrote 'If I shouldn't be alive / When the Robins come' with its admirable 'trying / With my Granite lip' and 'How many times these low feet staggered—/ Only the soldered mouth can tell'; but in the same year she wrote the sentimental piece with its bit of Scots—probably represented for her by Burns— 'Poor little Heart! / Did they forget thee? / Then dinna

care!' and the balladic repetition of 'That scalds me now
—that scalds me now' of no. 193. In 1861 she wrote
'There's a certain Slant of light' but also 'Why—do they
shut Me out of Heaven'—one of her 'little girl' pieces.
And in 'about 1865' she wrote the quatrain, of which I
italicize some words:

> To help our *Bleaker* Parts
> *Salubrious* Hours are given
> Which if they do not fit for Earth
> *Drill silently* for Heaven.—

She had written 'Arrange the Heart' and rejected it
for 'Drill silently'—an improvement both in sparing the
'Heart' and in giving the double-sensed *drill* (the martial
discipline; the carpenter's tool if not then the dentist's
also). Yet at the same time she wrote 'Let down the
Bars, Oh Death', a tritely sentimental sheep-and-
shepherd poem.

Emily added to her styles without subtracting; and in
maturity she wrote a new kind of poetry without
relinquishing the liberty of slipping back into her earlier
modes.

II

It used to be said of Emerson that his 'bad' rhymes were
due to a deficient ear—a theory once and for all dis-
proved by the publication, in the first volume of Rusk's
Letters, of the earliest poems of Emerson, written in
perfectly accurate heroic couplets. Even the early
Whitman could rhyme and metre acceptably. And
Emily's first known verses, written in the early 1850's,
demonstrate likewise that her subsequent deviation was
purposed. Her 'Valentine' poem faithfully rhymes
'swain' and 'twain', 'air' and 'fair'. But, having said that,
I have to add that none of them would have become

known as poets for these 'correct' productions. By intuition, and by relatively conscious theorizing, they had to create new kinds of poetry.

Like Whitman, Emily took off from Emerson, whose *Poems* and *Essays* she owned and knew; but Whitman took off from Emerson's theory of the poet and his rhetorical essays; Emily, from Emerson's own practice as a poet: his short-lined rhyming; his gnomic quatrains and gnomic short poems like 'Brahma'; his 'Hamatreya'.

This lineage from Emerson was blended with another lineage—that of the hymnal. Several times she quotes Isaac Watts's hymn beginning, 'There is a land of pure delight':

> Could we but climb where Moses stood
> And view the landscape o'er,
> Nor Jordan's stream, nor death's cold flood
> Should fright us from the shore;

and the stanza, with its alternating 4 and 3, remains one of her metrical favourites. She creates a counterpoint or descant on Watts, relaxing the rhyming of lines 1 and 3 and personalizing Watts's congregational pieces:

> 'Tis not the Dying hurts us so—
> 'Tis Living—hurts us more—
> But Dying—is a different way—
> A Kind behind the Door—

Short metre, long metre, common metre—the standard hymn stanzas—are her mould, not to break but to render pliant.

Emily's language is her own mixture of provincialisms, standard speech of her time, the concrete and the abstract, the words of young people and the theological words of orthodox preachers (e.g. infinite). Her use of language is almost unfailingly meditated and precise. Work-sheet drafts for a few of her poems provide the list of alternatives from which she chose. In the poem on the Bible (no. 1545), the epithet finally elected —'warbling'—was chosen out of these possible disyllables: 'typic, hearty, bonnie, breathless, spacious, tropic, warbling, ardent, friendly, magic, pungent, warbling, winning, mellow.' None of these disyllables seems inevitable; but 'warbling'—the unpremeditated singing of a bird or a rustic—seems the best candidate. Of a clergyman ('He preached upon "Breadth" till it argued him narrow') she asserts satirically that Jesus would not know how to 'meet so *enabled* a Man', choosing her epithet from a list which included 'learned, religious, accomplished, discerning, accoutred, established, conclusive'. Emily needs a trisyllabic word: but she certainly also distinguished it from 'able': to 'enable' is legally, as by authority, to make one what, by nature, he is *not*: it suggests the pretentiousness of borrowed righteousness or of learning extraneous to the personality.

Previous editions have printed the last stanza of 'I never saw a Moor' as

> I never spoke with God
> Nor visited in heaven—
> Yet certain am I of the spot
> As if the chart were given.

Johnson reads, for the conventional 'chart', the word 'checks', in the colloquial sense of railroad tickets, quoting in adequate support Emily's prose, 'My assurance of existence of Heaven is as great as though, having surrendered my checks to the conductor, I knew that I had arrived there.' In no. 391, 'A Visitor in Marl', Mme Bianchi's *Unpublished Poems* reads 'March' for 'Marl'. Neither here nor when, in a note, he cites Emily's writing of her dead father as 'lying in Marl', does Johnson gloss this unusual but accurate word. The 'Visitor' is Death; and the word 'Marl' means an earthy, crumbling deposit chiefly of clay, mixed with calcium carbonate, or earth (in the sense of clay): it means the cadaver. These two examples will illustrate that Emily used the words she meant, and the gain of their restoration.

III

As Allen Tate long ago remarked, Emily stands, among New Englanders, between Emerson and Hawthorne—of whom she wrote that he 'entices—appalls'. Her rearing was in Trinitarian Congregationalism—often in New England villages referred to as—in contrast to Unitarian heresy—the Orthodox Church. Unlike the rest of her family (some of whom capitulated early, some later), Emily never 'joined the church', never would fix the content of her belief; but she knew what her neighbours and her pastor believed, and—like Emerson in his attacks on Harvard College—had the personal comfort and poetic licence of cherishing favourite scepticisms without supposing that they would undermine, and hence render impossible of attack, the solid faith of others, the solid force of institutions. She lacks Hawthorne's sense of sin, and isolation for privacy is hardly an evil to her; the analogy to Hawthorne lies rather in her obsession with death and futurity—still more the sense of mystery: as in the remark (put on the lips of Holgrave), 'I begin to suspect that a man's bewilderment is the measure of his wisdom'. Her deepest poems are metaphysical or tragic; her mode of vision symbolist—thinking in analogies. Emerson (whose *Essays* an early 'tutor' gave her) may have flexed her mind, encouraged her speculations and her questionings of orthodoxy; but her mythology remains—what Hawthorne's was and Emerson's never—Biblical and Trinitarian. She is a rebel—but not, like Emerson, a schismatic.

A third ancestor comes often to my mind—Sir Thomas Browne, a writer dear to the nineteenth-century New Englanders, especially to the Concord men, and known and cited by Emily. 'For prose', she wrote Colonel Higginson, she had 'Mr. Ruskin, Sir Thomas Browne, and the *Revelations*'. These are very special kinds of prose certainly; and I don't hesitate to say that Emily's poetic style is not only that of some Emerson poems ('The Humble Bee', 'Hamatreya', 'Mithradates', 'Days') but that of Browne's *Religio* and *Christian Morals*. Her world view is the Brunonian sense of the natural world, so full of curious objects in the eyes of most men—though, as Browne remarks, he doesn't know how we call the toad ugly when it was made by the express design of God to assume that shape. Nor is Emily going to simplify the complexity of a God who made the bat. Of the bat, she writes (no. 1575):

> Deputed from what Firmament—
> Of what Astute Abode—
> Empowered with what Malignity
> Auspiciously withheld—
>
> To his adroit Creator
> Ascribe no less the praise—
> Beneficent, believe me,
> His Eccentricities——

Browne heaps up technical difficulties which beset the acceptance of the Bible and orthodox theology: he delights to list such difficulties as occasioned Bishop Colenso (of Arnoldian memory) the loss of his faith— the statistics of an Ark capable of holding all the creatures said to have entered.

Emily's most characteristic difficulties are with the

morals of the Bible, especially of the Old Testament—
which in her time and place had not been subjected to
the 'Higher Criticism'. She 'knew her Bible' well, the
total Bible: it was her prime mythology. She neither
rejects nor accepts it without question and reservation.
Its histories are rich and plausible human documents;
its doctrinal books, like St. Paul's epistles, are testi-
monials for consideration, propose questions and speculations for her theological sensibility to ponder. She would
have been shocked equally by having the Bible treated
as negligible, or even as 'literature', or by having it as
an infallible silencer of speculation.

Her famous 'The Bible is an antique Volume' was
originally written for her nephew Ned and given the
title, 'Diagnosis of the Bible, by a Boy'; but the boy was
not alien to the woman who understood his boredom
and his bafflement: the final version is hers.

> The Bible is an antique Volume—
> Written by faded Men
> At the suggestion of Holy Spectres—
> Subjects—Bethlehem
> Eden—the ancient Homestead—
> Satan—the Brigadier—
> Judas—the Great Defaulter—
> David—the Troubadour—
> Sin—a distinguished Precepice
> Others must resist—
> Boys that 'believe' are very lonesome—
> Other Boys are 'lost'—
> Had but the Tale a warbling Teller—
> All the Boys would come—
> Orpheus' sermon captivated—
> It did not condemn—

The sympathy with Satan and Judas is for rebels against
laws they don't understand, or it comes from a feeling

that, since sin must needs come into the world, and since the Crucifixion was foretold and necessary, we should not be too hard on the unhappy perpetrators. The mushroom is a 'Judas Iscariot' to the rest of Nature. Elsewhere (no. 120) she remarks that there are shocking instances of God's injustice: 'Moses wasn't fairly used; Ananias wasn't.' But it's temerarious to make such protestations. The same God who made the Lamb made the Lion: He who provided good and suffers the little ones to come unto Him also permits sin and evil—that 'where Sin abounded, Grace may much more abound'.

There have been times in which the pious felt the need to defend God, to prop Him up—as though it were our business to support the Rock and Word and Comforter. Emily is too orthodox—i.e. too inclusive— to forget that behind God the Son, Himself sturdy, is God the Father, the Creator of all things and the Abyss of Godhead, unexhausted by what His creatures understand of His ways: moving in a mysterious way His wonders to perform, and best known not defining Him.

Yet, in allowing for God's ways not being our ways, we musn't use language equivocally but apply our humanly highest standards. Writing on Abraham, Isaac, and God (no. 1317), Emily doesn't hesitate to identify God with 'tyranny' and to find the moral of the averted human sacrifice in the reflection that, even with a 'Mastiff', 'Manners may prevail'. The existence of a God Emily never doubts. The 'fop, the Carp, the Atheist' value the present moment, yet 'their commuted feet / The Torrents of Eternity / Do all but inundate'.

> The abdication of Belief
> Makes the Behavior small—
> Better an ignis fatuus
> Than no illume at all—

'Belief, it does not fit so well / When altered frequently.'

There must be a Heaven because there certainly are saints on earth; and sanctity argues its survival. But how prove a sky to a mole? *'Too much of proof affronts Belief.'* The turtle won't try to demonstrate to us that he can move—but, when we have turned our backs, he does. 'That oblique Belief which we call conjecture'—is the attempt to guess what Heaven is like—to picture 'What eye hath not seen'—what the 'mansions' of Heaven look like. Emily speculates on the state of the dead: whether they know what is happening to us or are too removed; or whether, on the contrary, they are nearer to us for the absence of their bodies. But these are conjectures unanswered by Scriptures. Straight belief is uncircumstantial; content to affirm what it cannot map or delineate. And, for Emily, belief is straight.

IV

I heartily wish that conjecture about Emily's lovers might cease as unprofitable. Of course her poems are all 'fragments of a great confession': of course she wrote out of her life, her life on various levels. But books on who her 'lover' was turn attention from the poems to the poet, and substitute detective work for criticism. Her readers of the 1890's did not require to know what 'who' or 'whos' gave her insight into love and renunciation, nor need we.

It is when the best of philosophers make blunders not inherent in their systems but extraneous to it—when Berkeley, in his neo-Platonic *Siris*, advocates the panacea of tar water—that we legitimately seek a biographical explanation. And when a good poet writes inferior poems we are concerned with the reason for the badness, in order to leave, inviolate, the goodness of the other poems. But the 'goodness' is not so to be explained.

One must distinguish biography from literary biography, distinguish between the study of the empirical person who wrote poems and that undeniable 'personality' present in poems which makes them recognizable as written by the same person. What is biographically peculiar to the empirical person is not relevant to the 'good poems', those intelligible to and valued by competent readers, which are elucidatory of our own experiences. To be sure, literary criticism can scarcely avoid a psychology of types—as it cannot dispense with a knowledge of the culture in which a poet was reared —and, certainly, cannot lack a close intimacy with the state of the language from which the poet makes artfully expressive deviations. But biographical studies and culture-history—for those who practise them, ends in themselves—are to be used by a critic with caution and delicacy. Scholarship as such restricts a great poet to her own time, place, and empirical self. Criticism must delicately 'clear' the poems for present use and evaluation—show what is for our time, or, more grandiosely, what is for all times.

I make these commonplaces of neoclassical and contemporary criticism, conscious that, in what immediately follows, I may seem to diverge from them. There is a 'lion in the way' of contemporary readers of Emily —the lion of biography. It has proved impossible not to pursue, to an extent, the facts gathered and the speculations offered by those who have sought to attach Emily's power as a poet of love and death to some single love and renunciation.

A widely informed and sensible work is Mrs. Bingham's *Emily Dickinson's Home: Letters of Edward Dickinson and his Family, with Documentation and Comment* (1955), which, as commentary, combines social history with family biography: I would commend specifically the chapters, 'The New England Way', 'Recreation', 'Funerals and Fears', 'Dickinson "Difference"'. The daughter of Mrs. Todd, Emily's first editor, takes in her stride the loves, real or imaginary; and she cites the testimony of Emily's brother, William Austin. A year his sister's senior, Austin was a collector of paintings and enamoured of shrubs, the honourable assumptor of his father's responsibilities to college, town, and family, yet a more flexible and troubled character. Austin, to whom, while he was away from Amherst, Emily wrote copious letters, who, in manhood, lived in the house next door in troubled marriage with 'Sister Sue', who was the affectionate brother, seems to me the most competent judge of his sister's personality. What was his judgement of the 'lovers'? Asked, after Emily's death, the direct question, 'Did she fall in love with the Rev. Mr. Wadsworth?' he thought not. He said that 'at different times' Emily 'had been devoted to several men'. He even went so far as to maintain that she had been several times in love, in her own way. But he denied that because of her devotion to any one man she forsook all others. Emily 'reached out eagerly, fervently even, toward anybody who lighted the spark. . .'

Wadsworth certainly mattered to Emily; and the time of his removal from Philadelphia to San Francisco, a distance prohibitive of prompt access to him by letter, coincides with significant alterations in her life and poetry. Yet this was a fantasy of love, constructed about a man whom she scarcely knew and who was doubtless never aware of her idealization. Her sense for what is real always won out over whatever presented attractive fantasy.

There were, I think, many loves in Emily's life, loves of varying kinds and durations. There were infatuations with Sister Sue and Kate Anthon, perhaps with Helen

Hunt Jackson—loves 'natural' enough and permitted by nineteenth-century standards. There was a succession of males to whom she attached her devotion: some of them, like Gould, Humphrey, and Newton, and Colonel Higginson, her 'teachers'; some more awesome characters.

Her father, Edward Dickinson, was a kind of version of God the Father: stern and implacable, yet a tower and rock of strength; mysterious in his ways, but doubtless always acting for the best; the man of moral rigidity who was none the less capable of ringing the church bell as for a fire so that his neighbours would emerge from their houses to share a magnificent sunset. Her feeling for her father was, I should guess, dominant. Her 'poems about God', the 'Papa in Heaven', are little-girl compounds of pertness and humility addressed to a powerful and puzzling big man, to Admirable Omnipotence. Her figures psychically distant and impressive —Father, the Rev. Mr. Wadsworth, Mr. Bowles, the Editor of the Springfield *Republican*, were all 'Fathers'; and God she made in their image and likeness.

It seems archetypally true of Emily to say that God was her Lover. The God whom she reverenced was not the Son, the 'Paragon of Chivalry', like her brother Austin and indeed herself, but God the Father, the Lover at once infinitely attractive and infinitely awesome, one partly revealed by the Son and His nature, but only partly revealed; finally, the unattainable God. 'He who loves God must not expect to be loved in return.'

All of Emily's lovers were unattainable: either members of her family or women or married men; and they were doubtless loved, in her way, precisely because they were unattainable—did not, could not, expose, even to herself, the nature of her dedication.

Emily's life is no riddle. New England had—and has—

many maiden ladies like her, and many widows who
are like maiden ladies. There are many who have loved
unsuccessfully or insuitably—whom fear or pride have
kept from the married state; many who have loved
'above them', could love in no other way, and who
prefer singleness to some democratic union. The father
who prefers his daughters not to marry, who needs
them at home with him, is matched by the daughter
so filial as to prefer the tried arrangement. There is
nothing monstrous—or even necessarily thwarted or
blighted—about such women. They have their friends
and their duties; they can nurture their own sensibilities
and spiritualities—grow sharper in consciousness for
their economy.

Many gradually withdraw from the world as Emily
did. The circumference shrinks as friends die or depart;
the pattern of life becomes more rigid. But the withdrawal can be gain if there is something to withdraw to.
Most spinsters have, like Emily, their brand of humour,
their mode of ritual—perhaps even their habitual way of
dressing; but what differentiates Emily is that she had
her poetry. She need not avert or circumvent woe save
by the stratagem of poetry. She need not keep her grief
to herself; she could give it to consciousness and to
paper—could face it by naming it.

Many richnesses sustained Emily—among them her
sense of 'degree', of status, of family. Of 'degree' she was
positively and negatively aware. When she wasn't a
little girl, to be fed a crumb, she was a Queen or an
Empress, jewelled and triumphant on a throne. At
once no man was 'good enough' for her to marry, and
those higher than she were so much higher as to seem
out of reach or, in fantasy, grandly, by their election, to
lift her to equality.

She was a Dickinson, the daughter of a 'Squire',

whose father had been one of the founders of Amherst College, whose brother was, if epigone, the honourable successor to greatness. The bonds between her and her family were such as to sustain her pride.

She was not, however she might seem to Boston, a rural poetess or spinster, but a princess. When Colonel Higginson proposed visits to Boston, access to her intellectual and literary 'peers' (Julia Ward Howe, for example, or Mrs. Sargent and her monthly convenings of paper-readers and polite disputants), Emily could not be moved from Amherst. She never came to Higginson: he, and other professed admirers, had to come to her, to her home, where she could set the tone and dictate the ritual. Emerson might leave Concord for the Saturday Club; like Thoreau, Emily stayed at home.

It has often been regretted that she did not, like Whitman, tender her poems to Emerson's sympathetic inspection rather than to Higginson's mixture of admiration and critical gentility; but Emerson, despite his elegant courtesy, his mode of listening to others, could not at once be heeded—and dismissed. Emerson was polished 'granite'—a master, like Emily herself, and (unlike her chosen mentors) a master in a domain too closely impinging on her own. In reputation 'above' her, she was a poet-in-verse such as he but adumbrated. He could not serve in the convenient capacity of Higginson nor incite the terror of forbidden presences.

How perceptive, how shrewd to estimate those who would serve, was this New England spinster. She seized upon what she needed, but seizure sufficed: she had no taste for neighbours.

V

After the fashion of nineteenth-century anthologies like Bryant's *Family Library of Poetry and Song* and

Emerson's *Parnassus*, Emily's poems were first published under the headings, 'Life', 'Nature', 'Love', and 'Time and Eternity'. But these categories are far from being mutually exclusive; indeed, they cannot be separated in any good poet or verse, and are not in Emily and Emily's—for a poet thinks analogically, thinks in terms of the interaction and interpenetration of these or any other spheres of being.

Nature, to Emily, is 'Animated'. She anthropomorphizes: bobolink, butterfly, rat, and the snake—no stranger to us, doubtless, than our fellows, whom, in turn, we metamorphose from the creatures. Inanimate Nature is also animate, like animal or person or ghostly presence.

> An awful Tempest mashed the air—
> The clouds were gaunt, and few—
> A Black—as of a Spectre's Cloak
> Hid Heaven and Earth from view.

Even the machine—the railroad train—is Animated Nature in the poem, one of a brilliant series in which, as in the Old English Riddle Poems, the object is characterized but never named, conceptualized. Her train is a mythological beast which first, catlike, *laps* the miles and *licks* the valleys up and which ends, horselike, by *neighing* and *stopping*, 'docile and omnipotent / At its own stable door'.

What moves is living; but death is immobile, and so are its approximations—loss, departures, removals.

Superficially, to be sure, Emily is in the line of those village versifiers whose function was to elegize the dead in broadside or for incision on slate or marble gravestones; and many of her poems were either composed, or later made to serve, as tributes to her deceased relatives, friends, Amherst acquaintances, the distant admired (Charlotte Brontë and George Eliot). Then, too, she was reared in a period in which poets like Poe, Bryant (who celebrated death from 'Thanatopsis' till his own), anthologies like Cheever's *Poets of America*, and newspaper poems, often cut out and preserved in scrapbooks, made the 'topic' appear particularly suited to verse. The frequency with which mortuary accounts appeared in her newspaper, the Springfield *Republican*, prompted Emily to ask a friend in 1853: 'Who writes those funny accidents, where railroads meet each other unexpectedly, and gentlemen in factories get their heads cut off quite informally?' It was Amherst custom, as it was elsewhere in New England, to visit cemeteries on Sunday afternoons. The local graveyard adjoined the Dickinson orchard on Pleasant Street; and, during her youth, funeral processions passed by the Dickinson house.

These circumstances supply a tradition and mollify, if not remove, suspicion of Emily's morbidity. But, if they elucidate, they do not explain Emily's death poems, which are unlike Poe's and unlike Bryant's.

To the most cursory scanner, Emily was 'much obsessed by Death'. 'Goings away', departures, whether to geographic distances or by felt disloyalties, spatial and psychic separations, absences from us, all disjunctions, can be felt, and were, by Emily, as deaths. In a rather usual pattern of reaction, she wrote her Death poems with a quality of magnitude almost proportioned to, for her, the unimportance of the intimated 'person in mind'—the *occasion* for a poem, not its motive or momentum.

Emily's 'white election', we know, began around the year 1862. This 'white election': could it not have been Emily's acceptance of Death? What 'facts' are supposed to explain the 'problem of Emily' point to some one, a Person unacknowledgeable to her consciousness. Her poems suggest compelled flights from impending, threatening consciousness of that person or persons.

How angry we feel when one whom we had loved, or protested we did, 'dies on us'. He or she has up and left us. Ashamed of anger towards the 'loved dead'—or those loved who have separated from us, one denies the feeling. Emily's 'white election' is not wholly devoid of moral blackmail, consequent guilts—rich pasture for poetry.

The poems about death are ranging in kind and tone. One says that Emily's poems about death are sometimes written from the point of view of the observer; in others, she is witnessing her own death by anticipation ('You'll be sorry when I'm dead' or 'I want to die'); in others she is contemplating present destitution by loss ('My life closed twice before its close'). The poems don't have to be in the first person to be self-regarding.

> On such a night, or such a night,
> Would anybody care
> If such a little figure
> Slipped quiet from its chair—

and ''Twas the old—road—through pain' and the other poems about the death of a little girl seem, unavoidably, Emily in such postures, quite as much as 'If I shouldn't be alive. . .'

Among all the poems about death one is temerarious in distinguishing the observed from the imagined or fictive. 'Looking at Death, is Dying' (no. 281) is a maxim to be attended—even though it occurs in a poem not about death but about loss.

The dead are variously conceived of—sometimes as in their graves, quiet despite the bustle of the day and of history. ('How many times these low feet staggered', 'Safe in their Alabaster Chambers'). 'I'm sorry for the

Dead-Today', light in tone, lightly pities the sleeping farmers and their wives who 'rest' while the festival of haying goes on in the village about them. In another poem, the grave is a cottage where a girl plays at 'Keeping house' and prepares 'marble tea'. And the gravestone is a kind of death-mask for the dead beneath it: it tries to thank those who gave the robin a 'Memorial crumb', and tries with 'Granite lip'.

Perhaps the most brilliant of the death-in-death poems is 'A Clock stopped— / Not the Mantel's', a master-piece in the employment of a conceit coterminous with the poem—a definition once proposed for Donne's poems but more accurately applied to such of Emily's as this. Most of what is said fits approximately both sides of the equation; and that intellectual work which is the conceit serves, as we know, to distance the poem.

Like a train, a clock may be felt near to animate. In fable, a clock stops when its owner dies; at any event, it measures the clock-time by which men live. The Doctor is a 'Shopman', a clock-repairer; but he cannot set the heart's pendulum to swinging again. To the dead, hours and minutes and 'Seconds' are alike now meaningless. They are meaningless compared with the 'Decades'—more than the metre can justify this under-statement for 'centuries'—the 'Decades of Arrogance' which separate 'Dial life' from the 'Degreeless Noon' of Eternity. The 'Trinket', the diminutively precious ob-ject, has gained the accrual of 'awe'; for the onlooker feels the 'Arrogance' of the dead—their unconcern for us.

This poem appears to take the stance of the onlooker; but does it? It can well be argued that the poet imagines herself at the lofty distance of death, envisages how those others will feel as they watch and witness. In a poem like this the distinction between the imagined and the imaginer becomes impossible to fix. In Emily's poems, the referent and its metaphoric referend are often difficult to distinguish.

'There's a certain Slant of light' is a poem ostensibly about winter afternoons with their 'Heavenly Hurt' and their 'Seal Despair'; when that winter light goes, 'tis like the Distance / On the look of Death'. In this poem 'Death' is a metaphor for winter light, and at the same time winter light is a metaphor for death: one inclines to say, preponderantly the latter. 'I like a look of Agony / Because I know it's true' invokes the glazing of the eyes in death; but 'Beads upon the Forehead' are invoked by 'Anguish'; and the death is not the death of the dead but of the living. 'A *Wounded* Deer—leaps highest' in the 'Extasy of *death*'; yet the next metaphors, the '*Smitten* Rock' and the '*trampled* Steel', are not death but, by anthropomorphic transfer, versions of that present anguish of which mirth is the cautious 'Mail'.

'It cant be "Dying"! It's too Rouge— / The Dead shall go in White' (no. 221) is a poem ostensibly about a sunset, a traditional symbol for death; but, by the familiar figure of suggesting by denying, she has occasion to speak of a kind of death. The reference to white suggests Emily's own habitual garb from this time on. In the Orient, as she may have known, white is the colour of lovers who have come through great tribulation and washed their robes (cf. no. 325; Revelation vii. 14) and is the colour of her 'blameless mystery'—perhaps in contrast to the blame-suspect black veil of Hawthorne's clergyman. White is the colour for her kind of death-in-life; and the poem seems dynamized by it, with the sunset metaphor.

Suggestion by negation is most powerfully used in 'It was not Death, for I stood up', a poem about death-in-life. The state deanimizes the self.

The Figures I have seen
Set orderly, for Burial,
Reminded me, of mine—

As if my life were shaven,
And fitted to a frame,
and could not breathe without a key . . .

It felt like the stopping of a clock, like frost-frozen ground
(deanimizing images); but most like chaos—chaos without 'even a Report of Land— / To justify—Despair'.

These poems about despair are probably the best
poems Emily ever wrote; but they cannot be taken as
her total 'message to the world'. Reading her work does
not induce despair. For herself first, and then for her
readers, the very articulation of despair is effectual movement towards its dispelling. The autonomy of Nature
and the 'creatures' constantly arouses her fascinated
apprehension of the variety and flexibility of nature. If
anger and fear paralyse, 'self-reliance' has its resources
unessayed without the felt need:

If your Nerve, deny you—
Go above your Nerve—
He can lean against the Grave,
If he fear to swerve—

.   .   .   .   .

'Tis so appalling—it exhilirates—
So over Horror, it half Captivates—
The Soul stares after it, secure—
To know the worst, leaves no dread more—

Then there are Emily's poems about immortality,
which she both doubted and affirmed—affirmed not
only on Bible testimony but from the argument that as
there are saints there must be a Heaven—as there is
grandeur, it cannot finally perish. These poems are
variously mythic: there is no Biblical warrant for 'flesh-

less lovers' meeting in Heaven. Whatever Emily's personal belief—centrally, a belief in belief—her after-death poems are readily translatable into other terms. As God is the resource, within or without, which transcends the resources we thought were our limits, so eternity is a name for ultimate definitions of the total personality:

> Of all the Souls that stand create—
> I have elected—One—
> When Sense from Spirit—files away—
> And Subterfuge—is done—

The final sense of Emily's total achievement is the power of poetry to register and master experience.

ALLEN TATE

1899–

THE MAN OF LETTERS IN THE MODERN WORLD

The Man of Letters in the Modern World, 1955

To the question, What should the man of letters be in our time?, we should have to find the answer in what we need him to do. He must do first what he has always done: he must re-create for his age the image of man, and he must propagate standards by which other men may test that image, and distinguish the false from the true. But at our own critical moment, when all languages are being debased by the techniques of mass-control, the man of letters might do well to conceive his responsibility more narrowly. He has an immediate responsibility, to other men no less than to himself, for the vitality of language. He must distinguish the difference between mere communication—of which I shall later have more to say—and the rediscovery of the human condition in the living arts. He must discriminate and defend the difference between mass communication, for the control of men, and the knowledge of man which literature offers us for human participation.

The invention of standards by which this difference may be known, and a sufficient minority of persons instructed, is a moral obligation of the literary man. But the actuality of the difference does not originate in the critical intelligence as such; it is exemplified in the specific forms of the literary arts, whose final purpose, the extrinsic end for which they exist, is not the control of other persons, but self-knowledge. By these arts, one means the arts without which men can live, but without which they cannot live well, or live as men. To keep alive the knowledge of ourselves with which the literary arts continue to enlighten the more ignorant portion of mankind (among whom one includes oneself), to separate them from other indispensable modes of knowledge, and to define their limits, is the intellectual and thus the social function of the writer. Here the man of letters is the critic.

The edifying generality of these observations is not meant to screen the difficulties that they will presently encounter in their particular applications. A marked difference between communication and communion I shall be at some pains to try to discern in the remarks that follow. I shall try to explore the assertion: Men in a dehumanized society may communicate, but they cannot live in full communion. To explore this I must first pursue a digression.

What happens in one mind may happen as influence or coincidence in another; when the same idea spreads to two or more minds of considerable power, it may eventually explode, through chain reaction, in a whole society; it may dominate a period or an entire epoch.

When René Descartes isolated thought from man's total being he isolated him from nature, including his own nature; and he divided man against himself. (The demonology which attributes to a few persons the calamities of mankind is perhaps a necessary convention of economy in discourse.) It was not the first time that man had been at war with himself: there was that first famous occasion of immemorial antiquity: it is man's permanent war of internal nerves. Descartes was only the new strategist of our own phase of the war. Men after the seventeenth century would have been at war with themselves if Descartes had never lived. He chose the new field and forged the new weapons. The battle is now between the dehumanized society of secularism, which imitates Descartes's mechanized nature, and the eternal society of the communion of the human spirit. The war is real enough; but again one is conscious of an almost mythical exaggeration in one's description of the combatants. I shall not condescend to Descartes by trying to be fair to him. For the battle is being fought, it has always been fought by men few of whom have heard of Descartes or any other philosopher.

Consider the politician, who as a man may be as good as his quiet neighbour. If he acts upon the assumption (which he has never heard of) that society is a machine to be run efficiently by immoral—or, to him, amoral—methods, he is only exhibiting a defeat of the spirit that he is scarcely conscious of having suffered. Now consider his fellow citizen, the knowing person, the trained man of letters, the cunning poet in the tradition of Poe and Mallarmé. If this person (who perhaps resembles ourselves) is aware of more, he is able to do less, than the politician, who does not know what he is doing. The man of letters sees that modern societies are machines, even if he thinks that they ought not to be: he is convinced that in its intractable Manicheism, society cannot be redeemed. The shadowy political philosophy of modern literature, from Proust to Faulkner, is, in its moral origins, Jansenist: we are disciples of Pascal, the merits of whose Redeemer were privately available but could not affect the operation of the power-state. While the politician, in his cynical innocence, uses society, the man of letters disdainfully, or perhaps even absent-mindedly, withdraws from it: a withdrawal that few persons any longer observe, since withdrawal has become the social convention of the literary man, in which society, in so far as it is aware of him, expects him to conduct himself.

It is not improper, I think, at this point, to confess that I have drawn in outline the melancholy portrait of the man who stands before you. Before I condemn him I wish to examine another perspective, an alternative to the double retreat from the moral centre, of the man of action and the man of letters, that we have completed in our time. The alternative has had at least the virtue of recommending the full participation of the man of letters in the action of society.

The phrase, 'the action of society', is abstract enough to disarm us into supposing that perhaps here and there in the past, if not uniformly, men of letters were hourly participating in it: the supposition is not too deceptive a paralogism, provided we think of society as the City of Augustine and Dante, where it was possible for men to find in the temporal city the imperfect analogue to the City of God. (The Heavenly City was still visible, to Americans, in the political economy of Thomas Jefferson.) What we, as literary men, have been asked to support, and what we have rejected, is the action of society as *secularism*, or the society that substitutes means for ends. Although the idolatry of the means has been egregious enough in the West, we have not been willing to prefer the more advanced worship that prevails in Europe eastward of Berlin, and in Asia. If we can scarcely imagine a society like the Russian, deliberately committing itself to secularism, it is no doubt because we cannot easily believe that men will prefer barbarism to civilization. They come to prefer the senility (which resembles the adolescence) and the irresponsibility of the barbarous condition of man without quite foreseeing what else they will get out of it. Samuel Johnson said of chronic drunkenness: 'He who makes a beast of himself gets rid of the pain of being a man.' There is perhaps no anodyne for the pains of civilization but savagery. What men may get out of this may be seen in the western world today, in an intolerable psychic crisis expressing itself as a political crisis.

The internal crisis, whether it precede or follow the political, is inevitable in a society that multiplies means without ends. Man is a creature that in the long run has got to believe in order to know, and to know in order to do. For doing without knowing is machine behaviour, illiberal and servile routine, the secularism with which man's specific destiny has no connexion. I take it that we have sufficient evidence, generation after generation, that man will never be completely or permanently enslaved. He will rebel, as he is rebelling now, in a shocking variety of 'existential' disorders, all over the world. If his *human* nature as such cannot participate in the action of society, he will not capitulate to it, if that action is inhuman: he will turn in upon himself, with the common gesture which throughout history has vindicated the rhetoric of liberty: 'Give me liberty or give me death'.

Man may destroy himself but he will not at last tolerate anything less than his full human condition. Pascal said that the 'sight of cats or rats is enough to unhinge the reason'—a morbid prediction of our contemporary existential philosophy, a modernized Dark Night of Sense. The impact of mere sensation, even of 'cats and rats' (which enjoy the innocence of their perfection in the order of nature)—a simple sense-perception from a world no longer related to human beings—will nourish a paranoid philosophy of despair. Blake's 'hapless soldier's sigh', Poe's 'tell-tale heart', Rimbaud's nature careening in a 'drunken boat', Eliot's woman 'pulling her long black hair', are qualities of the life of Baudelaire's *fourmillante Cité*, the secularism of the swarm, of which we are the present citizens.

Is the man of letters alone doomed to inhabit that city? No, we are all in it—the butcher, the baker, the candlestick-maker, and the banker and the statesman. The special awareness of the man of letters, the source at once of his Gnostic arrogance and of his Augustinian humility, he brings to bear upon all men alike: his hell has not been 'for those other people': he has reported his own. His report upon his own spiritual condition, in the last hundred years, has misled the banker and the statesman into the illusion that they have no hell because, as secularists, they have lacked the language to report it. What you are not able to name therefore does not exist —a barbarous disability, to which I have already alluded. There would be no hell for modern man if our men of letters were not calling attention to it.

But it is the business of the man of letters to call attention to whatever he is able to see: it is his function to create what has not been hitherto known and, as critic, to discern its modes. I repeat that it is his duty to render the image of man as he is in his time, which, without the man of letters, would not otherwise be known. What modern literature has taught us is not merely that the man of letters has not participated fully in the action of society; it has taught us that nobody else has either. It is a fearful lesson. The roll call of the noble and sinister characters, our ancestors and our brothers, who exemplify the lesson, must end in a shudder: Julien Sorel, Emma Bovary, Captain Ahab, Hepzibah Pyncheon, Roderick Usher, Lambert Strether, Baron de Charlus, Stephen Dedalus, Joe Christmas—all these and more, to say nothing of the precise probing of their, and our, sensibility, which is modern poetry since Baudelaire. Have men of letters perversely invented these horrors? They are rather the inevitable creations of a secularized society, the society of means without ends, in which nobody participates with the full substance of his humanity. It is the society in which everybody acts his part (even when he is most active) in the plotless drama of withdrawal.

I trust that nobody supposes that I see the vast populations of Europe and America scurrying, each man to his tree, penthouse, or cave, and refusing to communicate with other men. Humanity was never more gregarious, and never before heard so much of its own voice. Is not then the problem of communication for the man of letters very nearly solved? He may sit in a sound-proof room, in shirtsleeves, and talk at a metal object resembling a hornet's nest, throwing his voice, and perhaps also his face, at 587,000,000 people, more or less, whom he has never seen, and whom it may not occur to him that in order to love, he must have a medium even less palpable than air.

What I am about to say of communication will take it for granted that men cannot communicate by means of sound over either wire or air. They have got to communicate through love. Communication that is not also communion is incomplete. We *use* communication; we *participate* in communion. 'All the certainty of our knowledge', says Coleridge, 'depends [on this]; and this becomes intelligible to no man by the ministry of mere words from without. The medium, by which spirits understand each other, is not the surrounding air; but the *freedom* which they possess in common.' (The italics are Coleridge's.) Neither the artist nor the statesman will communicate fully again until the rule of love, added to the rule of law, has liberated him. I am not suggesting that we all have an obligation of *personal* love towards one another. I regret that I must be explicit about this matter. No man, under any political dispensation known to us, has been able to avoid hating other men by deciding that it would be a 'good thing' to love them; he loves his neighbour, as well as the man he has never seen, only through the love of God. 'He that saith that he is in the light, and hateth his brother, is in darkness even until now.'

I confess that to the otiose ear of the tradition of Poe and Mallarmé the simple-minded Evangelist may seem to offer something less than a solution to the problem of communication. I lay it down as a fact, that it is the only solution. 'We must love one another or die', Mr. Auden wrote more than ten years ago. I cannot believe that Mr. Auden was telling us that a secularized society cannot exist; it obviously exists. He was telling us that a society which has once been religious cannot, without risk of spiritual death, preceded by the usual agonies, secularize itself. A society of means without ends, in the age of technology, so multiplies the means, in the lack of anything better to do, that it may have to scrap the machines as it makes them; until our descendants will have to dig themselves out of one rubbish heap after another and stand upon it, in order to make more rubbish to make more standing-room. The surface of nature will then be literally as well as morally concealed from the eyes of men.

Will congresses of men of letters, who expect from their conversations a little less than mutual admiration, and who achieve at best toleration of one another's personalities, mitigate the difficulties of communication? This may be doubted, though one feels that it is better to gather together in any other name than that of Satan, than not to gather at all. Yet one must assume that men of letters will not love one another personally any better than they have in the past. If there has been little communion among them, does the past teach them to expect, under perfect conditions (whatever these may be), to communicate their works to any large portion of mankind? We suffer, though we know better, from an ignorance which lets us entertain the illusion that in the past great works of literature were immediately consumed by entire populations. It has never been so; yet dazzled by this false belief, the modern man of letters is bemused by an unreal dilemma. Shall he persist in his rejection of the existential 'cats and rats' of Pascal, the political disorder of the West that 'unhinges the reason'; or shall he exploit the new media of mass 'communication'—cheap print, radio, and television? For what purpose shall he exploit them?

The dilemma, like evil, is real to the extent that it exists as privative of good: it has an impressive 'existential' actuality: men of letters on both sides of the Atlantic consider the possible adjustments of literature to a mass audience. The first question that we ought to ask ourselves is: *What* do we propose to communicate to *whom*?

I do not know whether there exists in Europe anything like the steady demand upon American writers to 'communicate' quickly with the audience that Coleridge knew even in his time as the 'multitudinous Public, shaped into personal unity by the magic of abstraction'. The American is still able to think that he sees in Europe —in France, but also in England—a closer union, in the remains of a unified culture, between a sufficiently large public and the man of letters. That Alexis St.-Leger, formerly Permanent Secretary of the French Foreign Office, could inhabit the same body with St.-John Perse, a great living French poet, points to the recent actuality of that closer union; while at the same time, the two names for the two natures of the one person suggest the completion of the Cartesian disaster, the fissure in the human spirit of our age; the inner division creating the outer, and the eventual loss of communion.

Another way of looking at the question, *What* do we propose to communicate to *whom*? would eliminate the dilemma, withdrawal *or* communication. It disappears if we understand that literature has never communicated, that it cannot *communicate*: from this point of view we see the work of literature as a participation in communion. Participation leads naturally to the idea of the common experience. Perhaps it is not too grandiose a conception to suggest that works of literature, from the short lyric to the long epic, are the recurrent discovery of the human communion *as experience*, in a definite place and at a definite time. Our unexamined theory of literature as communication could not have appeared in an age in which communion was still possible for any appreciable majority of persons. The word communication presupposes the victory of the secularized society of means without ends. The poet, on the one hand, shouts to the public, on the other (some distance away), not the rediscovery of the common experience, but a certain pitch of sound to which the well-conditioned adrenals of humanity obligingly respond.

The response is not the specifically human mode of behaviour; it is the specifically animal mode, what is left of man after Occam's razor has cut away his humanity. It is a tragedy of contemporary society that so much of democratic social theory reaches us in the language of 'drive', 'stimulus', and 'response'. This is not the language of freemen, it is the language of slaves. The language of freemen substitutes for these words, respectively, *end*, *choice*, and *discrimination*. Here are two sets of analogies, the one sub-rational and servile, the other rational and free. (The analogies in which man conceives his nature at different historical moments are of greater significance than his political rhetoric.) When the poet is exhorted to communicate, he is being asked to speak within the orbit of an analogy that assumes that genuine communion is impossible: does not the metaphor hovering in the rear of the word 'communication' isolate the poet before he can speak? The poet at a microphone desires to sway, affect, or otherwise influence a crowd (not a community) which is then addressed as if it were permanently over *there*—not *here*, where the poet himself would be a member of it; he is not a member, but a mere part. He stimulates his audience— which a few minutes later will be stimulated by a newscommentator, who reports the results of a 'poll', as the Roman *pontifex* under Tiberius reported the colour of the entrails of birds—the poet thus elicits a response, in the context of the preconditioned 'drives' ready to be released in the audience. Something may be said to have been transmitted, or *communicated*; nothing has been shared, in a new and illuminating intensity of awareness.

One may well ask what these observations have to do with the man of letters in the modern world? They have nearly everything to do with him, since, unless I am wholly mistaken, his concern is with what has not been previously known about our present relation to an unchanging source of knowledge, and with our modes of apprehending it. In the triad of *end*, *choice*, and *discrimination*, his particular responsibility is for the last; for it is by means of discrimination, through choice, towards an end, that the general intelligence acts. The general intelligence is the intelligence of the man of letters: he must not be committed to the illiberal specializations that the nineteenth century has proliferated into the modern world: specializations in which means are divorced from ends, action from sensibility, matter from mind, society from the individual, religion from moral agency, love from lust, poetry from thought, communion from experience, and mankind in the community from men in the crowd. There is literally no end to this list of dissociations because there is no end yet in sight to the fragmenting of the western mind. The modern man of letters may, as a man, be as thoroughly the victim of it as his conditioned neighbour. I hope it is understood that I am not imputing to the man of letters a personal superiority; if he is luckier than his neighbours, his responsibility, and his capacity for the shattering peripeties of experience, are greater: he is placed at the precarious centre of a certain liberal tradition, from which he is as strongly tempted as the next man to escape. This tradition has only incidental connexions with political liberalism and it has none with the power-state; it means quite simply the freedom of the mind to discriminate the false from the true, the experienced knowledge from its verbal imitations. His critical responsibility is thus what it has always been—the recreation and the application of literary standards, which in order to be effectively literary, must be more than literary. His task is to preserve the integrity, the purity, and the reality of language wherever and for whatever purpose it may be used. He must approach his task through the letter—the letter of the poem, the letter of the politician's speech, the letter of the law; for the use of the letter is in the long run our one indispensable test of the actuality of our experience.

The letter then is the point to which the man of letters directs his first power, the power of discrimination. He will ask: Is there in this language genuine knowledge of our human community—or of our lack of it—that we have not had before? If there is, he will know that it is liberal language, the language of freemen, in which a choice has been made towards a probable end for man. If it is not language of this order, if it is the language of mere communication, of mechanical analogies in which the two natures of man are isolated and dehumanized, then he will know that it is the language of men who are, or who are waiting to be, slaves.

If the man of letters does not daily renew his dedication to this task, I do not know who else may be expected to undertake it. It is a task that cannot be performed today in a society that has not remained, in certain senses of the word that we sufficiently understand, democratic. We enjoy the privileges of democracy on the same terms as we enjoy other privileges: on the condition that we give something back. What the man of letters returns in exchange for his freedom is the difficult model of freedom for his brothers, Julien Sorel, Lambert Strether, and Joe Christmas, who are thus enjoined to be likewise free, and to sustain the freedom of the man of letters himself. What he gives back to society often enough carries with it something that a democratic society likes as little as any other: the courage to condemn the abuses of democracy, more particularly to *discriminate* the usurpations of democracy that are perpetrated in the name of democracy.

That he is permitted, even impelled by the democratic condition itself, to publish his discriminations of the staggering abuses of language, and thus of choices and ends, that vitiate the cultures of western nations, is in itself a consideration for the second thought of our friends in Europe. Might they not in the end ill prefer the upper millstone of Russia to the nether of the United States? Our formidable economic and military power— which like all secular power the man of letters must carry as his Cross; our bad manners in Europe; our ignorance of the plain fact that we can no more dispense with Europe than almighty Rome could have lived without a reduced Greece; our delusion that we are prepared to 'educate' Europe in 'democracy' by exporting dollars, gadgets, and sociology—to say nothing of the boorish jargon of the State Department—all this, and this is by no means all, may well tempt (in the words of Reinhold Niebuhr) 'our European friends to a virtual Manicheism and to consign the world of organization to the outer darkness of barbarism'. But it should be pointed out, I think, to these same European brothers, that the darkness of this barbarism still shows forth at least one light which even the black slaves of the Old South were permitted to keep burning, but which the white slaves of Russia are not: I mean the inalienable right to talk back: of which I cite the present discourse as an imperfect example.

The man of letters has, then, in our time a small but critical service to render to man: a service that will be in the future more effective than it is now, when the cult of the literary man shall have ceased to be an idolatry. Men of letters and their followers, like the *parvenu* gods and their votaries of decaying Rome, compete in the dissemination of distraction and novelty. But the true province of the man of letters is nothing less (as it is nothing more) than culture itself. The state is the mere operation of society, but culture is the way society lives, the material medium through which men receive the one lost truth which must be perpetually recovered: the truth of what Jacques Maritain calls the 'supra-temporal destiny' of man. It is the duty of the man of letters to supervise the culture of language, to which the rest of culture is subordinate, and to warn us when our language is ceasing to forward the ends proper to man. The end of social man is communion in time through love, which is beyond time.

YVOR WINTERS

1900–1968

MAULE'S CURSE OR HAWTHORNE AND THE PROBLEM OF ALLEGORY

In Defense of Reason, 1947

'At the moment of execution—with the halter about his neck and while Colonel Pyncheon sat on horseback, grimly gazing at the scene—Maule had addressed him from the scaffold, and uttered a prophecy, of which history as well as fireside tradition, has preserved the very words. "God," said the dying man, pointing his finger, with a ghastly look, at the undismayed countenance of his enemy, "God will give him blood to drink!" '

The House of the Seven Gables

OF Hawthorne's three most important long works— *The Scarlet Letter, The House of the Seven Gables*, and *The*

Marble Faun—the first is pure allegory, and the other two are impure novels, or novels with unassimilated allegorical elements. The first is faultless, in scheme and in detail; it is one of the chief masterpieces of English prose. The second and third are interesting, the third in particular, but both are failures, and neither would suffice to give the author a very high place in the history of prose fiction. Hawthorne's sketches and short stories, at best, are slight performances; either they lack meaning, as in the case of *Mr. Higginbotham's Catastrophe*, or they lack reality of embodiment, as in the case of *The Birthmark*, or, having a measure of both, as does *The Minister's Black Veil*, they yet seem incapable of justifying the intensity of the method, their very brevity and attendant simplification, perhaps, working against them; the best of them, probably, is *Young Goodman Brown*. In his later romances, *Septimius Felton*, *Dr. Grimshaw's Secret*, *The Ancestral Footstep*, and *The Dolliver Romance*, and in much of *The Blithedale Romance* as well, Hawthorne struggles unsuccessfully with the problem of allegory, but he is still obsessed with it.

Hawthorne is, then, essentially an allegorist; had he followed the advice of Poe and other well-wishers, contemporary with himself and posthumous, and thrown his allegorizing out the window, it is certain that nothing essential to his genius would have remained. He appears to have had none of the personal qualifications of a novelist, for one thing: the sombre youth who lived in solitude and in contemplation in Salem, for a dozen years or more, before succumbing to the charms and propinquity of Miss Sophia Peabody and making the spasmodic and only moderately successful efforts to accustom himself to daylight which were to vex the remainder of his life, was one far more likely to concern himself with the theory of mankind than with the chaos, trivial, brutal, and exhausting, of the actuality. Furthermore, as we shall see more fully, the Puritan view of life was allegorical, and the allegorical vision seems to have been strongly impressed upon the New England literary mind. It is fairly obvious in much of the poetry of Emerson, Emily Dickinson, Bryant, Holmes, and even Very—Whittier, a Quaker and a peasant, alone of the more interesting poets escaping; Melville, relatively an outsider, shows the impact of New England upon his own genius as much through his use of allegory as through his use of New England character; and the only important novelist purely a New Englander, aside from Hawthorne, that is, O. W. Holmes, was primarily concerned with the Puritan tendency to allegory, as its one considerable satirist, yet was himself more or less addicted to it.

These matters are speculative. That New England predisposed Hawthorne to allegory cannot be shown; yet the disposition in both is obvious. And it can easily be shown that New England provided the perfect material for one great allegory, and that, in all likelihood, she was largely to blame for the later failures.

The Puritan theology rested primarily upon the doctrine of predestination and the inefficaciousness of good works; it separated men sharply and certainly into two groups, the saved and the damned, and, technically, at least, was not concerned with any subtler shadings. This in itself represents a long step toward the allegorization of experience, for a very broad abstraction is substituted for the patient study of the minutiae of moral behaviour long encouraged by Catholic tradition. Another step was necessary, however, and this step was taken in Massachusetts almost at the beginning of the settlement, and in the expulsion of Anne Hutchinson became the basis of governmental action: whereas the wholly Calvinistic Puritan denied the value of the evidence of character and behaviour as signs of salvation, and so precluded the possibility of their becoming allegorical symbols—for the orthodox Calvinist, such as Mrs. Hutchinson would appear to have been, trusted to no witness save that of the Inner Light—it became customary in Massachusetts to regard as evidence of salvation the decision of the individual to enter the Church and lead a moral life.

The Puritans [says Parkes] were plain blunt men with little taste for mysticism and no talent for speculation. A new conception was formulated by English theologians, of whom William Ames was the most influential. The sign of election was not an inner assurance; it was a sober decision to trust in Christ and obey God's law. Those who made this sober decision might feel reasonably confident that they had received God's grace; but the surest proof of it was its fruit in conduct; complete assurance was impossible. It was assumed that all was the work of grace; it was God, without human co-operation, who caused the sober decision to be made. But in actual practice this doctrine had the effect of unduly magnifying man's ability to save himself, as much as Calvin's conception had unduly minimized it; conversion was merely a choice to obey a certain code of rules, and did not imply any emotional change, any love for God, or for holiness, or any genuine religious experience; religion in other words was reduced to mere morality.[1]

Objective evidence thus took the place of inner assurance, and the behaviour of the individual took on symbolic value. That is, any sin was evidence of damnation; or, in other words, any sin represented all sin. When Hester Prynne committed adultery, she committed

[1] 'The Puritan Heresy', by H. B. Parkes, *The Hound and Horn*, vol. ii, Jan.–Mar. 1932, pp. 173–4. See also *The Pragmatic Test*, by H. B. Parkes, The Colt Press, San Francisco.

an act as purely representative of complete corruption as the act of Faustus in signing a contract with Satan. This view of the matter is certainly not Catholic and is little short of appalling; it derives from the fact, that although, as Parkes states in the passage just quoted, there occurred an exaggeration of the will in the matter of practical existence, this same will was still denied in the matter of doctrine, for according to doctrine that which man willed had been previously willed by God.

The belief that the judgement of a man is predestined by God, and the corollary that the judgement of a good man, since all men are either good or bad, purely and simply, is the judgement of God, may lead in the natural course of events to extraordinary drama; and this the more readily if the actors in the drama are isolated from the rest of the world and believe that the drama in which they take part is of cosmic importance and central in human destiny. Andrews writes: 'The belief that God had selected New England as the chosen land was profoundly held by the Puritans who went there. Winthrop himself in 1640 wrote to Lord Saye and Sele of "this good land which God hath found and given to his people", adding that "God had chosen this country to plant his people in". Cotton in his sermon, *God's Promise to His Plantation* (London, 1634), devotes much space to the same idea—"This place is appointed me of God"'.[1] And Schneider writes on the same subject:

No one can live long in a Holy Commonwealth without becoming sensitive, irritable, losing his sense of values and ultimately his balance. All acts are acts either of God or of the devil; all issues are matters of religious faith; and all conflicts are holy wars. No matter how trivial an

[1] *The Colonial Period of American History*, by Charles M. Andrews, Yale University Press, 1934, vol. i, p. 386, n. 2.

opinion might appear from a secular point of view, it
became vital when promulgated as a theological dogma;
no matter how harmless a fool might be, he was intolerable if he did not fit into the Covenant of Grace; no matter
how slight an offence might be, it was a sin against Almighty God and hence infinite. Differences of opinion
became differences of faith. Critics became blasphemers,
and innovators, heretics.[1]

And again:

. . . the mind of the Puritan was singularly unified and
his imagination thoroughly moralized. The clergy were,
of course, the professional moral scientists, but the laymen
were no less dominated by such mental habits. The common
man and illiterate shared with the expert this interest in
divining God's purposes in the course of events. No event
was merely natural; it was an act of God and was hence
charged with that 'numinous' quality which gives birth to
both prophetic insight and mystic illumination.[2]

And again:

Nature was instructive to them only in so far as it
suggested the hidden mysterious operations of designing
agents. God and devil were both active, scheming, hidden
powers, each pursuing his own ends by various ministra-
tions, and natural events were therefore to be understood
only in so far as they showed evidence of some divine or
diabolical plot.[3]

Now according to the doctrine of predestination, if
we interpret it reasonably, Hester merely gave evidence,
in committing adultery, that she had always been one of
the damned. This point of view, if really understood,
could never have led to the chain of events which
Hawthorne described in *The Scarlet Letter*; neither could

---

[1] *The Puritan Mind*, by H. W. Schneider; Henry Holt, 1930,
pp. 51–52.
[2] Ibid., p. 48.   [3] Ibid., pp. 42–43.

it have led to the events of the actual history of New England. It is at this point that we must consider that fluid element, history, in connexion with dogma, for Hester, like the witches who so occupied the Mathers, was treated as if she had wilfully abandoned the ways of God for the ways of Satan. This final illogicality introduces the element of drama into the allegory of *The Scarlet Letter* and into the allegorical morality of the Puritans.

The English Puritans who settled Massachusetts were socially the product of centuries of the type of ethical discipline fostered by the Catholic and Anglo-Catholic Churches. They may have denied the freedom of the will and the efficaciousness of good works by lip, but by habit, and without really grasping the fact, they believed in them and acted upon them. Edwards exhorts sinners to repent while preaching the doctrine of the inability to repent; the Mathers wrestled with demons physically and in broad daylight, and quite obviously felt virtuous for having done so; in fact, to such a pass did Puritanism come, that Melville's Ahab, who wilfully embarks upon the Sea of Unpredictability in order to overtake and slay the Spirit of Evil—an effort in which he is predestined and at the end of which he is predestined to destruction—appears to us merely the heroic projection of a common Puritan type. The Puritan may be said to have conceived the Manicheistic struggle between Absolute Good and Absolute Evil, which he derived through the processes of simplification and misunderstanding which have already been enumerated, as a kind of preordained or mechanical, yet also holy combat, in which his own part was a part at once intense and holy and yet immutably regulated.

There were at least two motives in the new environment which tended to intensify the effect of habit in this connexion: one was the inevitable impulse given to the will by the exaltation attendant upon a new religious movement; the other was the impulse given by the supremely difficult physical surroundings in which the new colonies found themselves. Foster writes on these points: 'The first Puritans, sure in their own hearts that they were the elect of God, found the doctrine necessary to sustain them in the tremendous struggle through which they passed. . . Hence the doctrine nerved to greater activity; and it produced a similar effect during the first period of the promulgation of Calvinism, among every nation which accepted the system.'[1] The force of the will was strengthened at the beginning, then, at the same time that its existence was denied and that reliance upon its manner of functioning (that is, upon good works) was, from a doctrinal standpoint, regarded as sin. The will, highly stimulated, but no longer studied and guided by the flexible and sensitive ethical scholarship of the Roman tradition, might easily result in dangerous action.

Andrews speaks of this subject as follows:

The dynamic agency . . . the driving force which overrode all opposition, legal and otherwise, was the profound conviction of the Puritan leaders that they were doing the Lord's work. They looked upon themselves as instruments in the divine hand for the carrying out of a great religious mission, the object of which was the rebuilding of God's church in a land—the undefiled land of America—divinely set apart as the scene of a holy experiment that should renovate the church at large, everywhere corrupt and falling into ruins. This new and purified community was to be the home of a saving remnant delivered from the wrath to come and was to serve as an example to the mother church of a regenerated form of faith and wor-

[1] *A Genetic History of the New England Theology*, by Frank Hugh Foster, University of Chicago Press, 1907, p. 29.

ship. It was also to become a proselyting centre for the
conversion of the heathen and the extension of the true
gospel among those who knew it not. In the fulfilment of
this mission the Puritans counted obstacles, moral and
physical, of no moment. Theirs was a religious duty to
frustrate their enemies, to eradicate all inimical opinions,
religious and political, and to extend the field of their
influence as widely as possible. Once they had determined
on their rules of polity and conduct, as laid down in the
Bible and interpreted by the clergy, they had no doubts of
the justness and rightness of their course. The means employed might savour of harshness and inequity, but at all
costs and under all circumstances, error, sin, and idolatry,
in whatever form appearing and as determined by themselves, must be destroyed. In the process, as events were to
prove, a great many very human motives played an important part in interpreting the law of God, and personal
likes and dislikes, hypocrisy, prejudice, and passion got
badly mixed with the higher and more spiritual impulses
that were actively at work purging the church of its
errors.[1]

Over a long period, however, the doctrine of predestination would naturally lead to religious apathy; for
it offered no explicit motive to action; and this is precisely that to which it led, for after the Great Awakening
of the middle of the eighteenth century, itself a reaction
to previous decay in the Church, the Church lost power
rapidly, and by the opening of the nineteenth century
was succumbing on every hand to Unitarianism, a
mildly moralistic creed, in which the element of super-
naturalism was minimized, and which, in turn, yielded
rapidly among the relatively intellectual classes to
Romantic ethical theory, especially as propounded by
the Transcendentalists. 'It has never been a good way to
induce men to repent', says Foster, 'to tell them that they

[1] Charles M. Andrews, op. cit., vol. i, pp. 430–1.

cannot.'[1] Or at least the method has never been highly successful except when employed by a rhetorician of the power of Edwards, or by an orator of the effectiveness of Whitefield; and the effect can scarcely be expected long to outlive the immediate presence of the speaker. The Unitarians, in depriving the ethical life of the more impressive aspects of its supernatural sanction, and in offering nothing to take the place of that sanction, all but extinguished intensity of moral conviction, although their own conviction—we may see it protrayed, for example, in *The Europeans*, by Henry James, and exemplified in the lucid and classical prose of W. E. Channing—was a conviction, at least for a period, of the greatest firmness and dignity. Emerson eliminated the need of moral conviction and of moral understanding alike, by promulgating the allied doctrines of equivalence and of inevitable virtue. In an Emersonian universe there is equally no need and no possibility of judgement; it is a universe of amiable but of perfectly unconscious imbeciles; it is likewise a universe in which the art of the fictionist—or for that matter, any other art—can scarcely be expected to flourish. A fictionist who has been in any considerable measure affected by Emersonian or allied concepts, or even who is the product of the historical sequence which gave rise to Emerson, is likely to find himself gravely confused and may even find himself paralysed; and we have only to read such a document, to cite a single example, as *The New Adam and Eve*, to realize that Hawthorne's own moral ideas, in spite of his intense but conflicting moral sentiments, and in spite of his professed dislike for Emerson's philosophy, were much closer to the ideas of Emerson than to those of Edwards.

Now in examining Hawthorne, we are concerned

[1] Frank Hugh Foster, op. cit., p. 29.

with two historical centres: that of the first generation of Puritans in New England, in which occurs the action of *The Scarlet Letter*; and that of the post-Unitarian and Romantic intellectuals, in which was passed the life of Hawthorne.

Hawthorne, by nature an allegorist, and a man with a strong moral instinct, regardless of the condition of his ideas, found in the early history of his own people and region the perfect material for a masterpiece. By selecting sexual sin as the type of all sin, he was true alike to the exigencies of drama and of history. In the setting which he chose, allegory was realism, the idea itself; and his prose, always remarkable for its polish and flexibility, and stripped, for once, of all superfluity, was reduced to the living idea, it intensified pure exposition to a quality comparable in its way to that of great poetry.

The compactness and complexity of the allegory will escape all save the most watchful readers. Let us consider the following passage as a representative example. Hester has learned that the magistrates and clergy are considering whether or not she ought to be separated from her child, and she waits upon Governor Bellingham in order to plead with him:

On the wall hung a row of portraits, representing the forefathers of the Bellingham lineage, some with armour on their breasts, and others with stately ruffs and robes of peace. All were characterized by the sternness and severity which old portraits so invariably put on; as if they were the ghosts, rather than the pictures, of departed worthies and were gazing with harsh and intolerant criticism at the pursuits and enjoyments of living men.

At about the centre of the oaken panels, that lined the hall, was suspended a suit of mail, not, like the pictures, an ancestral relic, but of the most modern date; for it had been manufactured by a skilful armourer in London, the same year in which Governor Bellingham came over to New England. There was a steel head-piece, a cuirass, a gorget, and greaves, with a pair of gauntlets and a sword hanging beneath; all, especially the helmet and breast-plate, so highly burnished as to glow with white radiance, and scatter an illumination everywhere about the floor. This bright panoply was not meant for mere idle show, but had been worn by the Governor on many a solemn muster and training field, and had glittered, moreover, at the head of a regiment in the Pequot war. For, though bred a lawyer, and accustomed to speak of Bacon, Coke, Noye, and Finch as his professional associates, the exigencies of this new country had transformed Governor Bellingham into a soldier as well as a statesman and ruler.

Little Pearl—who was as greatly pleased with the gleaming armour as she had been with the glittering frontispiece of the house—spent some time looking into the polished mirror of the breast-plate.

'Mother,' cried she, 'I see you here. Look! Look!'

Hester looked, by way of humoring the child; and she saw that, owing to the peculiar effect of the convex mirror, the scarlet letter was represented in gigantic and exaggerated proportions, so as to be greatly the most prominent feature of her appearance. In truth, she seemed absolutely hidden behind it. Pearl pointed upward, also, at a similar picture in the head-piece; smiling at her mother with the elfish intelligence that was so familiar an expression on her small physiognomy. That look of naughty merriment was likewise reflected in the mirror, with so much breadth and intensity of effect, that it made Hester Prynne feel as if it could not be the image of her own child, but of an imp who was seeking to mold itself into Pearl's shape.

The portraits are obviously intended as an apology for the static portraits in the book, as an illustration of the principle of simplification by distance and by generalization; the new armour, on the other hand, is the new faith which brought the Puritans to New England, and which not only shone with piety—'especially the helmet and breast-plate', the covering of the head and heart—but supported them in their practical struggles with physical adversaries, and which in addition altered their view of the life about them to dogmatic essentials, so that Hester was obliterated behind the fact of her sin, and Pearl transformed in view of her origin. Governor Bellingham, in his combination of legal training with military prowess, is representative of his fellow colonists, who displayed in a remarkable degree a capacity to act with great strength and with absolutely simple directness upon principles so generalized as scarcely to be applicable to any particular moral problem, which mastered moral difficulties not by understanding them, but by crushing them out.

Historically and relatively considered, Richard Bellingham might conceivably have been spared this function in the story, for of his group he was one of the two or three most humane and liberal; but the qualities represented were the qualities of the group of which he was a leader, and were extremely evident in most of the actions of the colony. Perhaps the best—or in another sense, the worst—embodiment of these qualities is to be found in John Endecott, of whom Andrews gives the following characterization:

Endecott had few lovable qualities. He was stern, unyielding, and on some subjects a zealot. Johnson apostrophizes him as 'strong, valiant John', whom Christ had called to be his soldier, but the Old Planters, most if not all of whom were Anglicans and demanded service according to the Book of Common Prayer, deemed themselves slaves and took in very bad part his determination to suppress the Church of England in the colony. They preferred Roger Conant, who though a less forcible man was one much easier to get along with. Endecott's later career discloses his attitude toward those who differed with him—the heathen Indian, the Quaker, the prisoner before him for judgement, and the Brownes and other upholders of the Anglican service who were disaffected with the Puritan government. It also shows his dislike of forms and devices that offended him—the Book of Common Prayer, the cross of St. George, and the Maypole. He was hard, intolerant, and at times cruel. Even the Massachusetts government caused him 'to be sadly admonished for his offence' in mutilating the flag at Salem in 1635, charging him with 'rashness, uncharitableness, indiscretion, and exceeding the limits of his calling'; and again in the same year 'committed' him for losing his temper. Endecott once apologized to Winthrop for striking 'goodman Dexter', acknowledging that he was rash, but saying that Dexter's conduct 'would have provoked a very patient man'. The best that can be said of him has been said by Chapple ('The Public Service of John Endecott,' Historical Collections, Essex Institute), an essay in the best Palfrey manner. It is odd that Endecott should have chosen for his seal a skull and cross-bones.[1]

It is interesting to observe in such a passage, as in many others, that the Puritans cannot be discussed, nor can they discuss each other, without the language employed exceeding the limits proper to predestinarians and invoking the traditional morality of the older churches; yet the attempt to ignore this traditional morality as far as might be, and, in the matter of formal doctrine, to repudiate it, unquestionably had much to do with the formation of such characters as Professor Andrews here describes and as Hawthorne in the last passage quoted from him symbolizes. The imperceptive, unwavering brutality of many of the actions committed in the name of piety in the Massachusetts colonies more than justified the curse and prophecy uttered by Matthew

[1] Charles M. Andrews, op. cit., vol. i, p. 361, n. 3.

Maule, that God would give these Puritans blood to drink; in the name of God, they had violently cut themselves off from human nature; in the end, that is in Hawthorne's generation and in the generation following, more than one of them drank his own heart's blood, as Hawthorne himself must have done in his ultimate and frustrated solitude, and more than one of them shed it.

It is noteworthy that in this passage from *The Scarlet Letter* Hawthorne turns his instrument of allegory, the gift of the Puritans, against the Puritans themselves, in order to indicate the limits of their intelligence; it is noteworthy also that this act of criticism, though both clear and sound, is negative, that he nowhere except in the very general notion of regeneration through repentance establishes the nature of the intelligence which might exceed the intelligence of the Puritans, but rather hints at the ideal existence of a richer and more detailed understanding than the Puritan scheme of life is able to contain. The strength of *The Scarlet Letter* is in part safeguarded by the refusal to explore this understanding; the man who was able in the same lifetime to write *The New Adam and Eve*, to conceive the art-colony described in *The Marble Faun*, and to be shocked at the nude statues of antiquity, was scarcely the man to cast a clear and steady light upon the finer details of the soul.

The conception of the book in general is as cleanly allegorical as is the conception of the passage quoted. Hester represents the repentant sinner, Dimmesdale the half-repentant sinner, and Chillingworth the unrepentant sinner. The fact that Chillingworth's sin is the passion for revenge is significant only to the extent that this is perhaps the one passion which most completely isolates man from normal human sympathies and which therefore is most properly used to represent an unregenerate condition.

The method of allegorization is that of the Puritans themselves; the substance of the allegory remained in a crude form a part of their practical Christianity in spite of their Calvinism, just as it remained in their non-theological linguistic forms, just as we can see it in the language of the best poems of so purely and mystically Calvinistic a writer as Jones Very, a living language related to a living experience, but overflowing the limits of Calvinistic dogma; Hawthorne's point of view was naturally more enlightened than that of the Puritans themselves, yet it was insufficiently so to enable him to recover the traditional Christian ethics except in the most general terms and by way of historical sympathy, for had a more complete recovery been possible, he would not have been so narrowly bound to the method of allegory and the frustration of the later romances would scarcely have been so complete.

Once Hawthorne had reduced the problem of sin to terms as general as these, and had brought his allegory to perfect literary form, he had, properly speaking, dealt with sin once and for all; there was nothing further to be said about it. It would not serve to write another allegory with a new set of characters and a different sin as the motive; for the particular sin is not particular in function, but is merely representative of sin in general, as the characters, whatever their names and conditions may be, are merely representative of the major stages of sin—there is no escape from the generality so long as one adheres to the method. There was nothing further, then, to be done in this direction, save the composition of a few footnotes to the subject in the form of sketches.

The only alternative remaining was to move away from the allegorical extreme of narrative toward the specific, that is, toward the art of the novelist. The attempt was made, but fell short of success. In *The House of the Seven Gables* and in *The Marble Faun* alike the moral understanding of the action—and there is a serious attempt at such understanding, at least in *The Marble Faun*—is corrupted by a provincial sentimentalism ethically far inferior to the Manicheism of the Puritans, which was plain and comprehensive, however brutal. And Hawthorne had small gift for the creation of human beings, a defect allied to his other defects and virtues: even the figures in *The Scarlet Letter* are unsatisfactory if one comes to the book expecting to find a novel, for they draw their life not from simple and familiar human characteristics, as do the figures of Henry James, but from the precision and intensity with which they render their respective ideas; the very development of the story is neither narrative nor dramatic, but expository. When, as in *The Marble Faun* or *The House of the Seven Gables*, there is no idea governing the human figure, or when the idea is an incomplete or unsatisfactory equivalent of the figure, the figure is likely to be a disappointing spectacle, for he is seldom if ever a convincing human being and is likely to verge on the ludicrous. Hawthorne had not the rich and profound awareness of immediacy which might have saved a writer such as Melville in a similar predicament.

His effort to master the novelist's procedure, however, was not sustained, for his heart was not in it. In *The Blithedale Romance*, he began as a novelist, but lost himself toward the close in an unsuccessful effort to achieve allegory; the four unfinished romances represent similar efforts throughout.

His procedure in the last works was startlingly simple; so much so, that no one whom I can recollect has run the risk of defining it.

In *The Scarlet Letter* there occurs a formula which one might name the formula of alternative possibilities. In the ninth chapter, for example, there occurs the following passage:

The people, in the case of which we speak, could justify its prejudice against Roger Chillingworth by no fact or argument worthy of serious refutation. There was an aged handicraftsman, it is true, who had been a citizen of London at the period of Sir Thomas Overbury's murder, now some thirty years agone; he testified to having seen the physician, under some other name, which the narrator of the story had now forgotten, in company with Dr. Forman, the famous old conjuror, who was implicated in the affair of Overbury. Two or three individuals hinted, that the man of skill, during his Indian captivity, had enlarged his medical attainments by joining in the incantations of the savage priests; who were universally acknowledged to be powerful enchanters, often performing seemingly miraculous cures by their skill in the black art. A large number—many of them were persons of such sober sense and practical observation that their opinions would have been valuable in other matters —affirmed that Roger Chillingworth's aspect had undergone a remarkable change while he had dwelt in the town, and especially since his abode with Dimmesdale. At first, his expression had been calm, meditative, scholarlike. Now, there was something ugly and evil in his face, which they had not previously noticed, and which grew still more obvious to sight the oftener they looked upon him. According to the vulgar idea, the fire in his laboratory had been brought from the lower regions, and was fed with infernal fuel; and so, as might be expected, his visage was getting sooty with smoke.

In such a passage as this, the idea conveyed is clear enough, but the embodiment of the idea appears far-fetched, and Hawthorne offers it whimsically and apologetically, professing to let you take it or leave it. Another example occurs in the eighteenth chapter;

Dimmesdale and Hester are sitting in the forest, planning the flight which ultimately is never to take place, and Pearl, the symbolic offspring of the untamed elements of human nature, and hence akin to the forest, which, in the Puritan mind, was ruled by Satan in person, plays apart:

A fox, startled from his sleep by her light footstep on the leaves, looked inquisitively at Pearl, as doubting whether it were better to steal off or renew his nap on the same spot. A wolf, it is said—but here the tale has surely lapsed into the improbable—came up and smelt of Pearl's robe, and offered his savage head to be patted by her hand. The truth seems to be, however, that the mother-forest, and these wild things which it nourished, all recognized a kindred wildness in the human child.

Similarly, in *The Marble Faun*, one never learns whether Donatello had or had not the pointed ears which serve throughout the book as the physical symbol of his moral nature; the book ends with the question being put to Kenyon, who has had opportunities to observe, and with his refusing to reply.

This device, though it becomes a minor cause of irritation through constant recurrence, is relatively harmless, and at times is even used with good effect. If we reverse the formula, however, so as to make the physical representation perfectly clear but the meaning uncertain, we have a very serious situation; and this is precisely what occurs, in some measure toward the close of *The Blithedale Romance*, and without mitigation throughout the four unfinished romances. We have in the last all of the machinery and all of the mannerisms of the allegorist, but we cannot discover the substance of his communication, nor is he himself aware of it so far as we can judge. We have the symbolic footprint, the symbolic spider, the symbolic elixirs and poisons, but we have not that of which they are symbolic; we have the hushed, the tense and confidential manner, on the part of the narrator, of one who imparts a grave secret, but the words are inaudible. Yet we have not, on the other hand, anything approaching realistic fiction, for the events are improbable or even impossible, and the characters lack all reality. The technique neither of the novelist nor of the allegorist was available to Hawthorne when he approached the conditions of his own experience: he had looked for signals in nature so long and so intently, and his ancestors before him had done so for so many generations, that, like a man hypnotized, or like a man corroded with madness, he saw them; but he no longer had any way of determining their significance, and he had small talent for rendering their physical presence with intensity.

Percy Boynton,[1] in quoting the following passages from *Septimius Felton*, refers to it as a self-portrait:

As for Septimius, let him alone a moment or two, and then they would see him, with his head bent down, brooding, brooding, his eyes fixed on some chip, some stone, some common plant, any commonest thing, as if it were the clew and index to some mystery; and when, by chance startled out of these meditations, he lifted his eyes, there would be a kind of perplexity, a dissatisfied, foiled look in them, as if of his speculations he found no end.

It is in this generation and the next that we see most clearly and bitterly the realization of Maule's prophecy. These men were cut off from their heritage, from their source of significance, and were abnormally sensitive to the influence of European Romanticism. In Emerson[2]

---

[1] *Literature and American Life*, by Percy H. Boynton, Ginn and Co., 1936, p. 518.

[2] This subject is fully discussed by H. B. Parkes, *The Hound and Horn*, vol. iv, July–Sept. 1932, pp. 581–601, and *The Pragmatic Test*.

the terms of New England mysticism and of Romantic amoralism were fused and confused so inextricably that we have not yet worked ourselves free of them. In Poe, a man born without a background, New England or any other, Romantic doctrine was introduced directly, in a form free of theological terminology, but in a form none the less which would tend in the long run to support the influence of Emerson. In Melville, the greatest man of his era and of his nation, we find a writer superior at certain points in his career—in books such as *Moby Dick* and *Benito Cereno*, for example—to the confusion and apparently understanding it; at other points—in books like *Mardi* and *Pierre*—succumbing to the confusion; at all points in his career made to suffer for the confusion of contemporary literary taste; and at the end, settling himself in silence, a figure more difficult to face than the later Hawthorne—more difficult, because more conscious, more controlled, and more nearly indifferent.

In Henry Adams we see the curse at work most clearly: intellectual but inconsecutive, unable to justify any principle of action, yet with a character of the highest, a character which demanded not only just action but its justification, he was damned to a kind of restless torment; in which, though an historian of great learning and of high academic distinction, he transformed the Middle Ages by a process of subtle falsification, into a symbol of his own latter-day New England longing; in which, though a stylist of great power and precision, he propounded the aesthetic theory that modern art must be confused to express confusion;[1] in which, though a philosopher of a sort, he created one of the most unphilosophical theories of history imaginable, as a poetic symbol of his own despair. In the suicide of Henry

[1] See the last three or four pages of *Mont Saint-Michel and Chartres*.

Adams's wife it is conceivable that we see the logical outcome of his own dilemma, an outcome in his own case prevented by the inheritance of character, which, like the inheritance of confusion, was bequeathed him by early New England.[1]

In *The Scarlet Letter*, then, Hawthorne composed a great allegory; or, if we look first at the allegorical view of life upon which early Puritan society was based, we might almost say that he composed a great historical novel. History, which by placing him in an anti-intellectual age had cut him off from the ideas which might have enabled him to deal with his own period, in part made up for the injustice by facilitating his entrance, for a brief time, into an age more congenial to his nature. Had he possessed the capacity for criticizing and organizing conceptions as well as for dramatizing them, he might have risen superior to his disadvantages, but like many other men of major genius he lacked this capacity. In turning his back upon the excessively simplified conceptions of his Puritan ancestors, he abandoned the only orderly concepts, whatever their limitations, to which he had access, and in his last work he is restless and dissatisfied. The four last romances are unfinished, and in each successive one he sought to incorporate and perfect elements from those preceding; the last, *The Dolliver Romance*, which he had sought to make the best, had he lived, is a mere fragment, but on the face of it is the most preposterous of all. His dilemma, the choice between abstractions inadequate or irrelevant to experience on the one hand, and experience on the other as far as practicable unilluminated by understanding, is tragically characteristic of the history of this country and of its literature; only a few scattered indi-

[1] This idea is very ably defended by Katherine Simonds, the *New England Quarterly*, Dec. 1936.

viduals, at the cost of inordinate labour, and often impermanently, have achieved the permeation of human experience by a consistent moral understanding which results in wisdom and in great art. If art is to be measured by the greatness of the difficulties overcome—and the measure is not wholly unreasonable, for there can scarcely be virtue without a comprehension of sin, and the wider and more careful the comprehension the richer the virtue—then these few writers are very great indeed. Hawthorne, when he reversed his formula of alternative possibilities, and sought to grope his way blindly to significance, made the choice of the later Romantics; and his groping was met wherever he moved by the smooth and impassive surface of the intense inane.

MORTON DAUWEN ZABEL

1901–1964

WILLA CATHER: THE TONE OF TIME

Craft and Character: Texts, Method, and Vocation in Modern Fiction, 1957

IN 1927, at fifty-four, Willa Cather, after three decades of steady and patient labour in her craft, stood at the height of her career, with fifteen years of her best work behind her and her most popular book, *Death Comes for the Archbishop*, claiming an unstinted admiration. When she died twenty years later,[1] she had already come to

---

[1] On 24 Apr. 1947. The date of Willa Cather's birth, long recorded as 1876, was discovered by E. K. Brown and Leon

appear as a survivor of a distant generation, remote from the talents of the past two anxious decades and the problems that had taxed them. This estrangement could have been no surprise to her. It was of her own choice and election. In 1936, in prefacing her collection of essays then called *Not Under Forty*, she had admitted that her writing could have 'little interest for people under forty years of age'. 'The world broke in two in 1922 or thereabouts', she said, and it was to 'the backward, and by one of their number', that her later books were addressed. She had, in fact, so addressed her work from the time she first found her real bearings in authorship with *O Pioneers!* in 1913. Backwardness was with her not only a matter of her material and temperament. It was the condition of her existence as an artist.

She was one of the last in the long line of commemorators and elegists of American innocence and romantic heroism that virtually dates from the beginnings of a conscious native artistry in American literature. Her books, once she found her natural voice and *métier*, and once she had put aside her Eastern subjects and earlier themes of rebellious protest, had become elegies, and Irving, Cooper, Hawthorne, Mark Twain, and Sarah Orne Jewett figure in their ancestry. When, on rare occasions, she praised her fellow craftsmen, from Miss Jewett to Katherine Mansfield, Thornton Wilder, Sigrid Undset, or Thomas Mann (who 'belongs immensely to the forward-goers. . . But he also goes back a long way, and his backwardness is more gratifying to the backward'), it was usually because they also turned to the past and rooted their values there.[1]

Edel in their biography of her (1953) to have been 7 Dec. 1873. Her book of essays, *Not Under Forty*, was retitled *Literary Encounters* when she included it in her collected edition in 1937.

[1] This sympathy in Willa Cather was confirmed in the last

She was quite aware of the false and bogus uses to which the historic sentiment had been put in American fiction. Its products surrounded her in the early 1900's when she was feeling her way toward her career: 'machine-made historical novels', 'dreary dialect stories', 'very dull and heavy as clay'—books by John Fox, Jr., James Lane Allen, Thomas Nelson Page, Mary Johnston, and their successful competitors, the memory of which she likened to 'taking a stroll through a World's Fair grounds some years after the show is over'. She knew

years of her life in a project she did not live to complete: 'to place the setting of a story straight across the world, quite far into the past—leaving America entirely—in the setting of medieval Avignon.' She was 'no longer at any pains to conceal her disillusion and aversion to most of the life about her'. An account of this project has been given by George N. Kates in an essay on 'Willa Cather's Unfinished Avignon Story', in *Five Stories* by Willa Cather (New York: Vintage Books, 1956). Mr. Kates says further of this story, whose title was to be *Hard Punishments*: 'Willa Cather reached first for the stars over the pure air of Nebraska, and then, when their light became obscured, would accept nothing less beautiful in their place simply because it was American.' Also: 'Like many people of plain origins, her first great need had been to be reassured, to still the youthful panic of seeming to possess only an inferior brand of everything that her more fortunate brothers and sisters took as naturally theirs. This was a prime need; but she had conquered it in her own way, which was the way of genius.'

Willa Cather's books were: *April Twilights*, poems (1903, new edition 1933); *The Troll Garden*, her early stories (1905); *Alexander's Bridge* (1912); *O Pioneers!* (1913); *The Song of the Lark* (1915, revised 1932); *My Ántonia* (1918); *Youth and the Bright Medusa*, stories (1920); *One of Ours* (1922); *A Lost Lady* (1923); *The Professor's House* (1925); *My Mortal Enemy* (1926); *Death Comes for the Archbishop* (1927); *Shadows on the Rock* (1931); *Obscure Destinies*, tales (1932); *Lucy Gayheart* (1935); *Not Under Forty*, essays (1936); *Sapphira and the Slave Girl* (1940). Posthumous volumes were *The Old Beauty*, three tales (1948) and *Willa Cather on Writing* (1949). A 'Library Edition' in thirteen volumes, with some revisions, appeared in 1937–41.

that Miss Jewett had shone like a star in that lustreless company; that Henry James's 'was surely the keenest mind any American had ever devoted to the art of fiction'; that Stephen Crane 'had done something real'. She also had to learn the secret of their distinction the hard way. She came out of the West attracted by the prairie girl's mirage of the East—its cities, salons, studios, opera houses, Beacon Hill sanctities, the fever and excitement of New York, the lure of Atlantic liners, with the shrines of Europe beckoning beyond. Her early stories, many of them never collected from magazines, are full of this worshipful glamour, and she was already past thirty-five when she tried to make something of it in her first novel, *Alexander's Bridge* of 1912, which combined a problem out of Edith Wharton, a setting and something of a manner out of Henry James, and an outsider's clumsiness in handling them, with inevitable results in self-conscious stiffness and crudity of tone.

Only then did she remember the advice Sarah Orne Jewett had once given her: 'The thing that teases the mind over and over for years, and at last gets itself put down on paper—whether little or great, it belongs to Literature.' 'Otherwise', as Miss Jewett had also said, 'what might be strength in a writer is only crudeness, and what might be insight is only observation; sentiment falls into sentimentality—you can write about life, but never life itself.' Willa Cather put Beacon Hill and Bohemia behind her. She returned to the Nebraska of her girlhood—to a prairie town trying hard not to be blown away in the blast of a winter wind. She found the local habitation of her talent, and with *O Pioneers!* her serious career in art began.

From that point she began her journey into lost time, going back beyond Nebraska, Colorado, and Kansas to colonial New Mexico, to eighteenth-century Quebec, and finally to the pre-Civil War Virginia of her family, every step taking her deeper into the values and securities she set most store by. She had, to help her, her rediscovered devotion to the scenes of her early youth, the Western fields and skies she called 'the grand passion of my life', her brilliant gift for rendering landscape and weather in the closest approximation to the poetic art of Turgenev and Gogol American fiction has seen, her retentive sympathy for the life of farms, small towns, prairie settlements, immigrant colonies, and South-western outposts and missions. In all the tales of regional or pioneer America that have been produced in the past half-century, nothing has exceeded her skill in evoking the place-spirit of rural America in her finest books—*My Ántonia*, *A Lost Lady*, *The Professor's House*, *Death Comes for the Archbishop*, and *Obscure Destinies*.

The pathos of distance by which she induced her special poetry into these scenes was, of course, stimulated by her feeling that the inspiring landscape of the prairies, deserts, and mountains, no less than the graceful charm of colonial Virginia or old New York, had been obliterated by a vulgar and cheapening modernity. The garage that had been built on Charles Street in Boston on the site of the house where Mrs. James T. Fields had once held court to 'Learning and Talent' was symptomatic for Willa Cather of a general and humiliating degradation. So too the old wagon roads of the West, 'roads of Destiny' that 'used to run like a wild thing across the open prairie', had been resurveyed and obliterated to make highways for tourist and motor traffic. The railways once 'dreamed across the mountains' by a race of Titans, highways in the heroic conquest of the West, were streamlined for commuters between

New York and California. Wooden houses and piazza'd mansions, once landmarks of pioneer fortitude and hospitality, came down and suburban Tudor or sham Château went up in their place. The frontier universities that had once fostered a scholarship of vision and historical passion yielded to academic power plants thick with politics and careerism. She despised such a world, whose literature itself she saw as 'mere statistics' and 'sensory stimuli', and apparently she preferred to be despised by it.

The interesting thing about Willa Cather's career is that it started in protest against and flight from the very world she ended by idealizing and mourning. It recapitulates a characteristic American pattern of rebellion and return, censure and surrender. The prairie and the small town, the Western hinterland and the neighbourly community, as she presented them in her best early stories—'A Wagner Matinée', 'Paul's Case', 'The Sculptor's Funeral', 'A Death in the Desert'—were objects of a moral reproach and castigation as severe as any she later directed against the vulgarizing influences of the modern world. She was in fact a pioneer in the twentieth-century 'revolt from the village', and she spared no scorn in describing the provincial spirit. It had created the life of a 'dunghill', of petty existences, of 'little people' and a small humanity, of stingy hates and warping avarice that made generous spirits shrivel and ardent natures die. The savagery of her indictment was perhaps the harshest feeling she ever summoned in her work. Her frontier in those days was not the West; it was the East and the world of art, with desire the goad of her heroes and heroines and the running theme of her stories, as much as it was of Dreiser's or later of Scott Fitzgerald's.

It was in young artists—the dreaming, headstrong,

fractious, or unstable young, fated to defeat or bad ends
by the materialism and hostility of their surroundings—
that she first envisaged the heroic ideal. Paul, Katharine
Gaylord, Harvey Merrick, and Don Hedger are the
defeated or dishonoured 'cases' that foreshadow the
contrasting and triumphant lives of Alexandra Bergson,
Thea Kronborg, Ántonia Shimerda, Archbishop Mache-
beuf, and Nancy Till, and that lend their note of desire
or vision to the middle terms of Willa Cather's argument—the inspired natures who do not succeed but who,
by some force of character or apartness of temperament,
lend significance to the faceless anonymity around them.
These characters—the 'lost lady' Marian Forrester,
Myra Henshawe of *My Mortal Enemy*, Tom Outland
and Professor St. Peter of *The Professor's House*, even
the slighter Lucy Gayheart of a later novel—are the
most persuasive of Miss Cather's creations, her nearest
claims to skill in a field where she was admittedly
inexpert and limited: complex and credible psychology.
But somehow she never succeeded in bringing her
opposites into full play in a novel. They remained
irreconcilably differentiated, dramatically intractable,
morally and socially incapable of convincing complexity.

The full-bodied and heavily documented novel was
never congenial to her. She rightly understood her art
to be one of elimination and selection, which eventually
meant that it was at basis an art of simplification and
didactic idealization. *The Song of the Lark* and *One of
Ours* drag with detail. *My Ántonia* and *A Lost Lady* are
her finest successes because there her selection defines,
suggests, and evokes without falsely idealizing. When
she seized a theme of genuine social and moral poten-
tiality in *The Professor's House* or *My Mortal Enemy*, she
pared away its fuller substance until she produced books
that must remain, to her serious admirers, and against

whatever penetration and suggestive force they succeed in achieving, disappointingly frugal versions of two of the most interesting subjects in the America of her time. And when she decided to model *Death Comes for the Archbishop* on the pallid two-dimensional murals of Puvis de Chavannes, she prepared the way for the disembodied idealization, making for inertness and passivity, that overtook her Quebec drama in *Shadows on the Rock*, weakest of her books and portent of the thinness that showed increasingly in her later volumes.

What overtook her plots and characters was the same inflexibility that overtook her version of American life and history. She could not bring her early criticism into effective combination with her later nostalgic sentiment. Her case is not an isolated one. The American writing of the forty years during which she came to her literary maturity—its fiction and verse, and more specifically its criticism—shows other instances of a similar kind: of writers who began by vigourously but dispropor-tionately castigating the idealistic or materialistic tradi-tions in American life and literature and who eventually arrived at a sentimentalization equally unbalanced and simplistic. So Willa Cather, having never mastered the problem of desire in its full social and moral condi-tioning, passed from her tales of ambitious artists and defeated dreamers, worsted by provincial mediocrity or careerism, to versions of the American faith and its defeat that never came to satisfactory grips with the conditions of social conflict and personal morality. As her lovers, her artists, her pioneers, and her visionary Titans became disembodied of complex thought or emotion, so her America itself became disembodied of its principles of growth, crisis, and historical maturity. There obviously worked in her temperament that 'poetic romanticism' to which Lionel Trilling has referred her problem: what Parrington called 'the inferior complex of the frontier mind before the old and established'; the pioneer's fear of failure but greater fear of the success which comes 'when an idea becomes an actuality'; the doctrine of American individualism to which F. J. Turner credited the pioneer's failure to 'understand the richness and complexity of life as a whole'.[1] So to Willa Cather's early veneration for the distant goals and shining trophies of desire, ambition, and art, there succeeded a veneration for lost or distant sanctities which gradually spelled her diminution as a dramatic and poetic craftsman. The village, the prairie, the West, the New Mexican missions, thus became in time abstractions as unworkable, in any critical or moral sense, as her simplified understanding of Thomas Mann's Joseph saga. Art itself, in her versions of Flaubert, Mann, or Katherine Mansfield, took on a remote ideality and aesthetic pathos that do much to explain her distaste for Balzac, Dostoevsky, and Chekhov. And the Church, to which she finally appealed as a human and historic constant, became in her detached and inexperienced view of it the most abstract of all her conceptions, a cultural symbol, not a human or historical actuality, and the least real of any of the standards she invoked in her judgements and criticism of the modern world.

She defended her art in an essay, 'The Novel Démeublé', in 1922, which belongs among the theorizings by artists which constituted for Henry James an 'accident' which is 'happiest, I think, when it is soonest over'. At best it shows Willa Cather's temerity in venturing

[1] Lionel Trilling, 'Willa Cather', in *After the Genteel Tradition: American Writers since 1910*, edited by Malcolm Cowley (1937); Vernon Louis Parrington in *Main Currents in American Thought* (1927–30); Frederick Jackson Turner in *The Frontier in American History* (1920).

into 'the dim wilderness of theory'; at its worst it must be taken as one of those ventures which justify themselves chiefly because they tell what a restricted view of art some writers must impose on themselves in order to get their own kind of work done. In 1922 it had some value as a warning against the excesses of realism and documentation in fiction, as a preference for feeling and insight over 'observation' and 'description'. But when it went on to assert that Balzac's material—not merely Paris and its houses but 'the game of pleasure, the game of business, the game of finance'—is 'unworthy of an artist', that the banking system and Stock Exchange are scarcely 'worth being written about at all', and that 'the higher processes of art are all processes of simplification', it set Miss Cather down as an aesthetic fundamentalist whose achievement was bound, by the nature of her beliefs, to be sharply curtailed and inhibited. She stood by the essay; she reprinted it unmodified in *Not Under Forty* and in her collected edition. And there it shows, *post factum*, how little a principle of deliberate simplification serves its believer if he is also an artist. Willa Cather set up a standard directly opposed to Zola's programme for naturalism—and similarly disabling in its literalness and exclusiveness. For both sensibility and naturalism arrive at the same impasse when they deny art its right to richness of thought and complexity. What such principles limit is not merely craftsmanship; it is substance and experience. She saw as little as Zola did that to inhibit craftsmanship or content is to inhibit or starve the sensibility and insight that nourish them, and to arrive at the sterility of high-mindedness and the infirmity of an ideal. As with Zola, her practice escaped the infirmity when it disobeyed her theory. It is artists who have denied their art and theory no possible risk, challenge, or complexity who have arrived at a surer lease on creative life; it is to James and Conrad, as to Yeats, Eliot, and Valéry, that we turn, in their theory no less than in their practice, for the more responsible clues to endurance and authority in modern literature.

Yet it was by means of such simplification, discipline, conscious curtailment, that Willa Cather made her own achievement possible and wrote the books of her best years—books which, if too often minor in substance, are wholly her own, and if elegiac in their version of American history, recall a past that was once, whatever its innocence, a reality, and that required, in its own delusions as much as in the heroic versions of it she created, the correction and resistance of a later realism. The boy who told the story of *My Ántonia*, finding himself transported from Virginia to the prairies of Nebraska, said: 'I had the feeling that the world was left behind, that we had got over the edge of it, and were outside man's jurisdiction. I had never before looked up at the sky when there was not a familiar mountain ridge against it.' For thirty years Willa Cather found her clue to the heroic values of life in that Western world of open plains and pioneer struggle, lying, with its raw earth, untested possibilities, and summons to heroic endeavour, beyond the familiar jurisdiction of codes and laws. But when, in her last novel, *Sapphira and the Slave Girl* in 1940, she at last turned back, for the first time in her literary career, from Nebraska to the Virginia of her birth and earliest memories, to a country of older laws and severer customs—to Back Creek Valley west of the Blue Ridge and to the house of Henry Colbert, the miller, and his wife Sapphira, a Dodderidge of Loudon County—she brought the air of the more primitive Western world, with its insistence on primary or primitive emotion, into it.

The story offered the familiar features of her prairie tales. There is the retreat to the past, now 1856, when human dignity and honour were not yet outlawed by the confused motives and vulgar comforts of modern times; there is the idealizing pathos of distance and lost beauty; there is an epilogue that brings the story twenty-five years nearer—but only to 1881—when time has dissolved old conflicts, relaxed old tensions, and healed old wounds by its touch of humility and disillusionment. There is a stoic husband, asking no questions of an unkind destiny, and an imperious wife who finds herself exiled in the rough country over the Blue Ridge as earlier heroines like Marian Forrester and Myra Henshawe were exiled in the rough country of the West, self-confounded by her pride and fear of truth, defeating herself rather than allow victory or happiness to others. There is also a young girl, the Negro slave Nancy, on whom Sapphira vents her disappointment and jealousy, another embodiment of the spirit of youth and natural grace which had already appeared in Alexandra, Thea, Ántonia, Tom Outland, and Lucy Gayheart—the pure in heart whom no evil can wholly defeat and on whom Willa Cather fixed for her faith in character in an age of warring egotisms and debasing ambition.

She thus risked not only a repetition of characters and effects in which her expertness had already passed from mastery to formulation. She duplicated her matter and her pathos so narrowly as to make unavoidable the impression that what was once a sincere and valid theme had been subjected to a further attenuation of sentimental argument and special pleading. This effect was emphasized by the insistent plainness and candour of manner to which she adhered—that conscious simplicity, fiction most decidedly and stubbornly *démeublé*, which at times (in *My Ántonia* and *A Lost Lady* or stories like 'Neighbour Rosicky' and 'Old Mrs. Harris') she raised to a point of conviction and lyric poignance that must remain her indisputable achievement as an artist, but which on other occasions (*One of Ours, Shadows on the Rock*, almost abjectly in 'The Old Beauty') she permitted to lapse either into a didactic dullness of sobriety or into a sentimentality that begs the whole question of creating and substantiating character by means of creative language, sensation, and observed detail.

Her devotion to the past and its perished beauty was sincere but inevitably limited by a didactic principle and threatened by the inflexibility of an idealistic convention. Only when her sentiment was toughened by personal or atmospheric realism did she bring off her pathos successfully, and only when her idealism was grounded in a hard sense of physical and regional fact was she able to avoid banality and abstraction. To reread the whole of her work today is to realize how deliberately she accepted her risks and limitations in order to win her prizes. It is to see that the subtlety and scope of her themes—*The Professor's House* remains the most significant case—could readily fail to find the structure and substance that might have given them a convincing force or redeemed them from the tenuity of a sketch. It is to realize also that her novels reduce to a single motive and pattern whose sincerity is undeniable but rudimentary and which eventually becomes threadbare. But it is also to admit, finally, that in her best work Willa Cather brought to a kind of climax and genuine epic vision the sensibility of the American women who had preceded her—Rose Terry Cooke, Sarah Jewett, Mary Wilkins Freeman—and that she sublimated to its essentials a conception of pioneer life and native energy which in other hands has generally lapsed into crass romanticism and the more blatant kinds of American eloquence.

It was her honesty and persistence in rendering this quality that made possible her real contribution to contemporary, and to American, writing, and permitted her to touch, across a century, the ancestors she defined for herself: Hawthorne, Thoreau, Mark Twain. She defined, like Dreiser, Scott Fitzgerald, and a few of her other contemporaries between 1910 and 1930, a sense of proportion in American experience. She knew what it meant to be raised in the hinterland of privation and harsh necessities; knew what it meant to look for escape to Chicago and the world beyond; knew how much has to be fought in one's youth and origins, what the privileges of the richer world mean when they are approached from the outposts of life, what has to be broken away from and what has to be returned to for later nourishment, and how little the world becomes when its romantic distances and remote promise are curtailed to the dimensions of the individual destiny. This sense of tragic limitation insures the saving leaven of realism and moral necessity in Dreiser's novels; it was given superb expression by Scott Fitzgerald in the last eight pages of *The Great Gatsby* and in *Tender is the Night*; it has been given another and classic version in the work of Katherine Anne Porter. Willa Cather unquestionably had something to do with preserving for such artists that proportion and perspective in American experience.

The space of seventy years is too short in human history, even in the headlong pace of modern history, to permit anyone to claim that he saw the world break in two during it. The measure of the human fate is not to be calculated so conveniently, even in a century of disturbance like the twentieth, and least of all in the moral perspective to which the serious artist or moralist must address himself. To do so is to impose a personal sentiment on something too large to contain it. It was to such sentiment, with its attendant resentment and in-flexibility, that Willa Cather came to submit. But it must also be granted that she lived through a cleavage and a crisis in something more than American life; that she saw 'the end of an era, the sunset of the pioneer'; that it 'was already gone, that age; nothing could ever bring it back'; and she defined the pathos, if not the challenge and moral imperative, its passing imposed on every survivor and writer concerned with it. She did not succeed in surmounting the confines of her special transition and the discomfort it induced in her, and she did not write the kind of books that assure the future or the energy of a literature. That opportunity she con-sciously rejected. Talents who came after her have written fiction that surpasses hers in conflict and com-prehension, as in difficulty and courage—Cummings in *The Enormous Room*, Hemingway in *In Our Time* and *The Sun Also Rises*, Fitzgerald in *Tender is the Night*, Caroline Gordon in *None Shall Look Back*, Robert Penn Warren in *All the King's Men*, Eudora Welty in *A Curtain of Green* and *Delta Wedding*, Katherine Anne Porter in *Flowering Judas* and *Pale Horse, Pale Rider*, Faulkner in *The Sound and the Fury* and *Light in August*. Yet she did something in a time of distraction and cultural inflation to make the way clear for them, as much by the end she defined for one tradition as by the example of fidelity and personal scruple she set for her-self. No one who read her books between 1915 and 1930 can forget their poetry of evocation and retrospective pathos—no sensitive reader can miss it today—particu-larly if he shared, as most Americans have shared whether intimately or by inheritance, any part of the experience that went into their making. And Willa Cather also did something the aspirant to permanent quality rarely achieves: she wrote a few books—*My Ántonia* and *A Lost Lady* chief among them—that are not only American elegies but American classics, and that can still tell us, in a time of sanctified journalism and irresponsible sophistication, how much of a lifetime it costs to make that rare and expensive article.

F. O. MATTHIESSEN
1902–1950

TRADITION AND THE INDIVIDUAL TALENT

The Achievement of T. S. Eliot, 1947

> It is part of the business of the critic . . . to see litera-ture steadily and to see it whole; and this is eminently to see it *not* as consecrated by time, but to see it beyond time; to see the best work of our time and the best work of twenty-five hundred years ago with the same eyes.—Introduction to *The Sacred Wood*.

IN *After Strange Gods: A Primer of Modern Heresy*, T. S. Eliot stated that his aim was to develop further the theme of 'Tradition and the Individual Talent', which is probably his best-known essay. Nearly thirty years have now elapsed since it was written—and over thirty since his first notable poem, 'The Love Song of J. Alfred Prufrock'—a detail which underscores the fact that it is no longer accurate to think of Eliot's work as new or experimental. Indeed, with younger readers 'Tradition and the Individual Talent' is now as much of a classic as Matthew Arnold's 'The Study of Poetry'; and putting those essays side by side one can observe that Eliot's is equally packed with trenchant remarks on the relation of present to past, as well as on the nature of poetry itself.

It is illuminating to go farther and juxtapose the whole range of these writers' achievements. For, by so doing, one becomes aware of the extent to which Eliot's criticism has quietly accomplished a revolution: that in it we have the first full revaluation of poetry since *Essays in Criticism* appeared in 1865. Arnold's observations on the historical course of English poetry, his classification of the romantics of the age just before him, his dismissal of Dryden and Pope as authors of an age of prose, his exaltation of Milton, and his depreciation of Chaucer on the score of lacking 'high seriousness' —all of these views, sensitively elaborated, not only persuaded his generation but also, as Eliot has remarked, largely remain as the academic estimates of today. It is worth noting that A. E. Housman, who professed not to be a critic, also held most of them in his widely read lecture of 1933, 'The Name and Nature of Poetry'. Housman's enthusiasms remained those of the time when he was an undergraduate: he could see nothing in the seventeenth-century metaphysicals but perverse over-intellectualization, and he almost paraphrased Arnold's remarks on the school of Dryden. Moreover, when one goes through the names of the principal English critics since Arnold's death and since the brief plunge into the dead alley of aestheticism in the nineties, it is apparent that such representative work as that of Saintsbury, Whibley, or Bradley, or even that of W. P. Ker, was historical rather than critical, in the sense that it was engaged with description and categorization, filling in the outlines traced by Arnold, and only incidentally, if at all, raising any new questions. In America, Irving Babbitt, also indebted to Arnold (more, perhaps, than he recognized), was concerned with the relation of the artist's thought to society, but not at all with the nature of art. In the years just before the First World War, the speculations of T. E. Hulme and Ezra Pound brought a new quickening of life which prepared the way for Eliot's own development; but there was no detailed intensive re-examination of the quality and function of poetry until the publication of *The Sacred Wood* in 1920.

It could not be wholly clear then, but it has become so now, that the ideas first arriving at their mature expression in that volume definitely placed their author in the main line of poet-critics that runs from Ben Jonson and Dryden through Samuel Johnson, Coleridge, and Arnold. In fact, what has given the note of authority to Eliot's views of poetry is exactly what has made the criticism of the other writers just named the most enduring in English. They have not been merely theorists, but all craftsmen talking of what they knew at first hand. When Dryden writes about Chaucer, or Coleridge about Wordsworth, or Eliot about Donne, we may not agree on all points, but we take them seriously since we can observe at once their intimate understanding of what they are saying. With the generation of readers since the First World War, Donne has assumed the stature of a centrally important figure for the first time since the seventeenth century; and his rise has been directly connected with the fact that Eliot has enabled us to see him with fresh closeness, not only by means of his analysis of the method of metaphysical poetry but also because he has renewed that method in the rhythms and imagery of his own verse.

When Eliot is thought of in connexion with Arnold, probably the first thing that comes to mind is his reaction to the famous statement that the poetry of Dryden and Pope was 'conceived and composed in their wits, genuine poetry is conceived . . . in the soul'; his brief retort about poetry 'conceived and composed in the soul of a mid-century Oxford graduate'. In addition, one has the impression of deft, if inconspicuous sniping, kept up over quite a few years. What Eliot has attacked principally is not the conception of poetry as criticism of life; indeed, no one lately has taken that phrase very seriously except in so far as it throws light on Arnold's own poetry. The main offensive has been against certain jaunty inadequacies in Arnold's thought and, in particular, against his loose identification of poetry with religion. And yet, in his most recent remarks about Arnold, Eliot has recognized him as a friend, if not as a master; as one whose work at its best, both in verse and in criticism, has more to say to us than that of any other poet of his time.

Consequently, in any effort to gauge Eliot's achievement, to indicate just what traditions have entered into the shaping of his talent, it is important to remind oneself of the actual closeness of these two writers in the qualities of mind which they value. It might almost be either who remarks that 'Excellence dwells among rocks hardly accessible, and a man must almost wear his heart out before he can reach her'. For certainly there is in each a full understanding of the unremitting discipline for the critic in learning 'to see the object as it is'; an equal insistence on the current of fresh ideas in which a society must move as a primary condition for the emergence of mature art; an equal veneration for French intelligence; and, again and again, a similar scoring, not by logic, but by flexibility, resilience, and an intuitive precision. In addition, in more than one notable passage, such as those which reflect on the lonely relation of the thinker to society, there is almost an identical tone. When Arnold realizes that in a sense the critic's goal is never reached, that it is kept in sight only by unending vigilance, he says: 'That promised land it will not be ours to enter, and we shall die in the wilderness: but to have desired to enter it, to have saluted it from afar, is already, perhaps, the best distinction among contemporaries; it will certainly be the best title to esteem with posterity.' And Eliot takes up the echoing theme:

It is not to say that Arnold's work was vain if we say that it is to be done again; for we must know in advance, if we are prepared for that conflict, that the combat may have truces but never a peace. If we take the widest and wisest view of a Cause, there is no such thing as a Lost Cause because there is no such thing as a Gained Cause. We fight for lost causes because we know that our defeat and dismay may be the preface to our successors' victory, though that victory itself will be temporary; we fight rather to keep something alive than in the expectation that anything will triumph.

Although Eliot relates to the central values stressed by Arnold to a degree which has not heretofore been recognized, it would be misleading to slur over the equally marked divergences between them. The chief difference separating in quality both their criticism and verse is suggested in Eliot's remark that 'Arnold's poetry has little technical interest'. With Arnold, in so far as you can make such a division, the emphasis is on substance rather than on form. Such emphasis led him into his attempted definition of poetry as criticism of life, a phrase which would apply equally well to a novel as to a poem, and which wholly fails to suggest the created vision of life which constitutes the essence of all art.

The same emphasis also runs through Arnold's essays, where he gives us estimates of the value to the human spirit of poetry and of individual poets, but, although he frequently refers to 'the laws of poetic beauty and poetic truth', no detailed or even incidental examination of the precise nature of those laws emerges. With Eliot, the emphasis is on form. His essays on various Elizabethan dramatists, for example, are not concerned with the full-length rounded estimate, but with close technical annotation of detail. It is possible that he may sometimes regret his too sharp reversal: 'The spirit killeth, but the letter giveth life'; and yet it represents the intensity of dissatisfaction with the copious expansiveness of Arnold's age, with Swinburne and Tennyson far more than with Arnold himself. In thoughtful reaction, Eliot's method is spare and economical. He watches with the trained eye of the hawk, and then swoops on the one point that will illustrate the quality of the whole. His brief essays present in clearest outline the segment of the curve from which the complete circle can be constructed.

It is this preoccupation with craftmanship that has enabled him to relish so fully the virtues of Dryden. But Dryden's power has been, so to speak, simply one of Eliot's incidental discoveries. The principal elements entering into his revaluation of poetry can be most briefly described in terms of the poets who have left the deepest and most lasting mark on his own work: the seventeenth-century English metaphysicals, the nineteenth-century French symbolists, and Dante. Such a combination of interests, which he possessed even before his earliest published work, might at first glance seem not only unlikely but exotic for a young man of New England stock, born in St. Louis and educated at Milton and Harvard. But actually they are not so. They relate organically to his background, though an adequate demonstration of that fact would require a still unwritten chapter of American intellectual history, and might even surprise Eliot himself. Yet it is not to be forgotten that the symbolist movement has its roots in the work of the most thoroughly conscious artist in American poetry before Eliot, Edgar Poe; and that, therefore, in Eliot's taste for Baudelaire and Laforgue as well as for Poe, the wheel has simply come full circle. It is increasingly apparent that the renaissance of the New England mind, from Emerson and Thoreau to Emily Dickinson felt a deep kinship with the long-buried modes of thought and feeling of the seventeenth century; in fact, Emily Dickinson's poetry, especially, must be described as metaphysical. I do not suggest that Eliot is directly indebted to any of these writers; indeed, he once remarked to me both of his sustained distaste for Emerson, and of the fact that he had never read Miss Dickinson.

It must be noted, however, if only by way of parenthesis, that there is one author who grew out of the New England tradition to whom Eliot is greatly indebted. When he first began to write he could find among living artists of the older generation no poet who satisfied him, but, as Ezra Pound has remarked, it was Henry James, as well as Conrad, who taught them both 'that poetry ought to be as well written as prose'. In Eliot's case James taught him even more than that. In his tribute shortly after the novelist's death, Eliot spoke of him as 'the most intelligent man of his generation', by which he meant that, undistracted by 'ideas', James had maintained a point of view and had given himself wholly to the perfection of his craft, and that he had reflected on the novel as an art 'as no previous English novelist had done'. In addition, Eliot was fascinated by the way in which James did not simply relate but made the reader co-operate; by the richness of his 'references'; by the way, for example, in *The Aspern Papers*, he managed to give the whole feeling of Venice by the most economical strokes. Indeed, Eliot has said that the method in this story—'to make a place real not descriptively but by something happening there'—was what stimulated him to try to compress so many memories of past moments of Venice into his dramatic poem, superficially so different from James, 'Burbank with a Baedeker: Bleistein with a Cigar'. And what is even more significant, Eliot has perceived that James's 'real progenitor' was Hawthorne, that he cannot be understood without Hawthorne, that the essential strain common to them both was 'their indifference to religious dogma at the same time as their exceptional awareness of spiritual reality', their 'profound sensitiveness to good and evil', their extraordinary power to convey horror.

This brings us back to the point that no more than Henry James can Eliot be understood without reckoning with the Puritan mind. Its special mixture of passion overweighed by thought (as well as the less attractive combination of high moral idealism restrained by practical prudence that was probed by Santayana in 'The Genteel Tradition'); its absorption in the problem of belief and its trust in moments of vision; its dry, unexpected wit; its dread of vulgarity, as perplexing to the creator of 'Sweeney Erect' as to Henry James; its consciousness of the nature of evil, as acute in 'The Turn of the Screw' as in 'Ethan Brand' or 'Gerontion'; its full understanding of the dark consequences of loneliness and repression which are expressed in 'The Love Song of J. Alfred Prufrock' as well as in *The Scarlet Letter*; its severe self-discipline and sudden, poignant tenderness, to be found alike in Jonathan Edwards and in the author of *Ash Wednesday*—such attributes and preoccupations are common to the whole strain to which Eliot inextricably belongs. The natural relation of Dante to many elements in that strain is at once apparent. It need only be added that from Longfellow through Charles Eliot Norton, Santayana, and Charles Grandgent there was an unbroken line of Dante scholarship at Harvard. It may be that in the end Eliot gained a more challenging insight into the technical excellences of *The Divine Comedy* through conversations with Ezra Pound, but, at all events, in the preface to his own introduction to Dante he lists as his principal aids all the names which I have just mentioned.

To arrive not only at Eliot's debt to tradition but at an understanding of what he has himself added to it, it is essential at least to suggest more specific reasons why he has been attracted to these particular poets, and the exact use he has made of them. The need is more real in Eliot's case than it would be in most, since his own verse bears everywhere evidence of how his reading has been carried alive into his mind, and thus of his conception of poetry 'as a living whole of all the poetry that has ever been written'. Holding such a conception of the integral relation of the present to an alive past, believing that it is necessary for the poet to be conscious, 'not of what is dead, but of what is already living', he naturally also believes that one of the marks of a mature poet is that he should be 'one who not merely restores a tradition which has been in abeyance, but one who in his poetry re-twines as many straying strands of tradition as possible'. Perhaps the process would have been more compellingly described as 'fusing together' rather than 're-twining'; for only by some such process can the poet's work gain richness and density.

It is hardest to suggest in brief compass the extent of
Eliot's feeling for Dante, since he has himself devoted
many careful pages to defining exactly what he means
by calling him the most universal poet in a modern
language. That he does so regard him is of considerable
significance in throwing light on what qualities Eliot
most values in poetry, especially since he dwells chiefly
on the power of Dante's precision of diction, and of his
clear, visual images. He does not hesitate to say that he
believes Dante's simple style, his great economy of
words, makes him the most valuable master for anyone
trying to write poetry himself. That he does not believe
this style simple to attain is indicated by his laconic
sentence: 'In twenty years I have written about a dozen
lines in that style successfully; and compared to the
dullest passage of the "Divine Comedy", they are "as
straw".' It is also apparent, in view both of 'The Hollow
Men' and of the direction towards which he has been
moving since *Ash Wednesday*, that although he carefully
avoids saying that either Shakespeare or Dante is the
'greater', he is himself drawn more closely to the latter,
who, though he did not embrace so wide an 'extent and
variety of human life', yet understood 'deeper degrees of
degradation and higher degrees of exaltation'. It would
be glib to say that in *The Waste Land* and 'The Hollow
Men' Eliot wrote his *Inferno*, and that since then his
poems represent various stages of passing through a
Purgatorio; still such a remark may possibly illuminate
both his aims and achievement.

It is easier to illustrate the impact made upon Eliot by
the more restricted qualities of seventeenth-century
metaphysical poetry, particularly since they have also
appealed to many other readers of today. For it is not
accidental that the same people who respond to Proust
and Joyce have also found something important in

Donne. The remark that we have in the work of this
poet 'the fullest record in our literature of the disintegrat-
ing collision in a sensitive mind of the old tradition and
the new learning' might very well have been made about
The Waste Land. For, as has been frequently observed,
Donne's poetry also was born in part out of an increase
of self-consciousness. His probing, analytic mind was
keenly aware of the actual complexity of his feelings,
their rapid alterations and sharp antitheses; and our
more complete awareness of the sudden juxtapositions
of experience, of, in Eliot's phrase, 'the apparent irrelevance and unrelatedness of things', has drawn us strongly
to him. The jagged brokenness of Donne's thought has
struck a responsive note in our age, for we have seen a
reflection of our own problem in the manner in which
his passionate mind, unable to find any final truth in
which it could rest, became fascinated with the process
of thought itself. Eliot's earlier enthusiasm for this
element in Donne's mind is now considerably qualified
in view of his own growing desire for order and coherence; as is also some of his first response to the realization that we have in Donne the expression of an age that
'objects to the heroic and sublime and objects to the
simplification and separation of the mental faculties'.
But that such qualities have been deeply felt by a whole
generation of readers since 1918 is demonstrated by the
fact that even a character in Hemingway's *Farewell to
Arms* could quote from a metaphysical poem. It may
be that in reaction against Donne's previous neglect our
generation has gone to the extreme of exaggerating his
importance; and yet it would be hard to overestimate
the value of his discoveries as an artist. What he strove
to devise was a medium of expression that would correspond to the felt intricacy of his existence, that would
suggest by sudden contrasts, by harsh dissonances as well

as by harmonies, the actual sensation of life as he had himself experienced it. In sharp revolt against the too superficial beauty of *The Faerie Queene* and the purely 'literary' conventions of the sonneteers, he knew that no part of life should be barred as 'unpoetic', that nothing in mature experience was too subtly refined or too sordid, too remote or too commonplace to serve as material for poetry. His great achievement lay in his ability to convey 'his genuine whole of tangled feelings', as in 'The Extasie', the extraordinary range of feeling—from the lightest to the most serious, from the most spiritual to the most sensual —that can inhere in a single mood. This 'alliance of levity and seriousness' by which, as Eliot has observed, the seriousness is not weakened but intensified, 'implies a constant inspection and criticism of experience'; it involves 'a recognition, implicit in the expression of every experience, of other kinds of experience which are possible'. Such recognition demands a mind that is at once maturely seasoned, wise and discerning—and imaginative, a combination sufficiently rare to cause Eliot to maintain that 'it is hardly too much to say that Donne enlarged the possibilities of lyric verse as no other English poet has done'.

But Donne's technical discoveries did not belong to him alone. They were a product of a whole mode of thought and feeling which has seemed to Eliot the richest and most varied that has ever come to expression in English. He has described this mode as a development of sensibility, 'a direct sensuous apprehension of thought, or a re-creation of thought into feeling', which means that for all the most notable poets of Donne's time there was no separation between life and thought, and that their way of feeling 'was directly and freshly altered by their reading'. Such interweaving of emotions and thought exists in Chapman and Webster, and in the dense, masterful irregularity of the later plays of Shakespeare. It was as true for these poets as for Donne that 'a thought was an experience' which modified their capacity of feeling. As a result they could devour and assimilate any kind of experience, so that in their poetry passages of philosophical speculation stimulated by Montaigne or Seneca throb with as living a pulse as their own direct accounts of human passion. Indeed, one has only to turn to Montaigne and *Hamlet* and *Measure for Measure*, or to North's *Plutarch* and *Antony and Cleopatra* and *Coriolanus*, for complete examples of how reading as well as thought could be absorbed as vital experience.

How entirely Eliot believes such a capacity to be the only right state for the mature poet is emphasized by his extended comment that 'when a poet's mind is perfectly equipped for its work, it is constantly amalgamating disparate experience; the ordinary man's experience is chaotic, irregular, fragmentary. The latter falls in love, or reads Spinoza, and these two experiences have nothing to do with each other, or with the noise of the typewriter or the smell of cooking; in the mind of the poet these experiences are always forming new wholes.' That such a conviction concerning the creative process has sprung from one of Eliot's most recurrent discoveries about the nature of life is revealed when we find him writing, in a very different connexion: 'It is probable that men ripen best through experiences which are at once sensuous and intellectual; certainly many men will admit that their keenest ideas have come to them with the quality of a sense perception; and that their keenest sensuous experience has been "as if the body thought".' He was led to that reflection in contrasting the qualities of Henry James and Henry Adams, a contrast that brings out once more the elements that Eliot is continually stressing as characteristic of the greatest art. It also reveals a certain similarity that he felt between James and metaphysical poetry, thus making more apparent why he has been attracted to both and indicating the relations between two strands in his tradition. Deeply impressed by the acuteness of Adams's intelligence, Eliot yet felt a lack of full ripeness in his writing when compared with that of James. He expressed his distinction between them thus: 'There is nothing to indicate that Adams's senses either flowered or fruited . . . Henry James was not, by Adams's standards, "educated", but particularly limited; it is the sensuous contributor to the intelligence that makes the difference.'

In perhaps the most exciting phrase in all of his criticism, Eliot has called this rare fusion a way of feeling thought 'as immediately as the odour of a rose'. Such a capacity was possessed by later men in the seventeenth century, by Crashaw and Vaughan, and, in Eliot's account, found its last mature poetic voice in Andrew Marvell. The one thing common to the whole group, so diverse in their gifts and points of view, is, in Eliot's regard, 'that firm grasp of human experience, which is a formidable achievement of the Elizabethan and Jacobean poets'. He adds a further remark: 'This wisdom, cynical perhaps but untired (in Shakespeare, a terrifying clairvoyance), leads toward, and is only completed by, the religious comprehension'—a remark more heavily freighted with implications for his own development than would have been apparent at the time it was written, in 1921, the year before the publication of *The Waste Land*.

Similarities between Eliot's technical devices and those of Donne have been often observed: the conversational tone, the vocabulary at once colloquial and surprisingly strange—both of these a product of Eliot's belief in the relation of poetry to actual speech, and paralleling his use of 'non-poetic' material; the rapid association of ideas which demands alert agility from the reader; the irregular verse and difficult sentence structure as a part of fidelity to thought and feeling; and, especially, the flash of wit which results from the shock of such unexpected contrasts. But actually the manner in which sudden transitions are made in Eliot's verse owes much more to the method of the French symbolists. I. A. Richards has spoken of *The Waste Land* as 'a music of ideas', a phrase which suggests Eliot's particular attraction to Laforgue. By both poets connecting links are left out, as they are not by Donne, in an effort to utilize our recent closer knowledge of the working of the brain, of its way of making associations. That is to say, Eliot wants to suggest in the rhythms of his verse the movement of thought in a living mind, and thus to communicate the exact pattern of his meaning not so much by logical structure as by emotional suggestion. He is aware that such a method is dangerous, that it can easily lead into the false identity, 'Poésie, musique, c'est la même chose', which caused the vague obscureness of so much of Mallarmé's verse. But Eliot is equally sure that poetry can approach the condition of music without sacrificing its definite core of meaning so long as it has 'a definite emotion behind it'. He has understood the many-sided problem of the poet. He knows that he must not sacrifice either sense to sound, or sound to sense: 'Words are perhaps the hardest of all material of art: for they must be used to express both visual beauty and beauty of sound, as well as communicating a grammatical statement.'

In the preface to his translation of Perse's *Anabase* Eliot takes pains to point out that the French poet's suppression of 'explanatory and connecting matter' is not at all owing 'to incoherence, or to the love of crypto-gram', but to the deliberate belief that he can secure his most concentrated effect by the ordered compression of his sequence of images. Eliot is likewise convinced that 'there is a logic of the imagination as well as a logic of concepts', and, as he states elsewhere, that the one test of whether the sudden contrasts and juxtapositions of modern poetry are successful or not 'is merely a question of whether the mind is *serré* or *délié*, whether the whole personality is involved'. For, in words that take on greater significance the more one examines Eliot's own work, 'it is the unity of a personality which gives an indissoluble unity to his variety of subject'.

The principal quality which drew Eliot to the sym-bolists is one they possess in common with the meta-physicals, 'the same essential quality of transmuting ideas into sensations, of transforming an observation into a state of mind'. This quality might be defined more technically as 'the presence of the idea in the image', a definition with which I shall have more to do below. In both schools there is the demand for compression of statement, for centring on the revealing detail and elimi-nating all inessentials, and thus for an effect of compre-hensiveness to be gained by the bringing to bear of a great deal of packed experience on to a single moment of expression. In the symbolists there is an increased allusiveness and indirection, a flexibility in their verse designed to catch every nuance of their feeling. Such technical agility fascinated Eliot, especially in Laforgue, since it was coupled there with an unusual verbal adroitness—a combination of 'recondite words and simple phrasing', which is also to be found everywhere in Eliot's own early work; and likewise with a mocking-serious, worldly-aesthetic attitude which spoke directly to his own youthful sophistication. As a result, 'Prufrock', in the movement of its verse, its repetitions, and echoes, and even in its choice of theme, seems of all Eliot's poems to have been written most immediately under Laforgue's stimulus (though brought to a finished perfection of form which Laforgue's more impromptu verse scarcely attained); just as the verse of 'Gerontion' reveals the fullest impression of Eliot's mastery of the Jacobean dramatists.

The condensation of form that was demanded both by Donne and the symbolists logically builds its effects upon sharp contrasts, and makes full use of the element of surprise, which Eliot, as well as Poe, considers to have been 'one of the most important means of poetic effect since Homer'. It is always one of the prime functions of poetry to break through our conventional perceptions, to startle us into a new awareness of reality. As Hulme observed, 'poetry always endeavours to arrest you, and to make you continuously see a physical thing, to prevent you gliding through an abstract process'. In the poetry that Eliot most admires, poetry which has secured a union of thought and emotion, there will inevitably be an unexpected bringing together of material from seemingly disparate experiences. The reading of Spinoza and the smell of cooking will very possibly both enter into the full expression of a state of feeling, just as the most refined speculation from the Church fathers, a vivid detail from contemporary exploration, and the most coarsely sensual flash of wit unite in a single stanza of Donne's to make the expression of his love a concrete, living thing, very different from an abstract statement. Eliot's own kind of witty surprise is created in such a line as

I have measured out my life with coffee spoons.

'I have measured out my life'—the general, platitudinous

reflection is suddenly punctuated with an electric shock which flashes into the mind of the reader, in a single, concrete, ironic picture, Prufrock's whole futile way of existence.

But if the details of Eliot's style show everywhere the mark of his responsive mastery of the later symbolists, as well as of the metaphysicals, the impression of Baudelaire upon his spirit has been even more profound. The reason why he seems to have been stirred more deeply by *Les Fleurs du Mal* than by any other poetry written in the nineteenth century is, I think, suggested by the words which he has italicized in the sentence that indicates the nature of this debt:

It is not merely in the use of imagery of common life, not merely in the use of imagery of the sordid life of a great metropolis, but in the elevation of such imagery to the *first intensity*—presenting it as it is, and yet making it represent something much more than itself—that Baudelaire has created a mode of release and expression for other men.

For Baudelaire's intensity is the result of his having 'a sense of his own age', a quality not easy to analyse, but one which, as Eliot stresses it again and again in the course of discussing very different poets, is revealed to be one of his fundamental tests for great poetry. Such a sense is at an opposite pole from a familiarity with the surface details of a time, or from a sense of fashion. When Eliot finds that Blake possessed this sense as well as Villon, it is seen to consist in a condensed, bare honesty that can strike beneath the appearances of life to reality, that can grasp so strongly the intrinsic elements of life in the poet's own day that it likewise penetrates beneath the apparent variations of man from one epoch to another to his essential sameness. Eliot is quite aware that the degree of consciousness on the artist's part of such a sense has varied greatly in different ages, that whereas the great French novelists from Stendhal and Flaubert through Proust were deliberately occupied with analysing conditions of society as well as the individual, with chronicling 'the rise, the régime, and the decay of the upper bourgeoisie', on the other hand, it is in the very lack of such consciousness of social change and decay,

of corruptions and abuses peculiar to their own time, that the Elizabethan and Jacobean dramatists are blessed. We feel that they believed in their own age, in a way in which no nineteenth- or twentieth-century writer of the greatest seriousness has been able to believe in his age. And accepting their age, they were in a position to concentrate their attention, to their respective abilities, upon the common characteristics of humanity in all ages, rather than upon the differences.

But in any age the thing of highest importance for the poet is to 'express with individual differences the general state of mind, not as a *duty*, but simply because' —if he possesses that rare, unyielding honesty which alone will give his work depth—'he cannot help participating in it'. In such fashion Eliot dwells repeatedly on the integral relation of any poet's work to the society of which he is a part, to the climate of thought and feeling which give rise to his expression. In line with such reflections Eliot can say: 'The great poet, in writing himself, writes his time. Thus Dante, hardly knowing it, became the voice of the thirteenth century; Shakespeare, hardly knowing it, became the representative of the end of the sixteenth century, of a turning-point in history.'

In the case of Baudelaire, this ability to go beneath appearances to the most recurrently pervading elements in life was the result of the peculiar dogged strength with which he felt the torturing impact of the great modern city upon the lonely individual. For the very intensity of his suffering enabled him to see through the slogans of his age in a way that Victor Hugo, for example, could not; enabled him to cut beneath its 'bustle, programmes, platforms, scientific progress, humanitarianism, and revolutions which improved nothing' to a real perception of good and evil. Such a perception Eliot defines, in *After Strange Gods*, as 'the first requisite of spiritual life'. It is very close to Yeats's mature discovery that we begin to live only 'when we have conceived life as tragedy'. For both Yeats and Eliot recognize that there can be no significance to life, and hence no tragedy in the account of man's conflicts and his inevitable final defeat by death, unless it is fully realized that there is no such thing as good unless there is also evil, or evil unless there is good; that until this double nature of life is understood by a man, he is doomed to waver between a groundless, optimistic hopefulness and an equally chaotic, pointless despair. Eliot has learned from his own experience that the distinguishing feature of a human life consists in the occasions on which the individual most fully reveals his character, and that those are the moments of intense 'moral and spiritual struggle'. It is in such moments, rather than in the 'bewildering minutes' of passion 'in which we are all very much alike', that men and women come nearest to being real'—an affirmation which again underscores his inheritance of the central element in the Puritan tradition. And he has concluded that 'if you do away with this struggle, and maintain that by tolerance, benevolence, inoffensiveness, and a redistribution or increase of purchasing power, combined with a devotion on the part of an élite, to Art, the world will be as good as anyone could require, then you must expect human beings to become more and more vaporous'.

It is their penetration to the heart of this struggle between the mixed good and evil in man's very being, and thus to the central factors in human nature, which forms a common element between the three strains of poetry that have affected Eliot most deeply, between such writers as Dante, Webster, and Baudelaire. And consequently, when at the end of the first section of *The Waste Land*, Eliot's lines contain allusions to all three of these poets, he is not making a pastiche of his reading, or arbitrarily associating unrelated fragments:

Unreal City,
Under the brown fog of a winter dawn,
A crowd flowed over London bridge, so many,
I had not thought death had undone so many.
Sighs, short and infrequent, were exhaled,
And each man fixed his eyes before his feet.
Flowed up the hill and down King William Street,
To where Saint Mary Woolnoth kept the hours
With a dead sound on the final stroke of nine.
There I saw one I knew, and stopped him, crying:
    'Stetson!
'You who were with me in the ships at Mylae!
'That corpse you planted last year in your garden,
'Has it begun to sprout? Will it bloom this year?
'Or has the sudden frost disturbed its bed?
'Oh keep the Dog far hence, that's friend to men,
'Or with his nails he'll dig it up again!
'You! hypocrite lecteur!—mon semblable—mon frère!'

He wanted to present here the intolerable burden of his 'Unreal City', the lack of purpose and direction, the inability to believe really in anything and the resulting 'heap of broken images' that formed the excruciating contents of the post-war state of mind. But his city is Baudelaire's city as well, 'où le spectre en plein jour raccroche le passant'; it is the modern megalopolis dwarfing the individual. And it is given an additional haunting dimension as a realm of death in life by being linked with Dante's Limbo, the region of those dead who while on earth had 'lived without praise or blame', who had not been strong enough in will or passion either to do good or evil, and so were condemned for ever to wander aimlessly, in feverish, useless motion. And as this throng moves through the murky streets of wintry London, as dark at nine as at dawn, on its way, presumably, to jobs in shops and offices, the poet encounters one with whom he has shared experiences and now shares memories of war. The sense of the agonizing, since futile, effort to escape those memories, to bury those dead for good, is increased by a reminiscence of the dirge in *The White Devil*, one of the most poignantly terrifying passages in Webster's tragedy. And thus the three principal strains of poetry which have spoken so intimately to Eliot merge in a moment of acutely heightened consciousness. Eliot is not making mere literary allusions. He is not 'imitating' these poets; nor has he mistaken literature for life. Each of these references brings with it the weight of its special context, its authentic accent of reality, and thus enables Eliot to condense into a single passage a concentrated expression of tragic horror. And lest the reader think that such an awareness of the Unreal City is something special to the reading and experience of the poet, he, as well as Stetson, is reminded that it belongs both to Eliot and Baudelaire, and to himself, as part of the modern world, as well.

R. P. BLACKMUR

1904–1965

AN ADJUNCT TO THE MUSES' DIADEM: A NOTE ON E. P.

Language as Gesture, 1952

'IN the gloom, the gold gathers the light against it.'
It does not matter much what source the gloom has in
folly and misjudgement and human dark, if within the
gloom the gold still gathers the light against it. The line
occurs in Pound's eleventh Canto, one of those dealing
with Sigismondo Malatesta, written about 1922, and
thus, I think, at the heart of that period of Pound's work
which shows most light because there was most gold to
gather it, the period between 1918 and 1928: the period
of Propertius in Pound's remaking, of the translations
from the Provençal, of *Hugh Selwyn Mauberley*, and of
the first *Thirty Cantos*. Let us see, knowing the dimness
is only of time, what is (in Marianne Moore's phrase)
'not now more magnificent than it is dim'.

Take the line itself once more—'In the gloom, the
gold gathers the light against it'; does it not commit itself
in the memory by coming at an absolute image, good
anywhere the writs of language run, by the most ordinary possible means, the fused sequences of two trains
of alliteration, the one guttural and the other dental?
Does it not also, and more important, clinch the alliteration and the image by displaying itself, as Pound used to
argue all verse ought to display itself, in the sequence,
not of the metronome, but of the musical phrase? Do
we not come, thus, on a true blank-verse line where
something, which we here call music, lasts when the

words have stopped, and which locks, or gears, the words together when they are spoken? Nobody knows whether the words discover the music or the music discovers the unity in the words; nobody but a craftsman skilled at this particular job of work knows how to make words and music work in common with so little contextual or environmental force; without a drama or a situation; nobody, that is, but a craftsman skilled in the details of other men's work. 'In the gloom, the gold gathers the light against it.'

In the eighth Canto there is a running version of Malatesta's own lines beginning *O Spreti che gia fusti in questy regny*, which reads as follows:

> Ye spirits who of olde were in this land
> Each under Love, and shaken,
> Go with your lutes, awaken
> The summer within her mind,
> Who hath not Helen for peer
>   Yseut nor Batsabe.

Here again it is composition in the sequence of the musical phrase which lifts this most commonplace and traditional notion to the direct freshness of music, and without, as in songs actually sung, any disfigurement or blurring of the words. We resume, by the skill of the words and their order, not only the tradition but also the feeling that gave rise to the tradition, but we in no way repeat the localized version of the tradition that Malatesta himself used in (what would be) bad English of the twentieth century pretending to be fifteenth. Another example, the 'Alba' from *Langue d'Oc*, carries this variety of composition about as far as Pound, as craftsman, could force it. It is again translation.

> When the nightingale to his mate
> Sings day-long and night late
> My love and I keep state

> In bower,
> In flower,
> 'Till the watchman on the tower
> Cry:
>   'Up! Thou rascal, Rise,
>   I see the white
>   Light
>   And the night
>   Flies.'

Here, it is true, we are nearer both the regular or metro-
nomic pattern and an actual singing tune, but we are
there by exactly the means of musical composition; we
have only to think how Swinburne would have done it,
to see the delicacy and absoluteness of Pound's musical
phrase, and the difference is to be named by thinking of
what Pound called, and here made present, the 'prose
tradition in verse'. That tradition, that verse ought to be
at least as well written as prose, is exemplified, when one
has caught its idiosyncrasy of movement, in passage
after passage of the *Homage to Sextus Propertius*, nowhere
better for purposes of quotation than the opening of the
sixth selection.

> When, when, and whenever death closes our eyelids,
> Moving naked over Acheron
>   Upon the one raft, victor and conquered together,
> Marius and Jugurtha together,
>   one tangle of shadows.

The third and fourth lines in this passage are not at all
the same thing as what Propertius wrote, nor do they
need to have been for what Pound was doing.

> Victor cum victis pariter miscebitur umbris:
>   consule cum Mario, capte Iugurtha, sedes

is magnificent formal Latin with the special kind of
finality that goes with that mode of language and that

kind of musical creation in language. Pound used what he could catch of the mood in Propertius' mind—not the mode of his language—and responded to it with what he could make out of the best current mood and mode of his own time; that is why his versions of Propertius are called a Homage, and that is why they seem written in a mode of language (the prose tradition combined with composition in the musical phrase) which is an addition to the language itself. One more passage should suggest the characteristics of that mode. But for something to read in normal circumstances? For a few pages brought down from the forked hill unsullied?

> I ask a wreath which will not crush my head.
>   And there is no hurry about it;
> I shall have, doubtless, a boom after my funeral,
> Seeing that long standing increases all things
>   regardless of quality.

This and the 'Alba' quoted above are the extremes in opposite directions to which Pound brought his special mode; his very best work, the extreme of his own accomplishment, comes about when his mode is running in both directions at once, sometimes in the *Cantos*, sometimes in the two groups of poems called *Hugh Selwyn Mauberley*, and it is from these groups that we may select four examples. One is the fifth and concluding passage from the 'Ode pour l'Élection de son Sépulcre'.

> There died a myriad,
> And of the best, among them,
> For an old bitch gone in the teeth,
> For a botched civilization,
>
> Charm, smiling at the good mouth,
> Quick eyes gone under earth's lid,
>
> For two gross of broken statues,
> For a few thousand battered books.

'In the gloom, the gold gathers the light against it.'
There is no better poem of the other war, and it may
well come to be that there is no better poem to herald
the war just over, when we see what has happened in it.
One feels like addressing Pound as Williams addressed
the morning star: 'Shine alone in the sunrise, towards
which you lend no part.' The central distich, once the
context, both that before and the concluding distich, has
been mastered, makes both epitaph and epigraph, both
as near breathless and as near sound as words can be. It
is Propertius *and* the poets of the Langue d'Oc that wrote
them, the sequence of the musical phrase *and* the prose
tradition in verse, but leaning a little more strongly
toward Propertius and prose than Arnaut and music.

A little nearer to Arnaut, but not much, is a quatrain
from the preceding section of the same ode, but only by
reason of the rhymes. It needs no context:

> Faun's flesh is not to us,
> Nor the saint's vision.
> We have the Press for wafer;
> Franchise for circumcision.

It is prose in syntax; generalized or commonplace in
thought; but it is prose and commonplace moving into
music through a combination of its alliterative sequence
—its ear for syllabic relations and their development—
and the sequence of the idiomatic phrase. We can see—
or hear—this more clearly if we put it next to two
quatrains from 'Medallion', where the syllabic play is
as complex in English as Arnaut or Bertrans in Provençal, and where the rhyming is Pound's own.

> Luini in porcelain!
> The grand piano
> Utters a profane
> Protest with her clear soprano.

> The sleek head emerges
> From the gold-yellow frock
> As Anadyomene in the opening
> Pages of Reinach.

Eliot says that we must not be deceived by the roughness of the rhyme in these poems, but I do not see how anybody could see anything rough about a metric and syllabic practice which keep, as these lines do, all their sounds in the ear at once without blur or whir or anything but their own clear creation, as in this:

> Go, dumb-born book,
> Tell her that sang me once that song of Lawes:
> Hadst thou but song
> As thou hast subjects known,
> Then were there cause in thee that should condone
> Even my faults that heavy upon me lie
> And build her glories their longevity.

> Tell her that sheds
> Such treasure in the air,
> Recking naught else but that her graces give
> Life to the moment,
> I would bid them live
> As roses might, in magic amber laid,
> Red overwrought with orange and all made
> One substance and one colour
> Braving time.

These are the first two stanzas of the 'Envoi (1919)' to the first part of *Hugh Selwyn Mauberley*, and they are quoted last in our series of examples because, at least in the context here provided for them, they show almost perfectly the combination wanted—of the prose tradition and the musical phrase; and because, too, with some alteration of the pronouns, they are lines that might well be addressed to Pound himself—except on those occasions when he gave up his song (the subjects he had mastered as music) for the sake of subjects so called (songs which he had not mastered); for when he tried such subjects his poems are left so many

> Mouths biting empty air,
> The still stone dogs,
> Caught in metamorphosis, were
> Left him as epilogues;

just as when he kept to the songs he knew, he produced 'Ultimate affronts to human redundancies'—than which a poet of Pound's class can do nothing more.

But what is Pound's class, and how can it be described without any contemptuousness in the description and without giving the effect of anything contemptible in the class; for it is an admirable class and ought to be spoken of with admiration. Essentially it is the class of those who have a care for the purity of the tongue as it is spoken and as it sounds and as it changes in speech and sound, and who know that that purity can only exist in the movement of continuous alternation between the 'faun's flesh and the saint's vision', and who know, so, that the movement, not the alternatives themselves, is the movement of music.

It is the purity of language conceived as the mind's agency for creation or discovery, not merely manipulation or communication, that this class of poet works for; it is, so to speak, a pitch or condition of speech almost without reference to its particular content in a given work. The class is common enough, short of the work; it is the class of those everywhere who talk and read for the sake of talking and reading, the class of spontaneous appreciators; but it is a very uncommon class at the level of active work, and it is the active workers who make appreciation possible by providing immediate examples to train taste. It is executive work; it shows what can be done with the instrument by skill and continuous practice, and it reminds us, in terms of new prospects, of what has been done. But even more than those who read, those who write need the continuous example of poets supreme in the executive class or they would not know either what they ought to do or what it is possible for them to do in the collaboration between their conceptions and their language. Poets like Pound are the executive artists for their generation; he does not provide a new way of looking, and I think Eliot is mistaken in thinking his work an example of Arnold's criticism of life, but he provides the *means* of many ways of looking. If you criticize Pound for what he has said you come on the ancient commonplace refreshed through conventions that are immediately available; without his craftsmanship he would be a 'popular' poet in the pejorative sense: the convention is always interposed *between* the actuality and his reaction to it; even his best verse is only applicable to *other* situations, it never creates its own. But that is precisely what makes him so valuable to other poets, both good and bad; his executive example helps them to unite reaction and actuality directly in a convention—the necessary working together—of language and conception, not now a commonplace but a commonplace to come; and his work affords that help because it does not intrude any conception or contortion of conception of its own. Thus he differs from poets like Hopkins or Rimbaud or Swinburne or Whitman, whose innovations represented sometimes weaknesses and sometimes purposes of their own, which when imitated substitute for weaknesses in their imitators. Thus also, he differs from poets like Shakespeare or Dante or Wordsworth, from whom the modern poet learns less the means of his trade than he learns habits of feeling to transpose and habits of insights to translate and habits of architecture—of large composition—of which he will probably be incapable except in intent. He is like, rather, poets like Cavalcanti, Arnaut, Gautier (his own chosen example), Marlowe, Greene, and Herrick; all of whom strike the living writer as immediately useful in his trade, but in no way affecting the life he puts into his trade.

In short, poets of the class in which Pound shines are of an absolute preliminary necessity for the continuing life of poetry. What he meant by composition in the sequence of the musical phrase and by the prose tradition in verse, both as he taught them in his criticism and as he exhibited them in his translations and original verses, were not only necessary in 1912 or 1918, but are necessary now and have always been necessary if the work done by man's mind in verse is not to fall off and forget its possibilities. 'In the gloom, the gold gathers the light against it.' If the first word in the last line is taken in the opposite sense, as in his easy irony he meant it to be taken, we can apply to Pound once more in our own context, the following verses which he once applied to himself:

> His true Penelope was Flaubert,
> He fished by obstinate isles;
> Observed the elegance of Circe's hair
> Rather than the mottoes on sun-dials.
>
> Unaffected by 'the march of events,'
> He passed from men's memory in *l'an trentiesme
> De son eage;* the case presents
> No adjunct to the Muses' diadem.

ROBERT PENN WARREN

1905–

WILLIAM FAULKNER

Selected Essays, 1958

AT the age of fifty-three William Faulkner has written nineteen books which for range of effect, philosophical weight, originality of style, variety of characterization, humour, and tragic intensity are without equal in our time and country. Let us grant, even so, that there are grave defects in Faulkner's work. Sometimes the tragic intensity becomes mere sensationalism, the technical virtuosity mere complication, the philosophical weight mere confusion of mind. Let us grant that much, for Faulkner is a very uneven writer. The unevenness is, in a way, an index to his vitality, his willingness to take risks, to try for new effects, to make new explorations of material and method. And it is, sometimes at least, an index to a very important fact about Faulkner's work. The fact is that he writes of two Souths: he reports one South and he creates another. On one hand he is a perfectly straight realistic writer, and on the other he is a symbolist.

Let us speak first of that realistic South, the South which we can recognize by its physical appearance and its people. In this realistic way we can recognize that county which Faulkner calls Yoknapatawpha County, the county in which most of his stories occur and most of his people live. Jefferson, the county seat of Yoknapatawpha County, is already the most famous county seat in the nation, and is as solidly recognizable as anybody's home town. There is Miss Emily's house, the big squarish frame house, once white, decorated with cupolas and spires and scrolled balconies, in the heavily lightsome style of the seventies, once on the most select street but now surrounded by garages and cotton gins, lifting its stubborn and coquettish decay above the cotton wagons and gasoline pumps. There is Uncle Gavin's law office. There is the cedar-bemused cemetery. There is the jail where a hundred years ago, or near, the jailer's daughter, a young girl, scratched her name with a diamond on a window-pane. There are the neat, small, new one-story houses designed in Florida and California, set with matching garages in their neat plots of clipped grass and tedious flower beds. Then beyond that town where we recognize every item, the country stretches away, the plantation houses, the cotton fields, the back country of Frenchman's Bend, where Snopeses, and Varners live, the Beat Four section, where the Gowrie clan holds the land and brawls and makes whisky in the brush.

We know everything about Yoknapatawpha County. Its 2,400 square miles lie between the hills of north Mississippi and the rich black bottom lands. No land in all fiction lives more vividly in its physical presence than this county of Faulkner's imagination—the pine-winey afternoons, the nights with a thin sickle of moon like the heel print of a boot in wet sand, the tremendous reach of the big river in flood, yellow and sleepy in the afternoon, and the little piddling creeks, that run backward one day and forward the next and come busting down on a man full of dead mules and hen houses, the ruined plantation which was Popeye's hang-out, the swamps and fields and dusty roads, the last remnants of the great original forests, 'green with gloom' in summer, 'if anything actually dimmer than they had been in November's gray dissolution, where even at noon the sun fell only in windless dappling upon earth which never completely dried'. A little later I shall speak of what the physical world means to Faulkner, but for the moment I wish only to insist on its vividness, its recognizability.

This county has a population of 15,611 persons, who spill in and out of Faulkner's books with the startling casualness of life, not explaining themselves or asking to be explained, offering their being with no apology, as though we, the readers, were the intruders on their domain. They compose a society with characters as various as the Bundrens of *As I Lay Dying*; the Snopeses of *The Hamlet* and several stories; the Gowries of *Intruder in the Dust*; Ike McCaslin of 'The Bear' and 'Delta Autumn'; Percy Grimm, the gun-mad Nazi prototype of *Light in August*; Temple Drake, the dubious little heroine of *Sanctuary*; the Compsons, the ruined great family; Christmas, the tortured and self-torturing mulatto of *Light in August*; Dilsey, the old Negro woman, heroic and enduring, who stands at the centre of *The Sound and the Fury*; Wash, the no-good poor-white; and Sutpen, the violent bearer of the great design which the Civil War had brought to nothing, in *Absalom, Absalom*; and the tall convict of *The Wild Palms*. No land in all fiction is more painstakingly analysed from the sociological point of view. The descendants of the old families, the descendants of bush-whackers and carpetbaggers, the swamp rats, the Negro cooks and farm hands, the bootleggers and gangsters, tenant farmers, college boys, county-seat lawyers, country storekeepers, pedlars—all are here in their fullness of life and their complicated interrelations. The marks of class, occupation, and history are fully rendered, and we know completely their speech, food, dress, houses, manners, and attitudes.

Faulkner not only gives us the land and the people as

we can see them today; he gives us glimpses of their history. His stories go back to the time when the Indians occupied Yoknapatawpha County and held slaves, and the first Compson came with a small, light-waisted, strong-hocked mare that could do two furlongs in under a half-minute, and won all the races from Ikke-motubbe's young braves until Ikkemotubbe swapped him a square mile of that land for the little mare. We know how Sartorises, the aristocrats, and Sutpens, name-less, driven, rancorous, ambitious men, seized the land, created a society, fought a war to defend that society, lost the war, and watched their world change and the Snopeses arise. The past is dramatized in situation after situation, in its full complication. It is a recognizable past, not a romanticized past, though we find many characters in Faulkner who are themselves romantics about that past, Quentin of *The Sound and the Fury* or Hightower of *Light in August*.

The land, the people, and their history—they come to us at a realistic level, at the level of recognition. This realistic, recognizable world is one of the two Souths about which Faulkner writes. As a realist he knows this world; it is the world he lives in and carries on his daily business in. To represent this world with full fidelity is in itself a great achievement, and I would not underrate it. But this achievement is not Faulkner's claim to our particular attention. That claim is the world he creates out of the materials of the world he presents. Yoknapatawpha County, its people and its history, is also a parable—as Malcolm Cowley has called it, a legend.

We can approach the significance of this legend by thinking of the land and its history as a fate or doom—words that are often on Faulkner's page. From the land itself, from its rich soil yearning to produce, and from history, from an error or sin committed long ago and compounded a thousand times over, the doom comes. That is, the present is to be understood, and fully felt, only in terms of the past.

The men who seized the land from the Indians were determined to found an enduring and stable order. They brought to this project imagination and rectitude and strength and integrity and cunning and endurance, but their project—or their great 'design', to use Sutpen's word from *Absalom, Absalom*—was doomed from the first. It was 'accurst'—to use one of Faulkner's favourite words—by chattel slavery. There is a paradox here. The fact of slavery itself was not a single, willed act. It was a natural historical growth. But it was an evil, and all its human and humane mitigations and all its historical necessity could not quiet the bad conscience it engendered. The Civil War began the fulfilment of the doom. The war was fought with courage and fortitude and strength but with divided conscience. Not that the enemy was the bearer of light—the enemy was little better than a blind instrument of doom or fate. After the Civil War the attempt to rebuild according to the old plan and for the old values was defeated by a combination of forces: the carpetbaggers, the carriers of Yankee exploitation—or better, a symbol of it, for the real exploiters never left their offices 1,500 miles away—and the Snopeses, a new exploiting indigenous class descended from the bushwhackers and landless whites.

Meanwhile, most of the descendants of the old order are in various ways incompetent. For one thing, in so far as they carry over into the new world the code of behaviour prescribed by the old world, some sense of honour and honesty, they are at a disadvantage in dealing with the Snopeses, who have no code, who are pure pragmatists. But often the descendant of the old order clings to the letter of his tradition and forgets the spirit. George Marion O'Donnell, in one of the first perceptive essays ever published on Faulkner, pointed out the story 'There Was a Queen' as an example of this. The heroine, in order to get possession of certain obscene and insulting letters written her by a Snopes, gives herself to a detective who has blackmailed her. That is, to protect her reputation, she is willing to perform the act which will render the reputation a mere sham.

We find something of the same situation with the whining Mrs. Compson, the mother in *The Sound and the Fury*, who with her self-pity and insistence on her 'tradition' surrenders all the decency which the tradition would have prescribed, the honour and courage. Or the exponents of the tradition may lose all contact with reality and escape into a dream world of alcohol or rhetoric or madness or sexual dissipation. Or they fall in love with defeat and death, like Quentin Compson, who commits suicide at Harvard. Or they lose nerve and become cowardly drifters. Or, worst of all, they try to come to terms with reality by adopting Snopesism, like the last Jason of *The Sound and the Fury*, whose portrait is one of the most terrifying in all literature—the paranoidal self-deceiver, who plays the cotton market and when he loses, screams about those 'kikes' in New York who rob him, who himself robs the daughter of his sister Caddy over the years and in the end makes her into the desperate and doomed creature she becomes, who under the guise of responsibility for his family— the ailing mother, the idiot brother, the wild niece— tortures them all with an unflagging sadistic pleasure.

The point to insist on here is that you do not characteristically have noble examples of antique virtue beset by little and corrupt men. There are a few such examples of the antique virtue—old Ike McCaslin, for example, whom we shall come to later—but the ordinary situation is to find the descendant of the old order contributing, actively or passively, to his own ruin and degradation. He is not merely a victim, and he frequently misunderstands his own tradition.

Over against these people there stand, as we have said, the forces of 'modernism', embodied in various forms. There are, of course, the Snopeses, the pure exploiters, descendants of barn-burners and bushwhackers, of people outside of society, belonging to no side, living in a kind of limbo, not even having the privilege of damnation, reaching their apotheosis in Flem Snopes, who becomes a bank president in Jefferson. But there is also Popeye, the gangster of *Sanctuary*, with eyes like 'rubber knobs', a creature with 'that vicious depthless quality of stamped tin', the man who 'made money and had nothing he could do with it, spend it for, since he knew that alcohol would kill him like poison, who had no friends and had never known a woman'. Popeye is a kind of dehumanized robot, a mere mechanism, an abstraction, and as such he is a symbol for what Faulkner thinks of as modernism, for the society of finance capitalism.

It is sometimes said that Faulkner's theme is the disintegration of the Southern traditional life. For instance, Malcolm Cowley, in his fine introduction to the *Portable Faulkner*, says that the violence of Faulkner's work is 'an example of the Freudian method turned backward, being full of sexual nightmares that are in reality social symbols. It is somehow connected in the author's mind with what he regards as the rape and corruption of the South.' And Maxwell Geismar, whose lack of comprehension of Faulkner strikes me as monumental, interprets Faulkner's work as merely Southern apologetics, as 'the extreme hallucinations' of a 'cultural psychosis'.

It is true that Faulkner deals almost exclusively with the Southern scene, it is true that the conflict between past and present is a constant concern for him, it is true that the Civil War is always behind his work as a kind of backdrop, and it is true, or at least I think it is true, that in Faulkner's work there is the implication that Northern arms were the cutting edge of modernism. But granting all this, I should put the emphasis not in terms of South and North, but in terms of issues common to our modern world.

The Faulkner legend is not merely a legend of the South but of a general plight and problem. The modern world is in moral confusion. It does suffer from a lack of discipline, of sanction, of community of values, of a sense of mission. We don't have to go to Faulkner to find that out—or to find that it is a world in which self-interest, workableness, success provide the standards of conduct. It was a Yankee who first referred to the bitch goddess Success. It is a world in which the individual has lost his relation to society, the world of the power state in which man is a cipher. It is a world in which man is the victim of abstraction and mechanism, or at least, at moments, feels himself to be. It can look back nostalgically upon various worlds of the past, Dante's world of the Catholic synthesis, Shakespeare's world of Renaissance energy, or the world of our grandfathers who lived before Shiloh and Gettysburg, and feel loss of traditional values and despair in its own aimlessness and fragmentation. Any of those older worlds, so it seems now, was a world in which, as one of Faulkner's characters puts it, men 'had the gift of living once or dying once instead of being diffused and scattered creatures drawn blindly from a grab bag and assembled' —a world in which men were, 'integer for integer,' more simple and complete.

At this point we must pause to consider an objection. Someone will say, and quite properly, that there never was a golden age in which man was simple and complete. Let us grant that. But we must grant that even with that realistic reservation man's conception of his own role and position has changed from time to time. It is un-historical to reduce history to some dead level, and the mere fact that man in the modern world is worried about his role and position is in itself significant.

Again, it may be objected, and quite properly, that any old order that had satisfied human needs would have survived; that it is sentimental to hold that an old order is killed from the outside by certain wicked people or forces. But when this objection is applied to Faulkner it is based on a misreading of his work. The old order, he clearly indicates, did *not* satisfy human needs, did *not* afford justice, and therefore was 'accurst' and held the seeds of its own ruin. But the point is this: the old order, even with its bad conscience and confusion of mind, even as it failed to live up to its ideal, cherished the concept of justice. Even in terms of the curse, the old order as opposed to the new order (in so far as the new order is equated with Snopesism) allowed the traditional man to define himself as human by setting up codes, ideas of virtue, however mistaken; by affirming obligations, however arbitrary; by accepting the risks of humanity. But Snopesism has abolished the concept, the very possibility of entertaining the idea of virtue. It is not a question of one idea and interpretation. It is simply that no idea of virtue is conceivable in the world in which practical success is the criterion.

Within the traditional world there had been a notion of truth, even if man in the flow of things could not readily define or realize his truth. Take, for instance, a passage from 'The Bear'.

'All right,' he said. 'Listen,' and read again, but only one stanza this time and closed the book and laid it on the table. 'She cannot fade, though thou hast not thy bliss,' McCaslin said: 'Forever wilt thou love, and she be fair.'

'He's talking about a girl,' he said.

'He had to talk about something,' McCaslin said. Then he said, 'He was talking about truth. Truth is one. It doesn't change. It covers all things which touch the heart —honor and pride and pity and justice and courage and love. Do you see now?'

The important thing, then, is the presence of the concept of truth—that covers all things which touch the heart and define the effort of man to rise above the mechanical process of life.

When it is said, as it is sometimes said, that Faulkner is 'backward-looking', the answer lies, I think, in the notion expressed above. The 'truth' is neither of the past nor of the future. Or rather, it is of both. The constant ethical centre of Faulkner's work is to be found in the glorification of human effort and human endurance, which are not confined to any one time. It is true that Faulkner's work contains a savage attack on modernity, but the values he admires *are* found in our time. The point is that they are found most often in people who are outside the stream of the dominant world, the 'loud world', as it is called in *The Sound and the Fury*. Faulkner's world is full of 'good' people—Byron Bunch, Lucas Beauchamp, Dilsey, Ike McCaslin, Uncle Gavin, Benbow, the justice of the peace in *The Hamlet*, Ratliff of the same book, Hightower of *Light in August*—we could make an impressive list, probably a longer list from Faulkner than from any other modern writer. 'There are good men everywhere, at all times', Ike McCaslin says in 'Delta Autumn'.

It is not ultimately important whether the traditional order (Southern or other) as depicted by Faulkner fits exactly the picture which critical historical method provides. Let it be granted that Faulkner does simplify the matter. What remains important is that his picture of the traditional order has a symbolic function in contrast to the modern world which he gives us. It is a way of embodying his values—his 'truth'.

In speaking of the relation of the past to the present, I have mentioned the curse laid upon the present, the Southern present at least, by slavery. But also, as I have said, Faulkner is not concerned ultimately with the South, but with a general philosophical view. Slavery merely happens to be the particular Southern curse. To arrive at his broader philosophical view, we can best start with his notions of nature.

For one thing, one of the most impressive features of Faulkner's work is the vivid realization of the natural background. It is accurately observed, as accurately as in Thoreau, but observation provides only the stuff from which Faulkner's characteristic effects are gained. It is the atmosphere that counts, the infusion of feeling, the symbolic weight. Nature provides a backdrop—of lyric beauty, as in the cow episode of *The Hamlet*; of homely charm, as in the trial scene after the spotted horses episode of the same book; of sinister, brooding force, as in the river episodes from *The Wild Palms*—a backdrop for the human action and passion.

Nature is, however, more than a backdrop. There is an interrelation between man and nature, something not too unlike the Wordsworthian communion. At least, at moments, there is the communion, the interrelation. The indestructible beauty is there, beyond man's frailty. 'God created man', Ike McCaslin says in 'Delta Autumn', 'and He created the world for him to live in and I reckon He created the kind of world He would have wanted to live in if He had been a man.'

Ideally, if man were like God, as Ike McCaslin puts it, man's attitude toward nature would be one of pure contemplation, pure participation in nature's great forms and appearances, pure communion. The appropriate attitude for this communion is love, for with Ike McCaslin, who is as much Faulkner's spokesman as any other character, the moment of love is equated with godhood. But since man 'wasn't quite God himself', since he lives in the world of flesh, he must be a hunter, user, and violator. To return to McCaslin's words: God

put them both here: man and the game he would follow and kill, foreknowing it. I believe He said, 'So be it'. I reckon He even foreknew the end. But He said, 'I will give him his chance. I will give him warning and fore-knowledge too, along with the desire to follow and the power to slay. The woods and the fields he ravages and the game he devastates will be the consequence and signa-ture of his crime and guilt, and his punishment.'

There is, then, a contamination implicit in the human condition—a kind of Original Sin, as it were—the sin of use, exploitation, violation. So slavery is but one of the many and constant forms of that Original Sin. But it is possible—and necessary if man is to strive to be human—to achieve some measure of redemption through love. For instance, in 'The Bear', the great legendary beast which is pursued from year to year to the death is also an object of love and veneration, and the symbol of virtue; and the deer hunt of 'Delta Autumn' is for old Ike McCaslin a ritual of renewal. Those who have learned the right relationship to nature—'the pride and humility' which Ike as a boy learns from the half-Negro, half-Indian Sam Fathers (he learns it appro-priately from an outcast)—are set over against those who do not have it. In 'The Bear', General Comp-son speaks up to Cass McCaslin to defend the wish of the boy Ike McCaslin to stay an extra week in the woods:

You've got one foot straddled into a farm and the other foot straddled into a bank; you aint even got a good hand-hold where this boy was already an old man long before you damned Sartorises and Edmondses invented farms and banks to keep yourselves from having to find out what this boy was born knowing and fearing too maybe but without being afraid, that could go ten miles on a compass because he wanted to look at a bear none of us had ever got near enough to put a bullet in and looked at the bear and came the ten miles back on the compass in the dark; maybe by God that's the why and the wherefore of farms and banks.

The Sartorises and Edmondses, according to General Compson, have in their farms and banks something of the contamination, they have cut themselves off from the fundamental truth which young Ike already senses. But the real contamination is that of the pure exploiters, the apostles of abstractionism, those who have the wrong attitude toward nature and therefore toward other men.

We have a nice fable of this in the opening of *Sanctuary*, in the contrast between Benbow, the traditional man, and Popeye, the symbol of modernism. While the threat of Popeye keeps Benbow crouching by the spring, he hears a Carolina wren sing, and even under these circumstances tries to recall the local name for it. And he says to Popeye: 'And of course you dont know the name of it. I dont suppose you'd know a bird at all, without it was singing in a cage in a hotel lounge, or cost four dollars on a plate.' Popeye, as we may remember, spits in the spring (he hates nature and must foul it), is afraid to go through the woods ('Through all them trees?' he demands when Benbow points out the short cut), and when an owl whisks past them in the twilight, he claws at Benbow's coat with almost hysterical fear. 'It's just an owl', Benbow explains. 'It's nothing but an owl.'

The pure exploiters are, however, caught in a paradox. Though they may gain ownership and use of a thing, they never really have it. Like Popeye, they are impotent. For instance, Flem Snopes, the central character and villain of *The Hamlet*, who brings the exploiter's mentality to the quiet country of Frenchman's Bend, finally marries Eula Varner, a kind of fertility goddess or earth goddess; but his ownership is meaningless, for she never refers to him as anything but 'that man'—she does not even have a name for him—and he had got her only after she had given herself willingly to one of the hot-blooded boys of the neighbourhood. In fact, nothing can, in one sense, be 'owned'. Ike McCaslin, in 'The Bear,' says of the land which had come down to him:

It was never Father's and Uncle Buddy's to bequeath to me to repudiate because it was never Grandfather's to bequeath them to bequeath me to repudiate because it was never old Ikkemotubbe's to sell to Grandfather for bequeathment and repudiation. Because it was never Ikkemotubbe's fathers' fathers' to bequeath Ikkemotubbe to sell to Grandfather or any man because on the instant when Ikkemotubbe discovered, realized, that he could sell it for money, on that instant it ceased ever to have been his forever, father to father to father, and the man who bought it bought nothing.

In other words, reality cannot be bought. It can only be had by love.

The right attitude toward nature and man is love. And love is the opposite of the lust for power over nature or over other men, for God gave the earth to

man, we read in 'The Bear', not 'to hold for himself
and his descendants inviolable title forever, generation
after generation, to the oblongs and squares of the
earth, but to hold the earth mutual and intact in the
communal anonymity of brotherhood, and all the fee
He [God] asked was pity and humility and sufferance
and endurance and the sweat of his face for bread'. It
is the failure of this pity that curses the earth and
brings on the doom. For the rape of nature and the
rape of man are always avenged. Mere exploitation
without love is always avenged because the attitude
which commits the crime in itself leads to its own punishment, so that man finally punishes himself. It is along
this line of reasoning that we can read the last page of
'Delta Autumn':

> This land which man has deswamped and denuded and
> derivered in two generations so that white men can own
> plantations and commute every night to Memphis and
> black men own plantations and ride in jim crow cars to
> Chicago to live in millionaires' mansions on Lakeshore
> Drive, where white men rent farms and live like niggers
> and niggers crop on shares and live like animals, where
> cotton is planted and grows man-tall in the very cracks of
> the sidewalks, and usury and mortgage and bankruptcy
> and measureless wealth, Chinese and African and Aryan
> and Jew, all breed and spawn together until no man has
> time to say which one is which nor cares . . . No wonder
> the ruined woods I used to know dont cry for retribution!
> he thought: The people who have destroyed it will
> accomplish its revenge.

Despite the emphasis on the right relation to nature,
and the communion with nature, the attitude toward
nature in Faulkner's work does not involve a sinking
into nature. In Faulkner's mythology man has 'suzerainty
over the earth', he is not of the earth, and it is the
human virtues that count—'pity and humility and

endurance'. If we take even the extreme case of the idiot Snopes and his fixation on the cow in *The Hamlet* (a scene whose function in the total order of the book is to show that even the idiot pervert is superior to Flem), a scene in which the human being appears as close as possible to the 'natural' level, we find that the scene is the most lyrical in Faulkner's work: even the idiot is human and not animal, for only human desires, not animal desires, must clothe themselves in poetry. I think that George Marion O'Donnell is right in pointing to the humanism–naturalism opposition in Faulkner's work, and over and over again we find that the point of some story or novel has to do with the human effort to break out of the mechanical round of experience at the merely 'natural' level—'not just to eat and evacuate and sleep warm', as Charlotte Rittenmeyer says in *The Wild Palms*, 'so we can get up and eat and evacuate in order to sleep warm again', or not just to raise cotton to buy niggers to raise cotton to buy niggers, as it is put in another place. Even when a character seems to be caught in the iron ring of some compulsion, of some mechanical process, the effort may be discernible. And in Quentin's attempt in *The Sound and the Fury* to persuade his sister Caddy, who is pregnant by one of the town boys of Jefferson, to confess that she has committed incest with him, we find among other things the idea that 'the horror' of the crime and the 'clean flame' of guilt would be preferable to the meaninglessness of the 'loud world'. More is at stake in Quentin's attitude than the snobbery of a Compson, which would prefer incest to the notion that his sister has had to do with one of the underbred town boys.

And that leads us to the question of class and race. There is a current misconception on this point, the notion that Faulkner's Snopesism is a piece of snobbery.

It is true that the Snopeses are poor whites, descendants of bushwhackers (those who had no side in the Civil War but tried to make a good thing out of it), but any careful reader should realize that a Snopes is not to be equated with a poor white. For instance, the book most fully about the poor white, *As I Lay Dying*, is charged with sympathy and poetry. There are a hundred touches like that in Cash's soliloquy about the phonograph:

> I reckon its a good thing we ain't got ere a one of them. I reckon I wouldn't never get no work done a-tall for listening to it. I don't know if a little music ain't about the nicest thing a fellow can have. Seems like when he comes in tired of a night, it ain't nothing could rest him like having a little music played and him resting.

Or like the long section devoted to Addie Bundren, a section full of eloquence like that of this paragraph:

> And then he died. He did not know he was dead. I would lie by him in the dark, hearing the dark land talking of God's love and His beauty and His sin; hearing the dark voicelessness in which the words are the deeds, and the other words that are not deeds, that are just the gaps in peoples' lacks, coming down like the cries of geese out of the wild darkness in the old terrible nights, fumbling at the deeds like orphans to whom are pointed out in a crowd two faces and told, That is your father, your mother.

The whole of *As I Lay Dying* is based on the heroic effort of the Bundren family to fulfil the promise to the dead mother to take her body to Jefferson; and the fact that Anse Bundren, after the effort is completed, immediately gets him a new wife, 'the duck-shaped woman', does not negate the heroism of the effort or the poetry in which it is clothed. We are told by one critic that 'what should have been the drama of the Bundrens thus becomes in the end a sort of brutal farce', and that we are 'unable to feel the tragedy because the author has refused to accept the Bundrens, as he did accept the Compsons, as tragic'. Rather, I should say, the Bundrens come off a little better than the latter-day Compsons, the whining, self-deluding mother, the promiscuous Caddy, the ineffectual Quentin, and the rest, including the vile Jason. The Bundrens at least are capable of the heroic effort. What the conclusion indicates is that even such a fellow as Anse Bundren, in the grip of an idea, in terms of promise or code, can rise above his ordinary level; Anse falls back at the end, but only after the prop of the obligation has been removed. And we can recall that Wash Jones has been capable of some kind of obscure dream, as his attachment to Sutpen indicates, and that in the end, in his murder of Sutpen, he achieves dignity and manhood.

The final evidence that the Snopeses are not to be equated with 'poor white' comes in *The Hamlet*. The point of the book is the assault made by the Snopes family on a community of plain, hard-working small farmers. And if the corruption of Snopesism does penetrate into the community, there is no one here, not even Flem Snopes, who can be compared to Jason of *The Sound and the Fury*, the Compson who has embraced Snopesism.

As for the poor white, there has been a grave misconception in some quarters concerning the Negro in Faulkner's work. In one of Faulkner's books it is said that every white child is born crucified on a black cross, and remarks like this have led to the notion that Faulkner 'hates' Negroes—or at least all Negroes except the favoured black servitors. For instance, we find Maxwell Geismar exclaiming what a 'strange inversion' it is to take the Negro, who is the 'tragic consequence', and to exhibit him as the 'evil cause' of the failure of the old order in the South. But all this is to misread the text. It is slavery, not the Negro, which is defined quite flatly as the curse, and the Negro is the black cross in so far as he is the embodiment of the curse, the reminder of the guilt, the incarnation of the problem. The black cross is, then, the weight of the white man's guilt, the white man who now sells salves and potions to 'bleach the pigment and straighten the hair of Negroes that they might resemble the very race which for two hundred years had held them in bondage and from which for another hundred years not even a bloody civil war would have set them completely free'. The curse is still operative, as the crime is still compounded.

The actual role of the Negro in Faulkner's fiction is consistently one of pathos or heroism. There is Dilsey, under whose name in the Compson genealogy Faulkner writes, 'They endured', and whose role in *The Sound and the Fury* is to be the very ethical centre of the book, the vessel of virtue and compassion. Then there is the Negro in 'Red Leaves', the slave held by Indians who is hunted down to be killed at the funeral of the chief. When he is overtaken, one of the Indians says to him, 'You ran well. Do not be ashamed', and when he walks among the Indians, he is 'the tallest there, his high, close, mud-caked head looming above them all'. And old Sam Fathers is the fountain of the wisdom which Ike McCaslin, Faulkner's philosopher, finally gains, and the repository of the virtues central for Faulkner—'an old man, son of a Negro slave and an Indian king, inheritor on the one hand of the long chronicle of a people who had learned humility through suffering and learned pride through the endurance which survived the suffering, and on the other side the chronicle of a people even longer in the land than the first, yet who now existed there only in the solitary brotherhood of an old and childless Negro's alien blood and the wild and invincible spirit of an old bear'. Even Christmas in *Light in August* is a mixture of pathos and heroism. With his mixed blood, he is the lost, suffering, enduring creature, and even the murder he commits at the end is a fumbling attempt to define his manhood, an attempt to break out of the iron ring of mechanism, for the woman whom he kills has become a figure of the horror of the human which has surrendered human attributes.

Or for a general statement let us take a passage from 'The Bear':

'Because they will endure. They are better than we are. Stronger than we are. Their vices are vices aped from white men or that white men and bondage have taught them: improvidence and intemperance and evasion—not laziness: evasion: of what white men had set them to, not for their aggrandisement or even comfort but his own—' and McCaslin

'All right. Go on: Promiscuity. Violence. Instability and lack of control. Inability to distinguish between mine and thine—' and he

'How distinguish, when for two hundred years mine did not even exist for them?' and McCaslin

'All right. Go on. And their virtues—' and he

'Yes. Their own. Endurance—' and McCaslin

'So have mules:' and he

'—and pity and tolerance and forbearance and fidelity and love of children—' and McCaslin

'So have dogs:' and he

'—whether their own or not or black or not. And more: what they got not only from white people but not even despite white people because they had it already from the old free fathers a longer time free than us because we have never been free—'

It is in *Intruder in the Dust*, however, that his views of the Negro are most explicit and best dramatized. Lucas

Beauchamp, the stiff-necked and high-nosed old Negro man, is accused on good evidence of having shot a white man in the back, and is lodged in the Jefferson jail with a threat of lynching. The lynching is averted and Lucas's innocence established by a boy and an old lady. But what is important about the book is twofold: First, there is the role of Lucas as hero, the focus of dignity and integrity. Second, there is the quite explicit and full body of statement, which comes to us through the lips of Gavin, the lawyer-uncle of the boy who saves Lucas. To quote Gavin:

> . . . the postulate that Sambo is a human being living in a free country and hence must be free. That's what we are really defending [against the North]: the privilege of setting him free ourselves: which we will have to do for the reason that nobody else can since going on a century ago now the North tried it and have been admitting for seventy-five years now that they failed. So it will have to be us. Soon now this sort of thing [the lynching] wont even threaten anymore. It shouldn't now. It should never have. Yet it did last Saturday and it probably will again, perhaps once more, perhaps twice more. But then no more, it will be finished; the shame will still be there of course but then the whole chronicle of man's immortality is in the suffering he has endured, his struggle toward the stars in the stepping-stones of his expiations. Someday Lucas Beauchamp can shoot a white man in the back with the same impunity to lynch-rope or gasoline as a white man; in time he will vote anywhen and anywhere a white man can and send his children to the same school anywhere the white man's children go and travel anywhere the white man travels as the white man does it. But it won't be next Tuesday. . . .

This is not the whole passage, or even the burden of the whole passage, but it merits our lingering. The motive behind the notion of 'defending' against the

North is not merely resentment at easy Phariseeism. It is something else, two other things in fact. First, the realization that legislation in itself never solves a really fundamental question. Legislation can only reflect a solution already arrived at. Second, the problem is finally one of understanding and, in a sense, conversion: conversion and, as the passage puts it, expiation. That is, the real problem is a spiritual and moral one. The story of *Intruder in the Dust* is, in a sense, the education of the boy, and the thing he learns is a lesson in humanity. This can be brought to focus on two parallel episodes. He sees Lucas on the street one day, and Lucas walks past him without recognition. Later he realizes that Lucas had been grieving for his dead wife. Again, in the cemetery where the body of a Gowrie had been exhumed, he sees old Stub Gowrie, the father of the man Lucas had presumably killed, and realizes that this head of the brawling, mean, lawless Gowrie clan is grieving, too. The recognition of grief, the common human bond, that is his education.

That is the central fact in Faulkner's work, the recognition of the common human bond, a profound respect for the human. There are, in one way, no villains in his work, except those who deny the human bond. Even some of the Snopes family are, after all, human: the son of the barn-burner in the story 'Barn-Burning', or Mink in *The Hamlet*. The point about the Gowries in *Intruder in the Dust* is the same: the Gowries seem to be the enemy, the pure villains, but in the end there is the pure grief on old Stub's face, and he is human, after all.

If respect for the human is the central fact of Faulkner's work, what makes that fact significant is that he realizes and dramatizes the difficulty of respecting the human. Everything is against it, the savage egotism, the blank appetite, stupidity and arrogance, even virtues sometimes, the misreading of our history and tradition, our education, our twisted loyalties. That is the great drama, however, the constant story. His hatred of 'modernism'—and we must quote the word to give it his special meaning—arises because he sees it as the enemy of the human, as abstraction, as mechanism, as irresponsible power, as the cipher on the ledger or the curve on a graph.

And the reference to modernism brings us back to the question of the past and the present. But what of the future? Does Faulkner come to a dead end, setting up traditional virtues against the blank present, and let the matter stand there? No, he does not. But he holds out no easy solutions for man's 'struggle toward the stars in the stepping-stones of his expiations'. He does, however, give a sense of the future, though as a future of struggle in working out that truth referred to in 'The Bear'. We can remember that old Ike McCaslin, at the end of 'Delta Autumn' gives General Compson's hunting horn to the mulatto girl who has been deserted by her young kinsman, saying, 'We will have to wait'. And *The Sound and the Fury*, which is Faulkner's *Waste Land*, ends with Easter and the promise of resurrection.

LIONEL TRILLING

1905–

HUCKLEBERRY FINN

Introduction to Rinehart edition, 1948: The Liberal Imagination, 1951

IN 1876 Mark Twain published *The Adventures of Tom Sawyer* and in the same year began what he called 'another boys' book'. He set little store by the new venture and said that he had undertaken it 'more to be at work than anything else'. His heart was not in it—'I like it only tolerably well as far as I have got', he said, 'and may possibly pigeonhole or burn the MS. when it is done.' He pigeonholed it long before it was done and for as much as four years. In 1880 he took it out and carried it forward a little, only to abandon it again. He had a theory of unconscious composition and believed that a book must write itself; the book which he referred to as 'Huck Finn's Autobiography' refused to do the job of its own creation and he would not coerce it.

But then in the summer of 1883 Mark Twain was possessed by a charge of literary energy which, as he wrote to Howells, was more intense than any he had experienced for many years. He worked all day and every day, and periodically he so fatigued himself that he had to recruit his strength by a day or two of smoking and reading in bed. It is impossible not to suppose that this great creative drive was connected with—was perhaps the direct result of—the visit to the Mississippi he had made the previous year, the trip which forms the matter of the second part of *Life on the Mississippi*. His boyhood and youth on the river he so profoundly loved had been at once the happiest and most significant part of Mark Twain's life; his return to it in middle age stirred memories which revived and refreshed the idea of *Huckleberry Finn*. Now at last the book was not only ready but eager to write itself. But it was not to receive much conscious help from its author. He was always full of second-rate literary schemes and now, in the early weeks of the summer, with *Huckleberry Finn* waiting to complete itself, he turned his hot energy upon several of these sorry projects, the completion of which gave him as much sense of satisfying productivity as did his eventual absorption in *Huckleberry Finn*.

When at last *Huckleberry Finn* was completed and published and widely loved, Mark Twain became somewhat aware of what he had accomplished with the book that had been begun as journeywork and depreciated, postponed, threatened with destruction. It is his masterpiece, and perhaps he learned to know that. But he could scarcely have estimated it for what it is, one of the world's great books and one of the central documents of American culture.

Wherein does its greatness lie? Primarily in its power of telling the truth. An awareness of this quality as it exists in *Tom Sawyer* once led Mark Twain to say of the earlier work that 'it is *not* a boys' book at all. It will be read only by adults. It is written only for adults'. But this was only a manner of speaking, Mark Twain's way of asserting, with a discernible touch of irritation, the degree of truth he had achieved. It does not represent his usual view either of boys' books or of boys. No one, as he well knew, sets a higher value on truth than a boy. Truth is the whole of a boy's conscious demand upon the world of adults. He is likely to believe that the adult world is in a conspiracy to lie to him, and it is this belief, by no means unfounded, that arouses Tom and Huck and all boys to their moral sensitivity, their everlasting concern with justice, which they call fairness. At the same time it often makes them skilful and profound liars in their own defence, yet they do not tell the ultimate lie of adults: they do not lie to themselves. That is why Mark Twain felt that it was impossible to carry Tom Sawyer beyond boyhood—in maturity 'he would lie just like all the other one-horse men of literature and the reader would conceive a hearty contempt for him'.

Certainly one element in the greatness of *Huckleberry Finn*, as also in the lesser greatness of *Tom Sawyer*, is that it succeeds first as a boys' book. One can read it at ten

and then annually ever after, and each year find that it
is as fresh as the year before, that it has changed only in
becoming somewhat larger. To read it young is like
planting a tree young—each year adds a new growth
ring of meaning, and the book is as little likely as the
tree to become dull. So, we may imagine, an Athenian
boy grew up together with the *Odyssey*. There are few
other books which we can know so young and love so
long.

The truth of *Huckleberry Finn* is of a different kind
from that of *Tom Sawyer*. It is a more intense truth,
fiercer and more complex. *Tom Sawyer* has the truth of
honesty—what it says about things and feelings is never
false and always both adequate and beautiful. *Huckleberry
Finn* has this kind of truth, too, but it has also the truth
of moral passion; it deals directly with the virtue and
depravity of man's heart.

Perhaps the best clue to the greatness of *Huckleberry
Finn* has been given to us by a writer who is as different
from Mark Twain as it is possible for one Missourian to
be from another. T. S. Eliot's poem, 'The Dry Salvages',
the third of his *Four Quartets*, begins with a meditation
on the Mississippi, which Mr. Eliot knew in his St.
Louis boyhood:

I do not know much about gods; but I think that the river
Is a strong brown god . . .

And the meditation goes on to speak of the god as

                                  almost forgotten
By the dwellers in cities—ever, however, implacable,
Keeping his seasons and rages, destroyer, reminder of
What men choose to forget. Unhonoured, unpropitiated
By worshippers of the machine, but waiting, watching
    and waiting.

Huckleberry Finn is a great book because it is about a god —about, that is, a power which seems to have a mind and will of its own, and which to men of moral imagination appears to embody a great moral idea.

Huck himself is the servant of the river-god, and he comes very close to being aware of the divine nature of the being he serves. The world he inhabits is perfectly equipped to accommodate a deity, for it is full of presences and meanings which it conveys by natural signs and also by preternatural omens and taboos: to look at the moon over the left shoulder, to shake the tablecloth after sundown, to handle a snakeskin, are ways of offending the obscure and prevalent spirits. Huck is at odds, on moral and aesthetic grounds, with the only form of established religion he knows, and his very intense moral life may be said to derive almost wholly from his love of the river. He lives in a perpetual adoration of the Mississippi's power and charm. Huck, of course, always expresses himself better than he can know, but nothing draws upon his gift of speech like his response to his deity. After every sally into the social life of the shore, he returns to the river with relief and thanksgiving; and at each return, regular and explicit as a chorus in a Greek tragedy, there is a hymn of praise to the god's beauty, mystery, and strength, and to his noble grandeur in contrast with the pettiness of men.

Generally the god is benign, a being of long sunny days and spacious nights. But, like any god, he is also dangerous and deceptive. He generates fogs which bewilder, and contrives echoes and false distances which confuse. His sand bars can ground and his hidden snags can mortally wound a great steamboat. He can cut away the solid earth from under a man's feet and take his house with it. The sense of the danger of the river is what saves the book from any touch of the sentimentality and moral ineptitude of most works which contrast the life of nature with the life of society.

The river itself is only divine; it is not ethical and good. But its nature seems to foster the goodness of those who love it and try to fit themselves to its ways. And we must observe that we cannot make—that Mark Twain does not make—an absolute opposition between the river and human society. To Huck much of the charm of the river life is human: it is the raft and the wigwam and Jim. He has not run away from Miss Watson and the Widow Douglas and his brutal father to a completely individualistic liberty, for in Jim he finds his true father, very much as Stephen Dedalus in James Joyce's *Ulysses* finds his true father in Leopold Bloom.[1] The boy and the Negro slave form a family, a primitive community—and it is a community of saints.

Huck's intense and even complex moral quality may possibly not appear on a first reading, for one may be caught and convinced by his own estimate of himself, by his brags about his lazy hedonism, his avowed preference for being alone, his dislike of civilization. The fact is, of course, that he is involved in civilization up to his ears. His escape from society is but his way of reaching what society ideally dreams of for itself. Responsibility is the very essence of his character, and it is perhaps to the point that the original of Huck, a boyhood companion of Mark Twain's named Tom Blenkenship, did, like Huck, 'light out for the Territory', only to become a justice of the peace in Montana, 'a good citizen and greatly respected'.

[1] In Joyce's *Finnegans Wake* both Mark Twain and Huckleberry Finn appear frequently. The theme of rivers is, of course, dominant in the book; and Huck's name suits Joyce's purpose, for Finn is one of the many names of his hero. Mark Twain's love of and gift for the spoken language make another reason for Joyce's interest in him.

Huck does indeed have all the capacities for simple happiness he says he has, but circumstances and his own moral nature make him the least carefree of boys—he is always 'in a sweat' over the predicament of someone else. He has a great sense of the sadness of human life, and although he likes to be alone, the words 'lonely' and 'loneliness' are frequent with him. The note of his special sensibility is struck early in the story: 'Well, when Tom and me got to the edge of the hilltop we looked away down into the village and could see three or four lights twinkling where there were sick folks, maybe; and the stars over us was sparkling ever so fine; and down by the village was the river, a whole mile broad, and awful still and grand.' The identification of the lights as the lamps of sick-watches defines Huck's character.

His sympathy is quick and immediate. When the circus audience laughs at the supposedly drunken man who tries to ride the horse, Huck is only miserable: 'It wasn't funny to me . . . ; I was all of a tremble to see his danger.' When he imprisons the intending murderers on the wrecked steamboat, his first thought is of how to get someone to rescue them, for he considers 'how dreadful it was, even for murderers, to be in such a fix. I says to myself, there ain't no telling but I might come to be a murderer myself yet, and then how would I like it'. But his sympathy is never sentimental. When at last he knows that the murderers are beyond help, he has no inclination to false pathos. 'I felt a little bit heavy-hearted about the gang, but not much, for I reckoned that if they could stand it I could.' His will is genuinely good and he has no need to torture himself with guilty second thoughts.

Not the least remarkable thing about Huck's feeling for people is that his tenderness goes along with the assumption that his fellow men are likely to be dangerous and wicked. He travels incognito, never telling the truth about himself and never twice telling the same lie, for he trusts no one and the lie comforts him even when it is not necessary. He instinctively knows that the best way to keep a party of men away from Jim on the raft is to beg them to come aboard to help his family stricken with smallpox. And if he had not already had the knowledge of human weakness and stupidity and cowardice, he would soon have acquired it, for all his encounters forcibly teach it to him—the insensate feud of the Graingerfords and Shepherdsons, the invasion of the raft by the Duke and the King, the murder of Boggs, the lynching party, and the speech of Colonel Sherburn. Yet his profound and bitter knowledge of human depravity never prevents him from being a friend to man.

No personal pride interferes with his well-doing. He knows what status is and on the whole he respects it—he is really a very *respectable* person and inclines to like 'quality folks'—but he himself is unaffected by it. He himself has never had status, he has always been the lowest of the low, and the considerable fortune he had acquired in *The Adventures of Tom Sawyer* is never real to him. When the Duke suggests that Huck and Jim render him the personal service that accords with his rank, Huck's only comment is, 'Well, that was easy so we done it.' He is injured in every possible way by the Duke and the King, used and exploited and manipulated, yet when he hears that they are in danger from a mob, his natural impulse is to warn them. And when he fails of his purpose and the two men are tarred and feathered and ridden on a rail, his only thought is, 'Well, it made me sick to see it; and I was sorry for them poor pitiful rascals, it seemed like I couldn't ever feel any hardness against them any more in the world'.

And if Huck and Jim on the raft do indeed make a

community of saints, it is because they do not have an ounce of pride between them. Yet this is not perfectly true, for the one disagreement they ever have is over a matter of pride. It is on the occasion when Jim and Huck have been separated by the fog. Jim has mourned Huck as dead, and then, exhausted, has fallen asleep. When he awakes and finds that Huck has returned, he is over-joyed; but Huck convinces him that he has only dreamed the incident, that there has been no fog, no separation, no chase, no reunion, and then allows him to make an elaborate 'interpretation' of the dream he now believes he has had. Then the joke is sprung, and in the growing light of the dawn Huck points to the debris of leaves on the raft and the broken oar.

Jim looked at the trash, and then looked at me, and back at the trash again. He had got the dream fixed so strong in his head that he couldn't seem to shake it loose and get the facts back into its place again right away. But when he did get the thing straightened around he looked at me steady without ever smiling, and says:

'What do dey stan' for? I'se gwyne to tell you. When I got all wore out wid work, en wid de callin' for you, en went to sleep, my heart wuz mos' broke bekase you wuz los', en I didn' k'yer no mo' what became er me en de raf'. En when I wake up en fine you back agin, all safe en soun', de tears come, en I could a got down on my knees en kiss yo' foot, I's so thankful. En all you wuz thinkin' 'bout wuz how you could make a fool uv ole Jim wid a lie. Dat truck dah is *trash*; en trash is what people is dat puts dirt on de head er dey fren's en makes 'em ashamed.'

Then he got up slow and walked to the wigwam, and went in there without saying anything but that.

The pride of human affection has been touched, one of the few prides that has any true dignity. And at its utter-ance, Huck's one last dim vestige of pride of status, his sense of his position as a white man, wholly vanishes:

'It was fifteen minutes before I could work myself up
to go and humble myself to a nigger; but I done it, and
I warn't sorry for it afterwards either.'

This incident is the beginning of the moral testing and
development which a character so morally sensitive as
Huck's must inevitably undergo. And it becomes a
heroic character when, on the urging of affection,
Huck discards the moral code he has always taken for
granted and resolves to help Jim in his escape from
slavery. The intensity of his struggle over the act suggests
how deeply he is involved in the society which he
rejects. The satiric brilliance of the episode lies, of course,
in Huck's solving his problem not by doing 'right' but
by doing 'wrong'. He has only to consult his conscience,
the conscience of a Southern boy in the middle of the
last century, to know that he ought to return Jim to
slavery. And as soon as he makes the decision according
to conscience and decides to inform on Jim, he has all
the warmly gratifying emotions of conscious virtue.
'Why, it was astonishing, the way I felt as light as a
feather right straight off, and my troubles all gone . . .
I felt good and all washed clean of sin for the first time
I had ever felt so in my life, and I knowed I could
pray now.' And when at last he finds that he cannot
endure his decision but must sacrifice the comforts of
the pure heart and help Jim in his escape, it is not because
he has acquired any new ideas about slavery—he believes
that he detests Abolitionists; he himself answers when
he is asked if the explosion of a steamboat boiler had
hurt anyone, 'No'm, killed a nigger', and of course
finds nothing wrong in the responsive comment, 'Well,
it's lucky because sometimes people do get hurt'. Ideas
and ideals can be of no help to him in his moral crisis.
He no more condemns slavery than Tristram and Lance-
lot condemn marriage; he is as consciously *wicked* as any

illicit lover of romance and he consents to be damned for a personal devotion, never questioning the justice of the punishment he has incurred.

Huckleberry Finn was once barred from certain libraries and schools for its alleged subversion of morality. The authorities had in mind the book's endemic lying, the petty thefts, the denigrations of respectability and religion, the bad language, and the bad grammar. We smiled at that excessive care, yet in point of fact *Huckleberry Finn* is indeed a subversive book—no one who reads thoughtfully the dialectic of Huck's great moral crisis will ever again be wholly able to accept without some question and some irony the assumptions of the respectable morality by which he lives, nor will ever again be certain that what he considers the clear dictates of moral reason are not merely the engrained customary beliefs of his time and place.

We are not likely to miss in *Huckleberry Finn* the subtle, implicit moral meaning of the great river. But we are likely to understand these moral implications as having to do only with personal and individual conduct. And since the sum of individual pettiness is on the whole pretty constant, we are likely to think of the book as applicable to mankind in general and at all times and in all places, and we praise it by calling it 'universal'. And so it is; but like many books to which that large adjective applies, it is also local and particular. It has a particular moral reference to the United States in the period after the Civil War. It was then when, in Mr. Eliot's phrase, the river was forgotten, and precisely by the 'dwellers in cities', by the 'worshippers of the machine'.

The Civil War and the development of the railroads ended the great days when the river was the central artery of the nation. No contrast could be more moving than that between the hot, turbulent energy of the river life of the first part of *Life on the Mississippi* and the melancholy reminiscence of the second part. And the war that brought the end of the rich Mississippi days also marked a change in the quality of life in America which, to many men, consisted of a deterioration of American moral values. It is, of course, a human habit to look back on the past and to find it a better and more innocent time than the present. Yet in this instance there seems to be an objective basis for the judgement. We cannot disregard the testimony of men so diverse as Henry Adams, Walt Whitman, William Dean Howells, and Mark Twain himself, to mention but a few of the many who were in agreement on this point. All spoke of something that had gone out of American life after the war, some simplicity, some innocence, some peace. None of them was under any illusion about the amount of ordinary human wickedness that existed in the old days, and Mark Twain certainly was not. The difference was in the public attitude, in the things that were now accepted and made respectable in the national ideal. It was, they all felt, connected with new emotions about money. As Mark Twain said, where formerly 'the people had desired money', now they 'fall down and worship it'. The new gospel was, 'Get money. Get it quickly. Get it in abundance. Get it in prodigious abundance. Get it dishonestly if you can, honestly if you must'.[1]

With the end of the Civil War capitalism had established itself. The relaxing influence of the frontier was coming to an end. Americans increasingly became 'dwellers in cities' and 'worshippers of the machine'. Mark Twain himself became a notable part of this new dispensation. No one worshipped the machine more

[1] *Mark Twain in Eruption*, edited by Bernard De Voto, p. 77.

than he did, or thought he did—he ruined himself by his devotion to the Paige typesetting machine, by which he hoped to make a fortune even greater than he had made by his writing, and he sang the praises of the machine age in *A Connecticut Yankee in King Arthur's Court*. He associated intimately with the dominant figures of American business enterprise. Yet at the same time he hated the new way of life and kept bitter memoranda of his scorn, commenting on the low morality or the bad taste of the men who were shaping the ideal and directing the destiny of the nation.

Mark Twain said of *Tom Sawyer* that it 'is simply a hymn, put into prose form to give it a worldly air'. He might have said the same, and with even more reason, of *Huckleberry Finn*, which is a hymn to an older America forever gone, an America which had its great national faults, which was full of violence and even of cruelty, but which still maintained its sense of reality, for it was not yet enthralled by money, the father of ultimate illusion and lies. Against the money-god stands the river-god, whose comments are silent—sunlight, space, uncrowded time, stillness, and danger. It was quickly forgotten once its practical usefulness had passed, but, as Mr. Eliot's poem says, 'The river is within us . . .'

In form and style *Huckleberry Finn* is an almost perfect work. Only one mistake has ever been charged against it, that it concludes with Tom Sawyer's elaborate, too elaborate, game of Jim's escape. Certainly this episode is too long—in the original draft it was much longer—and certainly it is a falling off, as almost anything would have to be, from the incidents of the river. Yet it has a certain formal aptness—like, say, that of the Turkish initiation which brings Molière's *Le Bourgeois Gentilhomme* to its close. It is a rather mechanical development of an idea, and yet some device is needed to permit Huck to return to his anonymity, to give up the role of hero, to fall into the background which he prefers, for he is modest in all things and could not well endure the attention and glamour which attend a hero at a book's end. For this purpose nothing could serve better than the mind of Tom Sawyer with its literary furnishings, its conscious romantic desire for experience and the hero's part, and its ingenious schematization of life to achieve that aim.

The form of the book is based on the simplest of all novel-forms, the so-called picaresque novel, or novel of the road, which strings its incidents on the line of the hero's travels. But, as Pascal says, 'rivers are roads that move', and the movement of the road in its own mysterious life transmutes the primitive simplicity of the form: the road itself is the greatest character in this novel of the road, and the hero's departures from the river and his returns to it compose a subtle and significant pattern. The linear simplicity of the picaresque novel is further modified by the story's having a clear dramatic organization: it has a beginning, a middle, and an end, and a mounting suspense of interest.

As for the style of the book, it is not less than definitive in American literature. The prose of *Huckleberry Finn* established for written prose the virtues of American colloquial speech. This has nothing to do with pronunciation or grammar. It has something to do with ease and freedom in the use of language. Most of all it has to do with the structure of the sentence, which is simple, direct, and fluent, maintaining the rhythm of the word-groups of speech and the intonations of the speaking voice.

In the matter of language, American literature had a special problem. The young nation was inclined to think that the mark of the truly literary product was a grandiosity and elegance not to be found in the common speech. It therefore encouraged a greater breach between its vernacular and its literary language than, say, English literature of the same period ever allowed. This accounts for the hollow ring one now and then hears even in the work of our best writers in the first half of the last century. English writers of equal stature would never have made the lapses into rhetorical excess that are common in Cooper and Poe and that are to be found even in Melville and Hawthorne.

Yet at the same time that the language of ambitious literature was high and thus always in danger of falseness, the American reader was keenly interested in the actualities of daily speech. No literature, indeed, was ever so taken up with matters of speech as ours was. 'Dialect', which attracted even our serious writers, was the accepted common ground of our popular humorous writing. Nothing in social life seemed so remarkable as the different forms which speech could take—the brogue of the immigrant Irish or the mispronunciation of the German, the 'affectation' of the English, the reputed precision of the Bostonian, the legendary twang of the Yankee farmer, and the drawl of the Pike County man. Mark Twain, of course, was in the tradition of humour that exploited this interest, and no one could play with it nearly so well. Although today the carefully spelled-out dialects of nineteenth-century American humour are likely to seem dull enough, the subtle variations of speech in *Huckleberry Finn*, of which Mark Twain was justly proud, are still part of the liveliness and flavour of the book.

Out of his knowledge of the actual speech of America Mark Twain forged a classic prose. The adjective may seem a strange one, yet it is apt. Forget the misspellings and the faults of grammar, and the prose will be seen to move with the greatest simplicity, directness, lucidity, and grace. These qualities are by no means accidental. Mark Twain, who read widely, was passionately interested in the problems of style; the mark of the strictest literary sensibility is everywhere to be found in the prose of *Huckleberry Finn*.

It is this prose that Ernest Hemingway had chiefly in mind when he said that 'all modern American literature comes from one book by Mark Twain called *Huckleberry Finn*'. Hemingway's own prose stems from it directly and consciously; so does the prose of the two modern writers who most influenced Hemingway's early style, Gertrude Stein and Sherwood Anderson (although neither of them could maintain the robust purity of their model); so, too, does the best of William Faulkner's prose, which, like Mark Twain's own, reinforces the colloquial tradition with the literary tradition. Indeed, it may be said that almost every contemporary American writer who deals conscientiously with the problems and possibility of prose must feel, directly or indirectly, the influence of Mark Twain. He is the master of the style that escapes the fixity of the printed page, that sounds in our ears with the immediacy of the heard voice, the very voice of unpretentious truth.

CLEANTH BROOKS

1906–

WHAT DOES POETRY COMMUNICATE?

The Well Wrought Urn, 1947

CORINNA'S GOING A MAYING

Get up, get up for shame, the Blooming Morne
Upon her wings presents the god unshorne.
  See how *Aurora* throwes her faire
  Fresh-quilted colours through the aire:
  Get up, sweet-Slug-a-bed, and see
  The Dew-bespangling Herbe and Tree.
Each Flower has wept, and bow'd toward the East,
Above an houre since; yet you not drest,
  Nay! not so much as out of bed?
  When all the Birds have Mattens seyd,
  And sung their thankfull Hymnes: 'tis sin,
  Nay, profanation to keep in,
When as a thousand Virgins on this day,
Spring, sooner than the Lark, to fetch in May.

Rise; and put on your Foliage, and be seene
To come forth, like the Spring-time, fresh and greene;
  And sweet as *Flora*. Take no care
  For Jewels for your Gowne, or Haire:
  Feare not; the leaves will strew
  Gemms in abundance upon you:
Besides, the childhood of the Day has kept,
Against you come, some *Orient Pearls* unwept:
  Come, and receive them while the light
  Hangs on the Dew-locks of the night:
  And *Titan* on the Eastern hill
  Retires himselfe, or else stands still
Till you come forth. Wash, dresse, be briefe in praying:
Few Beads are best, when once we goe a Maying.

Come, my *Corinna*, come; and comming, marke
How each field turns a street; each street a Parke
　　Made green, and trimm'd with trees: see how
　　Devotion gives each House a Bough,
　　Or Branch: Each Porch, each doore, ere this,
　　An Arke a Tabernacle is
Made up of white-thorn neatly enterwove;
As if here were those cooler shades of love.
　　Can such delights be in the street,
　　And open fields, and we not see't?
　　Come, we'll abroad; and let's obay
　　The Proclamation made for May:
And sin no more, as we have done, by staying;
But my *Corinna*, come, let's goe a Maying.

There's not a budding Boy, or Girle, this day,
But is got up, and gone to bring in May.
　　A deale of Youth, ere this, is come
　　Back, and with *White-thorn* laden home.
　　Some have dispatcht their Cakes and Creame,
　　Before that we have left to dreame:
And some have wept, and woo'd, and plighted Troth,
And chose their Priest, ere we can cast off sloth:
　　Many a green-gown has been given;
　　Many a kisse, both odde and even:
　　Many a glance too has been sent
　　From out the eye, Loves Firmament:
Many a jest told of the Keyes betraying
This night, and Locks pickt, yet w'are not a Maying.

Come, let us goe, while we are in our prime;
And take the harmlesse follie of the time.
　　We shall grow old apace and die
　　Before we know our liberty.
　　Our life is short; and our dayes run
　　As fast away as do's the Sunne:
And as a vapour, or a drop of raine
Once lost, can ne'er be found againe:

So when or you or I are made
A fable, song, or fleeting shade;
All love, all liking, all delight
Lies drown'd with us in endless night.
Then while time serves, and we are but decaying;
Come, my *Corinna*, come, let's goe a Maying.

THE question of what poetry communicates, if anything, has been largely forced upon us by the advent
of 'modern' poetry. Some of that poetry is admittedly
highly difficult—a very great deal of it is bound to
appear difficult to the reader of conventional reading
habits, even in spite of the fact—actually, in many cases,
because of the fact—that he is a professor of literature.

For this reason, the difficult moderns are often represented as untraditional and generally irresponsible. (The
War, incidentally, has encouraged the tendency: critics
who ought to know better lend themselves to the
popular plea that we should go back to the good old
days when a poet meant what he said and there was no
nonsense about it.)

The question, however, allows only one honest
answer: modern poetry (if it is really poetry, and, at its
best, it is really poetry) communicates whatever any
other poetry communicates. The fact is that the question
is badly asked. What does traditional poetry communicate? What does a poem like Herrick's 'Corinna's
going a Maying' communicate? The example is a
fair one: the poem has been long praised, and it is not
noted for its difficulty.

The textbook answer is easy: the poem is a statement
of the *carpe diem* theme. So it is, of course. But what does
the poem do with the theme—specifically: Does the
poet accept the theme? How seriously does he accept
it? Within what context? &c. These are questions of the
first importance, a point that becomes obvious when

we come to deal with such a matter as the following: after describing the joys of the May-day celebration, the poet prefaces his final invitation to Corinna to accept these joys by referring to them as 'the harmlesse follie of the time'. Unless we are absent-mindedly dictating a stock answer to an indifferent freshman, we shall certainly feel constrained to go further in describing what the poem 'says'.

Well, let us try again. Herrick's poem says that the celebration of nature is a beautiful but harmless folly, and his invitation to Corinna, thus, is merely playful, not serious. The Anglican parson is merely pretending for the moment that he is Catullus and that his Corinna is a pagan nymph. The poem is a pretence, a masquerade.

But there are the closing lines of the poem:

> Our life is short; and our dayes run
>   As fast away as do's the Sunne:
> And as a vapour, or a drop of raine
>   Once lost, can ne'er be found againe:
>   So when or you or I are made
>   A fable, song, or fleeting shade;
>   All love, all liking, all delight
>   Lies drown'd with us in endless night.
> Then while time serves, and we are but decaying;
> Come, my *Corinna*, come, let's goe a Maying.

Obviously, there is a sense in which the invitation is thoroughly serious.

Confronted with this apparent contradiction, we can conclude, if we like, that Herrick is confused; or, softening the censure, we can explain that he was concerned only with providing some sort of framework for a description of the Devonshire spring. But if Herrick is confused about what he is saying in the poem, he behaves very strangely for a man in that plight. Far from being unconscious of the contradictory elements in the poem, he quite obviously has them in mind. Indeed, he actually takes pains to stress the clash between the Christian and pagan world views; or, rather, while celebrating the pagan view, he refuses to suppress references to the Christian. For instance, for all the dew-besprinkled description of the morning, he makes the ominous, unpagan word 'sin' run throughout the poem. While the flowers are rejoicing and the birds are singing their hymns of praise, it is a 'sin' and a 'profanation' for Corinna to remain within doors. In the second stanza, the clash between paganism and Christianity becomes quite explicit: Corinna is to be 'briefe in praying: / Few Beads are best' on this morning which is dedicated to the worship of the nature god. And in the third stanza, paganism becomes frankly triumphant. Corinna is to

. . . sin no more, as we have done, by staying . . .

Moreover, a great deal that is usually glossed over as decoration or atmosphere in this poem is actually used by the poet to point up this same conflict. Herrick persists (with a shrewdness worthy of Sir James Frazer) in seeing the May Day rites as religious rites, though, of course, those of a pagan religion. The flowers, like worshippers, bow to the east; the birds sing 'Mattens' and 'Hymnes'; and the village itself, bedecked with greenery, becomes a cluster of pagan temples:

Devotion gives each House a Bough,
Or Branch: Each Porch, each doore, ere this,
An Arke a Tabernacle is . . .

The religious terms—'devotion', 'ark', 'tabernacle'— appear insistently. Corinna is actually being reproached for being late to church—the church of nature. The village itself has become a grove, subject to the laws of nature. One remembers that the original sense of 'pagan' was 'country-dweller' because the worship of the old gods and goddesses persisted longest there. On this May morning, the country has come into the village to claim it, at least on this one day, for its own. Symbolically, the town has disappeared and its mores are superseded.

I cannot see how we can avoid admitting that all this is communicated by the poem. Here it is in the poem. And its repercussions on the theme (if we still want to view the poem as a communication of a theme) are important. Among other things, they qualify the theme thus: the poem is obviously not a brief for the acceptance of the pagan ethic so much as it is a statement that the claims of the pagan ethic—however much they may be overlaid—exist, and on occasion emerge, as on this day.

The description of Corinna herself supplies another important qualification of the theme. The poet suggests that she properly falls under the dominion of nature as do the flowers and birds and trees. Notice the opening of the second stanza:

> Rise; and put on your Foliage . . .

And this suggestion that she is a part of nature, like a plant, is reinforced throughout the poem. The trees drenched in dew will shake down dew-drops on her hair, accepting her as a companion and equal. Her human companions, the boys and girls of the village, likewise are plants—

> There's not a budding Boy, or Girle, this day,
> But is got up, and gone to bring in May.

Indeed, as we go through the first three stanzas of the poem the old relationships gradually dissolve: the street itself turns into a park, and the boys and girls returning with their arms loaded with branches of white-thorn, merge into the plants themselves. Corinna, like them, is subject to nature, and to the claims of nature; and the season of springtime cannot, and ought not, to be denied. Not to respond is to 'sin' against nature itself.

All this is 'communicated' by the poem, and must be taken into account when we attempt to state what the poem 'says'. No theory of communication can deny that this is part of what the poem communicates, however awkwardly a theory of communication may be put to it to handle the problem.

We have still not attempted to resolve the conflict between the Christian and pagan attitudes in the poem, though the qualification of each of them, as Herrick qualifies each in the poem, may make it easier to discover possible resolutions which would have appealed to Herrick the Anglican parson who lived so much of his life in Devonshire and apparently took so much interest, not only in the pagan literature of Rome and Greece, but in the native English survivals of the old fertility cults.

Something of the nature of the poet's reconcilement of the conflicting claims of paganism and Christianity— and this, again, is part of what the poem communicates —is foreshadowed in the fourth stanza. The paganism with which the poem is concerned is clearly not an abstract and doctrinaire paganism. It comes to terms with the authoritative Christian mores, casually and without undue thought about the conflict—at least the paganism in action does: the village boys and the girls with their grass-stained gowns, coming to the priest to receive the blessing of the church.

> And some have wept, and woo'd, and plighted Troth,
> And chose their Priest, ere we can cast off sloth . . .

After the poet's teasing play between attitudes in the first three stanzas, we are apparently approaching some kind of viable relation between them in this most realistic stanza of the poem with its

> Many a jest told of the Keyes betraying
> This night, and Locks pickt . . .

The explicit resolution, of course, is achieved with a change of tone, in the last stanza, with its

> Come, let us goe, while we are in our prime;
> And take the harmlesse follie of the time.
> We shall grow old apace, and die . . .

I shall not try to indicate in detail what the resolution is. Here one must refer the reader to the poem itself. Yet one can venture to suggest the tone. The tone would be something like this: All right, let's be serious. Dismiss my pagan argument as folly. Still, in a sense, we are a part of nature, and are subject to its claims, and participate in its beauty. Whatever may be true in reality of the life of the soul, the body does decay, and unless we make haste to catch some part of that joy and beauty, that beauty—whatever else may be true—is lost.

If my clumsy paraphrase possesses any part of the truth, then this is still another thing which the poem communicates, though I shall hardly be able to 'prove' it. As a matter of fact, I do not care to insist upon this or any other paraphrase. Indeed it is just because I am suspicious of such necessarily abstract paraphrases that I think our initial question, 'What does the poem communicate?' is badly asked. It is not that the poem communicates nothing. Precisely the contrary. The poem communicates so much and communicates it so richly and with such delicate qualifications that the thing communicated is mauled and distorted if we attempt to convey it by any vehicle less subtle than that of the poem itself.

This general point is reinforced if we consider the function of particular words and phrases within the poem. For instance, consider

> Our life is short; and our dayes run
> As fast away as do's the Sunne:
> And as a vapour, or a drop of raine
> Once lost, can ne'er be found againe . . .

Why does the rain-drop metaphor work so powerfully? It is hardly because the metaphor is startlingly novel. Surely one important reason for its power is the fact that the poet has filled the first two stanzas of his poem with references to the dew. And the drops of dew have come to stand as a symbol of the spring and early dawn and of the youth of the lovers themselves. The dew-drops are the free gift of nature, spangling every herb and tree; they sparkle in the early light like something precious, like gems; they are the appropriate decoration for the girl; but they will not last—Corinna must hasten to enjoy them if she is to enjoy them at all. Thus, in the context of the poem they become a symbol heavily charged with meanings which no dictionary can be expected to give. When the symbol is revived at the end of the poem, even though in somewhat different guise, the effect is powerful; for the poet has made the little globule of moisture come to stand for the brief beauty of youth. And this too is part of what the poem says, though it is said indirectly, and the dull or lazy reader will not realize that it has been said at all.

The principle of rich indirection applies even to the individual word. Consider

> Then while time serves, and we are but decaying;
> Come, my *Corinna*, come, let's goe a Maying.

'While time serves' means loosely 'while there is yet time', but in the full context of the poem it also means 'while time serves us', while time is still servant, not master—before we are mastered by time. Again, mere recourse to the dictionary will not give us this powerful second meaning. The poet is exploiting the potentialities of language—indeed, as all poets must do, he is remaking language.

To sum up: our examination of the poem has not resulted in our locating an idea or set of ideas which the poet has communicated with certain appropriate decorations. Rather, our examination has carried us farther and farther into the poem itself in a process of exploration. As we have made this exploration, it has become more and more clear that the poem is not only the linguistic vehicle which conveys the thing communicated most 'poetically', but that it is also the sole linguistic vehicle which conveys the things communicated accurately. In fact, if we are to speak exactly, the poem itself is the *only* medium that communicates the particular 'what' that is communicated. The conventional theories of communication offer no easy solution to our problem of meanings: we emerge with nothing more enlightening than this graceless bit of tautology: the poem says what the poem says.

There is a further point that comes out of our examination: our examination tends to suggest that not only our reading of the poem is a process of exploration, but that Herrick's process of making the poem was probably a process of exploration too. To say that Herrick 'communicates' certain matters to the reader tends to falsify the real situation. The old description of the poet was better and less dangerous: the poet is a maker, not a communicator. He explores, consolidates, and 'forms' the total experience that is the poem. I do not mean that he fashions a replica of his particular experience of a certain May morning like a detective making a *moulage* of a footprint in wet clay. But rather, out of the experiences of many May mornings, and out of his experience of Catullus, and possibly out of a hundred other experiences, he fashions, probably through a process akin to exploration, the total experience which is the poem.

This experience is *communicable*, partially so, at least. If we are willing to use imaginative understanding, we can come to know the poem as an object—we can share in the experience. But the poet is most truthfully described as a *poietes* or maker, not as an expositor or communicator. I do not mean to split hairs. It is doubtless possible to elaborate a theory of communication which will adequately cover these points. I believe that I. A. Richards, if I understand him correctly, has attempted to qualify his theory in precisely this way. At any rate, the net effect of his criticism has been to emphasize the need of a more careful reading of poetry and to regard the poem as an organic thing.

But most proponents of poetry as communication have been less discerning, and have used this view of poetry to damn the modern poets. I refer to such typical critics as Max Eastman and F. L. Lucas. But perhaps the most hard-bitten and vindictive of all the adherents of the theory is a man to whom the phrase 'theory of communication' may seem novel and unfamiliar: I mean the average English professor. In one form or another, whether in a conception which makes poetry a romantic raid on the absolute, or in a conception of more didactic persuasion which makes poetry an instrument of edification, some form of the theory of communication is to be found deeply embedded in the average teacher's doctrine of poetry. In many contexts it does little or no harm; but it can emerge to becloud the issues thoroughly when one confronts poetry which is unfamiliar or difficult.

Much modern poetry is difficult. Some of it may be difficult because the poet is snobbish and definitely wants to restrict his audience, though this is a strange vanity and much rarer than Mr. Eastman would have us think. Some modern poetry is difficult because it is bad—the total experience remains chaotic and incoherent because the poet could not master his material and give it a form. Some modern poetry is difficult because of the special problems of our civilization. But a great deal of modern poetry is difficult for the reader simply because so few people, relatively speaking, are accustomed to reading *poetry as poetry*. The theory of communication throws the burden of proof upon the poet, overwhelmingly and at once. The reader says to the poet: Here I am; it's your job to 'get it across' to me—when he ought to be assuming the burden of proof himself.

Now the modern poet has, for better or worse, thrown the weight of the responsibility upon the reader. The reader must be on the alert for shifts of tone, for ironic statement, for suggestion rather than direct statement. He must be prepared to accept a method of indirection. He is further expected to be reasonably well acquainted with the general tradition—literary, political, philosophical, for he is reading a poet who comes at the end of a long tradition and who can hardly be expected to write honestly and with full integrity and yet ignore this fact. But the difficulties are not insuperable, and most of them can be justified in principle as the natural results of the poet's employment of his characteristic methods. For example, surely there can be no objection to the poet's placing emphasis on methods characteristic of poetry—the use of symbol rather than abstraction, of suggestion rather than explicit pronouncement, of metaphor rather than direct statement.

In stressing such methods, it is true, the modern poet

has not produced a poetry which easily yields manageable abstractions in the way that some of the older poetry seems to do. But this is scarcely a conclusion that is flattering to the antagonists of modern poetry. What does an 'older poem' like 'Corinna's going a Maying' say? What does this poem communicate? If we are content with the answer that the poem says that we should enjoy youth before youth fades, and if we are willing to write off everything else in the poem as 'decoration', then we can properly censure Eliot or Auden or Tate for not making poems so easily tagged. But in that case we are not interested in poetry; we are interested in tags. Actually, in a few years, when time has wrought its softening changes, and familiarity has subdued the modern poet's frightful mien, and when the tags have been obligingly supplied, we may even come to terms with our difficult moderns.

W. H. AUDEN

1907–

HENRY JAMES: THE AMERICAN SCENE

Introduction to Scribner edition, 1946

TWO of James's virtues, his self-knowledge, his awareness of just what he could and could not do, and his critical literary sense, his respect for the inalienable right of every subject to its own form and treatment, are nowhere more conspicuous than in *The American Scene*.

Of all possible subjects, travel is the most difficult for an artist, as it is the easiest for a journalist. For the latter, the interesting event is the new, the extraordinary,

the comic, the shocking, and all that the peripatetic
journalist requires is a flair for being on the spot where
and when such events happen—the rest is merely passive
typewriter thumping: meaning, relation, importance,
are not his quarry. The artist, on the other hand, is
deprived of his most treasured liberty, the freedom to
invent; successfully to extract importance from historical
personal events without ever departing from them, free
only to select and never to modify or to add, calls for
imagination of a very high order.

Few writers have had less journalistic talent than
James, and this is his defect, for the supreme masters
have one trait in common with the childish scribbling
mass, the vulgar curiosity of a police-court reporter.
One can easily imagine Stendhal or Tolstoy or Dostoevski
becoming involved in a bar-room fight, but James,
never. I have read somewhere a story that once, when
James was visiting a French friend, the latter's mistress,
unobserved, filled his top-hat with champagne, but I
do not believe it because, try as I will, I simply cannot
conceive what James did and said when he put his hat
on.

James was, of course, well aware of this limitation;
he knew that both his character and circumstances confined his residence to a certain kind of house or hotel,
his intimate acquaintance to a certain social class, and
that such confinement might be an insuperable obstacle
to writing a book of travel in which the author must try
to catch the spirit, not of a particular milieu, but of a
whole place, a whole social order. Nevertheless, the
challenge, perhaps just because it was, for him, so particularly formidable, fascinated James from the first, and
The American Scene is only the latest, most ambitious,
and best of a series of topographical writings, beginning
in 1870 with sketches of Saratoga and Newport.

Immature as these early American pieces are, they seem to me more satisfactory than the subsequent descriptions of England and Europe, even the charming 'A Little Tour in France (1886)'. Confronted with the un-American scene, he seems prim and a little amateurish, as if he were a conscientious father writing letters to an intelligent daughter of fourteen: as guide books, the European travelogues are incomplete, and as personal impressions, they are timid; the reader is conscious that the traveller must have seen and felt a great deal more than he says, and refrained either from a fear of shocking or from a lack of confidence in his own judgement; but even as a young man, James was unafraid of America as a subject: puzzled often, angry sometimes, yes, but quite certain of what he felt and of his right to say it.

In letters directly and in his novels by implication James makes many criticisms of the English, but he would never have been so outspoken about them as he is, for instance, about the habits of American children of whom he writes in 1870:

You meet them far into the evening, roaming over the piazzas and corridors of the hotels—the little girls especially —lean, pale, formidable. Occasionally childhood confesses itself, even when maternity resists, and you see at eleven o'clock at night some poor little bedizened precocity collapsed in slumber in a lonely wayside chair.

And again in 1906:

. . . there were ladies and children all about—though indeed there may have been sometimes *but* the lone breakfasting child to deal with; the little pale, carnivorous, coffee-drinking ogre or ogress, who prowls down in advance of its elders, engages a table—dread vision!—and has the 'run' of the bill of fare.

All who knew James personally have spoken of the

terror he could inspire when enraged, and one of the minor delights of *The American Scene* is that the stranger occasionally gets a glimpse, at a fortunately safe distance, of what these outbursts must have been like—the un-hurried implacable advance of the huge offensive periods, the overwhelming alliterative barrage, the an-nihilating adverbial scorn.

The freedoms of the young three—who were, by-the-way, not in their earliest bloom either—were thus bandied about in the void of the gorgeous valley without even a consciousness of its shelter, its recording echoes... The immodesty was too colossal to be anything but innocence, on the other hand, was too colossal to be anything but inane. And they were alive, the slightly stale three: they talked, they laughed, they sang, they shrieked, they romped, they scaled the pinnacle of publicity and perched on it flapping their wings; whereby they were shown in possession of many of the movements of life.

*   *   *   *   *

Whom were they constructed, such specimens, to talk with or to talk over, or to talk under, and what form of address or of intercourse, what uttered, what intelligible terms of introduction, of persuasion, of menace, what developed, what specific human process of any sort, was it possible to impute to them? What reciprocities did they imply, what presumptions did they, could they, create? What happened, inconceivably, when such Greeks met such Greeks, such faces looked into such faces, and such sounds, in especial, were exchanged with such sounds? What women did they live with, what women, living with them, could yet leave them as they were? What wives, daughters, sisters, did they in fine make credible; and what, in especial, was the speech, what the manners, what the general dietary, what most the monstrous morning meal, of ladies receiving at such hands the law or the license of life?

Just what, one asks with nostalgic awe, would James

have said if confronted with the spectacle of a drum-majorette?

In writing *The American Scene*, the 'facts' he selected to go on are, even for James, amazingly and, one would have thought, fatally few. Though he seems to have visited Chicago (and not to have 'liked' it) he confines his chapters to the East Coast from Boston to Miami. The Far West, the Mid West, the Deep South are totally ignored. This is a pity because the regional differences of the United States are significant though not, I think, so decisively significant as the professional regionalists insist. Today it would be quite fatal to neglect the states remoter from Europe, not so much as regions in themselves, but because some of the most essential and generally typical American facts, such as the film and automobile industries, the public power projects, the divorce mills, are regionally situated. Still, even in 1906, there were many things west of Massachusetts, the landscape of Arizona, the distinctive atmosphere of San Francisco, to mention only two of them, which would have 'amused' 'the restless analyst', and in whose amusement his readers would have been very glad to share.[1]

With the second limitation that James imposed upon himself, however—his decision to reject all second-hand information and sentiment, to stick to those facts, however few, which were felt by him, however mistakenly, to be important, to be unashamedly, defiantly subjective —one can only wholeheartedly agree. In grasping the character of a society, as in judging the character of an individual, no documents, statistics, 'objective' measurements can ever compete with the single intuitive glance. Intuition may err, for though its sound judgement is, as Pascal said, only a question of good eyesight, it must be

---

[1] James originally intended, it appears, to write a second volume dealing with the West and Middle West.

good, for the principles are subtle and numerous, and the omission of one principle leads to error; but documentation which is useless unless it is complete, must err in a field where completeness is impossible. James's eyesight was good, his mind was accurate, and he understood exactly what he was doing; he never confused his observation with his interpretation.

The fond observer is by his very nature committed everywhere to his impression—which means essentially, I think, that he is foredoomed, in one place as in another, to 'put in' a certain quantity of emotion and reflection. The turn his sensibility takes depends of course on what is before him; but when is it not in some manner exposed and alert? If it be anything really of a touchstone, it is more disposed, I hold, to easy bargains than to hard ones; it only wants to be *somehow* interested, and is not without the knowledge that an emotion is after all, at the best or the worst, but an emotion. All of which is a voluminous commentary, I admit, on the modest text that I perhaps made the University Hospital stand for too many things. That establishes at all events my contention—that the living fact, in the United States, *will* stand, other facts not preventing, for almost anything you may ask of it.

*   *   *   *   *

Where, in the United States, the interest, where the pleasure of contemplation is concerned, discretion is the better part of valor and insistence too often a betrayal. It is not so much that the hostile fact crops up as that the friendly fact breaks down. If you have luckily *seen*, you have seen; carry off your prize, in this case, instantly and at any risk. Try it again and you don't, you won't, see.

Yet, if the vision had, necessarily, to be brief, it was neither poor nor vague, and only the most leisurely and luxuriant treatment could do justice to its rich possibilities. In the novels and short stories of the previous decade, James had been evolving a style of metaphorical description of the emotions which is all his own, a kind of modern Gongorism, and in *The American Scene* this imagery, no longer inhibited by the restraining hand of character or the impatient tug of plot, came to its fullest and finest bloom.

Indeed, perhaps the best way to approach this book is as a prose poem of the first order, i.e. to suspend, for the time being, one's own conclusions about America and Americans, and to read on slowly, relishing it sentence by sentence, for it is no more a guide book than the 'Ode to a Nightingale' is an ornithological essay. It is not even necessary to start at the beginning or read with continuity; one can open it at almost any page. I advise, for instance, the reader who finds James's later manner a little hard to get into, to begin by reading the long paragraph about Lee's statue which concludes the chapter on Richmond: this is, admittedly, a purple patch, but there are many others which match it.

James's first-hand experiences were, necessarily, mostly those of a tourist, namely scenic objects, landscapes, buildings, the faces and behaviour of strangers, and his own reflections on what these objects stood for. Unlike his modern rival at conveying the sense of Place, D. H. Lawrence, James was no naturalist; one is not convinced that he knew one bird or flower from another. He sees Nature as a city-bred gentleman with a knowledge of the arts, and by accepting this fully, turns it to his advantage in his descriptive conceits.

. . . the social scene, shabby and sordid, and lost in the scale of space as the quotable line is lost in a dull epic or the needed name in an ageing memory.

* * * * *

The spread of this single great wash of winter from latitude to latitude struck me in fact as having its analogy in the vast vogue of some infinitely selling novel, one of

those happy volumes of which the circulation roars,
periodically, from Atlantic to Pacific and from great
windy state to state, in the manner as I have heard it
vividly put, of a blazing prairie fire; with as little possibility of arrest from 'criticism' in the one case as from the
bleating of lost sheep on the other.

*　　*　　*　　*　　*

. . . the hidden ponds where the season itself seemed to
bend as a young bedizened, a slightly melodramatic
mother, before taking some guilty flight, hangs over the
crib of her sleeping child.

But it is in his treatment of social objects and mental
concepts that James reveals most clearly his great and
highly original poetic gift. Outside of fairy tales, I know
of no book in which things so often and so naturally
become persons.

Buildings address James:

Un bon mouvement, therefore: you must make a dash for
it, but you'll see I'm worth it.

James addresses buildings:

You overdo it for what you are; you overdo it still
more for what you may be; and don't pretend above all,
with the object lesson supplied you, close at hand, by the
queer case of Newport, don't pretend, we say, not to
know what we mean.

Buildings address each other:

Exquisite was what they called you, eh? We'll teach
you, then, little sneak, to be exquisite! We'll allow none
of that rot round here.

At Farmington, the bullying railroad orders taste and
tradition

—off their decent avenue without a fear that they will
'stand up' to it.

From Philadelphia the alluring train,

disvulgarized of passengers, steams away, in disinterested empty form, to some terminus too noble to be marked in *our* poor schedules.

Again, since *The Faerie Queene*, what book has been more hospitable to allegorical figures?

At Mount Vernon,

the slight, pale, bleeding Past, in a patched homespun suit, stands there taking the thanks of the Bloated Present, having woundedly rescued from thieves and brought to his door the fat, locked pocket book of which that personage appears to be the owner.

At Baltimore the Muse of History descends in a quick white flash to declare that she has found that city 'a charming patient'.

In Richmond the Spirit of the South reveals herself for a vivid moment,

a figure somehow blighted and stricken discomfortably, impossibly seated in an invalid chair, and yet facing one with strange eyes that were half a defiance and half a deprecation of one's noticing, and much more of one's referring to, any abnormal sign.

In Florida the American Woman is waiting to state her case in the manner of a politician in Thucydides:

How can I do *all* the grace, all the interest, as I'm expected to? Yes, literally all the interest that isn't the mere interest in the money... All I want—that is all I need, for there is perhaps a difference—is, to put it simply, that my parents and my brothers and my male cousins should consent to exist otherwise than occultly, undiscoverably, or, as I suppose you'd call it, irresponsibly.

When 'the recent immigrant', to copy the Jamesian nomenclature, compares his own impressions with those of 'the restless analyst', he is immediately struck by how little, on the one hand, America has changed in any decisive way—the changes, great as they are, seem but extensions and intensifications of a pattern already observable thirty years ago—and by the irrevocable catastrophic alterations in Europe, on the other—what recognizable identity is there between the confident glittering hostess of those days and the bruised, beggared, debased, dead-beat harridan of ours? For has not what James called *The Margin* 'by which the total of American life, huge as it already appears, is still so surrounded as to represent for the mind's eye on a general view but a scant central flotilla huddled as for very fear of the fathomless depth of water, the too formidable future' become the contemporary ambience of Europe, with this difference, that, while its vague and vast fluidity still, on the whole, continues to affect the observer on this side of the Atlantic as being, if not positively friendly, at least neutral, to the observer on the other side it looms with the extreme of menace, charged with every foreboding of worse disasters to come?

The features of the American scene which most struck the analyst then are those which most strike the immigrant now, whether they are minor details like the magnificent boots and teeth, the heavy consumption of candy, 'the vagueness of separation between apartments, between hall and room, between one room and another, between the one you are in and the one you are not in', or major matters like the promiscuous gregariousness, the lack, even among the rich, of constituted privacy, the absence of forms for vice no less than for virtue, the 'spoiling' of women and their responsibility for the whole of culture, above all the elimination from the scene of the squire and the parson.[1] It takes the

[1] The immigrant would like to add one element, the excessses of the climate, which is either much too hot or much too cold

immigrant a little time to discover just why the United States seems so different from any of the countries he resentfully or nostalgically remembers, but the crucial difference is, I think, just this last elimination of 'the pervasive Patron' and 'the old ecclesiastical arrogance for which, oh! a thousand times, the small substitutes, the mere multiplication of the signs of theological enterprise, in the tradition and on the scale of commercial and industrial enterprise, have no attenuation worth mentioning'.

What in fact is missing, what has been consciously rejected, with all that such a rejection implies, is the *romanitas* upon which Europe was founded and which she has not ceased attempting to preserve. This is a point which, at the risk of becoming tedious, must be enlarged upon, since the issue between America and Europe is no longer a choice between social levelling and social distinctions. The levelling is a universal and inexorable fact. Nothing can prevent the liquidation of the European nations or any other nation in the great continents, Asia, Africa, America, the liquidation of the 'individual' (in the eighteenth-century liberal meaning of the word) in the collective proletariat, the liquidation of Christendom in the neutral world. From that there is no refuge anywhere. But one's final judgement of Europe and America depends, it seems to me, upon whether one thinks that America (or America as a symbol) is right to reject *romanitas* or that Europe is right in trying to find

or much too wet or much too dry or even, in the case of the Californian coast, much too mild, a sort of meteorological Back Bay. And then—oh dear!—the *insects*, and the *snakes*, and the *poison ivy* . . . The truth is, Nature never intended human beings to live here, and her hostility, which confined the Indian to a nomad life and forbids the white man to relax his vigilance and will for one instant, must be an important factor in determining the American character.

new forms of it suited to the 'democratized' societies of our age.

The fundamental presupposition of *romanitas*, secular or sacred, is that virtue is prior to liberty, i.e. what matters most is that people should think and act rightly; of course it is preferable that they should do so consciously of their own free will, but if they cannot or will not, they must be made to, the majority by the spiritual pressure of education and tradition, the minority by physical coercion, for liberty to act wrongly is not liberty but licence. The antagonistic presupposition, which is not peculiar to America and would probably not be accepted by many Americans, but for which this country has come, symbolically, to stand, is that liberty is prior to virtue, i.e. liberty cannot be distinguished from licence, for freedom of choice is neither good nor bad but the human prerequisite without which virtue and vice have no meaning. Virtue is, of course, preferable to vice, but to choose vice is preferable to having virtue chosen for one.

To those who make the first presupposition, both State and Church have the same positive moral function; to those who make the second, their functions differ: the function of the State becomes a negative one—to prevent the will of the strong from interfering with the will of the weak, or the wills of the weak with one another, even if the strong should be in the right and the weak in the wrong—and the Church, whether Catholic or Protestant, divorced from the State, becomes a witness, an offered opportunity, a community of *converts*. The real issue has been obscured, for both sides, by the historical struggle for social equality which made liberty seem the virtue—or licence the vice—of which equality was the prized or detested pre-condition. This was natural since, when the struggle began, the most glaring cause of the lack of liberty was the privileged position of the few and the unprivileged position of the many so that a blow struck for equality was, in most cases, at the same time a blow struck for liberty, but the assumed order of priority was false all the same. The possibility that De Tocqueville foresaw from an inspection of America in 1830, has become a dreadful reality in the Europe of 1946, namely, that *romanitas* is perfectly capable of adapting itself to an egalitarian and untraditional society; it can even drop absolute values and replace the priest by the social engineer without violating its essential nature (which is and always was not Christian but Manichean), which it reveals in its democratic form by its persecution of dissident minorities. And it was from America, the first egalitarian society, that it learned how to adapt itself. For instance, it took the technique of mass advertising, eliminated the competitive element and changed the sales object from breakfast foods to political passions; it took the egalitarian substitute for tradition, fashion, and translated it from the putting over of best-sellers and evening frocks to the selling of an ever-switching party line; it took the extra-legal vigilantes and put them into official uniforms; it took the inert evil of race prejudice and made it a dynamic evil. An America which does not realize the difference between equality and liberty is in danger, for, start with equality in order to arrive at liberty and the moment you come to a situation where inequality is or seems to you, rightly or wrongly, a stubborn fact, you will come to grief. For instance, the unequal distribution of intellectual gifts is a fact; since they refuse to face it, the institutions of Higher Learning in America cannot decide whether they are to be Liberal Arts Colleges for the exceptional few or vocational schools for the average many, and so fail to do their duty by either. On the other, more sinister, hand, the Southerner, rightly or wrongly, believes that the negro is his inferior; by putting equality before liberty, he then refuses him the most elementary human liberties, for example, the educational and economic liberties that are the only means by which the negro could possibly become the equal of the white, so that the latter can never be proven mistaken.

Democratic snobbery or race prejudice is uglier than the old aristocratic snobbery because the included are relatively so many and the excluded relatively so few. The exclusiveness, for instance, of Baron de Charlus is forgivable and even charming. If Charlus will speak to only half a dozen people, it cannot be supposed that the millions suffer severely from being unable to speak to Charlus; his behaviour is frankly irrational, a personal act from which, if anyone suffers, it is only himself. The exclusiveness of the American Country Club—I cannot share James's pleasure in that institution—is both inexcusable and vulgar, for, since it purports to be democratic, its exclusion of Jews is a contradiction for which it has to invent dishonest rationalizations.

As the issue between virtue first and liberty first becomes clearer, so does the realization that the cost to any society that accepts the latter is extremely high, and to some may seem prohibitive. One can no longer make the task look easier than it is by pretending, as the liberals of the Enlightenment believed, that men are naturally good. No, it is just as true as it ever was that man is born in sin, that the majority are always, relatively, in the wrong, the minority sometimes, relatively, in the right (every one, of course, is free at any time to belong to either), and all, before God, absolutely in the wrong, that all of the people some of the time and some of the people most of the time will abuse their liberty and treat it as the licence of an escaped slave. But if the principle is accepted, it means accepting this: it means accepting a State that, in comparison to its Roman rival, is dangerously weak (though realizing that, since people will never cease trying to interfere with the liberties of others in pursuing their own, the State can never wither away. Tyranny today, anarchy tomorrow is a neo-Roman daydream); it means accepting a 'Society', in the collective inclusive sense that is as neutral to values (liberty is not a value but the ground of value) as the 'Nature' of physics;[1] it means accepting an educational system in which, in spite of the fact that authority is essential to the growth of the individual who is lost without it, the responsibility for recognizing authority is laid on the pupil; it means accepting the impossibility of any 'official' or 'public' art; and, for the individual, it means accepting the lot of the Wandering Jew, i.e. the loneliness and anxiety of having to choose himself, his faith, his vocation, his tastes. The Margin is a hard taskmaster; it says to the individual: 'It's no good your running to me and asking me to make you into someone. You must choose. I won't try to prevent your choice, but I can't and won't help you make it. If you try to put your trust in me, in public opinion, you will become, not someone but no one, a neuter atom of the public.'

This situation of the individual has far-reaching consequences for the artist. With his usual uncannily accurate foresight, De Tocqueville wrote:

Poets living in democratic times will prefer the delineation of passions and ideas to that of persons and achievements... The destinies of mankind, man himself taken

---

[1] Is not the aesthetic effect of Rockefeller Centre due to the *completeness* with which, in its handling of material and its design as a public building, this double neutrality of 'Nature' and 'Society' is accepted?

aloof from his country and his age and standing in the presence of Nature and God, with his passions, his doubts, his rare prosperities and inconceivable wretchedness, will become the chief, if not the sole, theme of poetry . . . I do not fear that the poetry of democratic nations will prove insipid or that it will fly too near the ground. I rather apprehend that it will be forever losing itself in the clouds and that it will range at last to purely imaginary regions. I fear that the productions of democratic poets may often be surcharged with immense and incoherent imagery, with exaggerated descriptions and strange creations; and that the fantastic beings of their brain may sometimes make us regret the world of reality.

If one compares Americans with Europeans, those, that is, who grew up before the ruin of Europe, one might say, crudely and too tidily, that the mediocre American is possessed by the Present and the mediocre European is possessed by the Past. The task of overcoming mediocrity, that is of learning to possess instead of being possessed, is thus different in each case, for the American has to make the Present *his* present, and the European the Past *his* past. There are two ways of taking possession of the Present: one is with the help of the Comic or Ironic spirit. Hence the superiority of American (and Yiddish) humour. Compared with *The New Yorker*, how insufferably stuffy and provincial the comic papers of all other countries, even France, appear, and, politically and religiously, how incorrigibly shallow and naïve. The other way is to choose a Past, i.e. to go physically or in the spirit to Europe. James's own explanation of his migration—

To make so much money that you won't, that you don't 'mind', don't mind anything—that is absolutely, I think, the main American formula. Thus your making no money—or so little that it passes there for none—and being thereby distinctly reduced to minding, amounts to your being reduced to the knowledge that America is no place for you . . . The withdrawal of the considerable group of the pecuniarily disqualified seems, for the present, an assured movement; there will always be scattered individuals condemned to mind on a scale beyond any scale of making—

seems to me only partly true; better T. S. Eliot's observation in his essay on James:

It is the final consummation of an American to become, not an Englishman, but a European—something no born European, no person of European nationality can become.

It is from American critics like James and Eliot that we Europeans have learned to understand our social and literary traditions in a way we could never have learned by ourselves, for they, with natural ease, look at our past, as it is extremely difficult for us to look, with contemporary eyes. Eliot's criticism of Milton, for example, may be unjustified, but only an American could have made it in such a way that it deserves serious consideration from lovers of Milton; an Englishman might have criticized him, but it would have been for some personal reason, like annoying his father.

It is harder for an American than it is for a European to become a good writer, but if he succeeds, he contributes something unique; he sees something and says it in a way that no one before him has said it. Think of the important American writers of the past—Poe, Emerson, Hawthorne, Melville, Whitman, Emily Dickinson, Henry Adams, Henry James—or of any group of contemporary American poets—Eliot, Frost, Marianne Moore, Cummings, Wallace Stevens, Laura Riding—could any European country (except, possibly, Germany) produce writers who in subject-matter, temperament, language, are so utterly unlike one another or anybody else? (Blake and Hopkins are the only English poets I can think of who might have been Americans.) Further, without mentioning names, is there any country where discipleship is attended by such disastrously banal results, in contrast to Europe where apprenticeship is the normal and fruitful state for the beginner?

The great danger for the young American writer is impatience. A wise uncle would advise him thus: 'Publish nothing before you are thirty but study, absorb, experiment. Take at least three years over every book. Be very careful about your health and lead a life as regular as a commuter's. Above all, do not write your autobiography, for your childhood is literally the whole of your capital.'

The great danger for the European writer on the other hand is, or rather was, indolence. (For the present and future, as the novels of Kafka testify, his situation is probably to be the 'American' one.) It was easier for him to write fairly well, but much harder to write as well as he possibly could, because he was a cultural *rentier*. His problem was how to possess the past, to do which he had to choose a present, and he was always tempted to think that rebellion against the past was such a choice, which it was not, for the rebel is a mirror image of the conformist. He had in fact to become by art what the American writer is by nature, *isolated*, and perhaps the only advice as to how to achieve this that *his* wise uncle could have given was: 'Get out, or get drunk, or get ill.'

James wrote a short story, 'The Great Good Place', which has been praised by Mr. Fadiman and condemned by Mr. Matthiessen, in both instances, I think, for the wrong reason, for both take it literally. The former says, 'The Place is what our civilization could be... It is a hotel without noise, a club without newspapers. You even have to pay for service'. If this were true, then the latter would be quite right to complain, as he does, that it is the vulgar daydream of a rich bourgeois intellectual. I believe, however, that, in his own discreet way, James is writing a religious parable, that is, he is not describing some social utopia, but a spiritual state which is achievable by the individual now, that the club is a symbol of this state not its cause, and the money a symbol of the sacrifice and suffering demanded to attain and preserve it. Anyway, the story contains a passage of dialogue which seems relevant to *The American Scene*.

'Every man must arrive by himself and on his own feet —isn't that so? We're Brothers here for the time as in a great monastery, and we immediately think of each other and recognize each other as such: but we must have first got here as we can, and we meet after long journeys by complicated ways.'
'Where is it?'
'I shouldn't be surprised if it were much nearer than one ever suspected.'
'Nearer "town", do you mean?'
'Nearer everything—nearer everyone.'

Yes. Nearer everything. Nearer than James himself perhaps, suspected, to the 'hereditary thinness' of the American Margin, to 'the packed and hoisted basket' and 'the torture rooms of the living idiom', nearer to the unspeakable juke-boxes, the horrible Rockettes and the insane salads, nearer to the anonymous countryside littered with heterogeneous *dreck* and the synonymous cities besotted with electric signs, nearer to radio commercials and congressional oratory and Hollywood Christianity, nearer to all the 'democratic' lusts and licences, without which, perhaps, the analyst and the immigrant alike would never understand by contrast the nature of the Good Place nor desire it with sufficient desperation to stand a chance of arriving.

PHILIP RAHV

1908–

PALEFACE AND REDSKIN

Image and Idea, 1957

VIEWED historically, American writers appear to group themselves around two polar types. Paleface and redskin I should like to call the two, and despite occasional efforts at reconciliation no love is lost between them.

Consider the immense contrast between the drawing-room fictions of Henry James and the open-air poems of Walt Whitman. Compare Melville's decades of loneliness, his tragic failure, with Mark Twain's boisterous career and dubious success. At one pole there is the literature of the low-life world of the frontier and of the big cities; at the other the thin, solemn, semi-clerical culture of Boston and Concord. The fact is that the creative mind in America is fragmented and one-sided. For the process of polarization has produced a dichotomy between experience and consciousness—a dissociation between energy and sensibility, between conduct and theories of conduct, between life conceived as an opportunity and life conceived as a discipline.

The differences between the two types define themselves in every sphere. Thus while the redskin glories in his Americanism, to the paleface it is a source of endless ambiguities. Sociologically they can be distinguished as patrician *v.* plebeian, and in their aesthetic ideals one is drawn to allegory and the distillations of symbolism, whereas the other inclines to a gross, riotous naturalism. The paleface is a 'highbrow', though his mentality—as in the case of Hawthorne and James—is often of the kind that excludes and repels general ideas; he is at the same time both something more and something less than an intellectual in the European sense. And the redskin deserves the epithet 'lowbrow' not because he is badly educated—which he might or might not be—but because his reactions are primarily emotional, spontaneous, and lacking in personal culture. The paleface continually hankers after religious norms, tending toward a refined estrangement from reality. The redskin, on the other hand, accepts his environment, at times to the degree of fusion with it, even when rebelling against one or another of its manifestations. At his highest level the paleface moves in an exquisite moral atmosphere; at his lowest he is genteel, snobbish, and pedantic. In giving expression to the vitality and to the aspirations of the people, the redskin is at his best; but at his worst he is a vulgar anti-intellectual, combining aggression with conformity and reverting to the crudest forms of frontier psychology.

James and Whitman, who as contemporaries felt little more than contempt for each other, are the purest examples of this dissociation.[1] In reviewing *Drum Taps* in 1865 the young James told off the grand plebeian innovator, advising him to stop declaiming and go sit in the corner of a rhyme and metre school, while the innovator, snorting at the novelist of scruples and moral delicacy, said 'Feathers!' Now this mutual repulsion between the two major figures in American literature would be less important if it were mainly personal or aesthetic in reference. But the point is that it has a profoundly national and social-historical character.

[1] According to Edith Wharton, James changed his mind about Whitman late in life. But this can be regarded as a private fact of the Jamesian sensibility, for in public he said not a word in favour of Whitman.

James and Whitman form a kind of fatal antipodes. To this, in part, can be traced the curious fact about them that, though each has become the object of a special cult, neither is quite secure in his reputation. For most of the critics and historians who make much of Whitman disparage James or ignore him altogether, and vice versa. Evidently the high valuation of the one is so incongruous with the high valuation of the other that criticism is chronically forced to choose between them —which makes for a breach in the literary tradition without parallel in any European country. The aristocrat Tolstoy and the tramp Gorky found that they held certain values and ideas in common, whereas James and Whitman, who between them dominate American writing of the nineteenth century, cannot abide with one another. And theirs is no unique or isolated instance.

The national literature suffers from the ills of a split personality. The typical American writer has so far shown himself incapable of escaping the blight of one-sidedness: of achieving that mature control which permits the balance of impulse with sensitiveness, of natural power with philosophical depth. For the dissociation of mind from experience has resulted in truncated works of art, works that tend to be either naïve and ungraded, often flat reproductions of life, or else products of cultivation that remain abstract because they fall short on evidence drawn from the sensuous and material world. Hence it is only through intensively exploiting their very limitations, through submitting themselves to a process of creative yet cruel self-exaggeration, that a few artists have succeeded in warding off the failure that threatened them. And the later novels of Henry James are a case in point.

The palefaces dominated literature throughout the

nineteenth century, but in the twentieth they were overthrown by the redskins. Once the continent had been mastered, with the plebeian bourgeoisie coming into complete possession of the national wealth, and puritanism had worn itself out, degenerating into mere respectability, it became objectively possible and socially permissible to satisfy that desire for experience and personal emancipation which heretofore had been systematically frustrated. The era of economic accumulation had ended and the era of consumption had arrived. To enjoy life now became one of the functions of progress—a function for which the palefaces were temperamentally disqualified. This gave Mencken his opportunity to emerge as the ideologue of enjoyment. Novelists like Dreiser, Anderson, and Lewis—and, in fact, most of the writers of the period of 'experiment and liberation'—rose against conventions that society itself was beginning to abandon. They helped to 'liquidate' the lag between the enormous riches of the nation and its morality of abstention. The neo-humanists were among the last of the breed of palefaces, and they perished in the quixotic attempt to re-establish the old values. Eliot forsook his native land, while the few palefaces who managed to survive at home took to the academic or else to the 'higher' and relatively unpopular forms of writing. But the novelists, who control the main highway of literature, were, and still are, nearly all redskins to the wigwam born.

At present the redskins are in command of the situation, and the literary life in America has seldom been so deficient in intellectual power. The political interests introduced in the nineteen-thirties have not only strengthened their hold but have also brought out their worst tendencies; for the effect of the popular political creeds of our time has been to increase their habitual

hostility to ideas, sanctioning the relaxation of standards and justifying the urge to come to terms with semi-
literate audiences.

The redskin writer in America is a purely indigenous
phenomenon, the true-blue offspring of the western
hemisphere, the juvenile in principle and for the good of
the soul. He is a self-made writer in the same way that
Henry Ford was a self-made millionaire. On the one
hand he is a crass materialist, a greedy consumer of
experience, and on the other a sentimentalist, a half-
baked mystic listening to inward voices and watching
for signs and portents. Think of Dreiser, Lewis, Anderson, Wolfe, Sandburg, Caldwell, Steinbeck, Farrell,
Saroyan: all writers of genuine and some even of
admirable accomplishments, whose faults, however, are
not so much literary as faults of raw life itself. Unable
to relate himself in any significant manner to the cultural
heritage, the redskin writer is always on his own; and
since his personality resists growth and change, he must
continually repeat himself. His work is ridden by compulsions that depress the literary tradition, because they
are compulsions of a kind that put a strain on literature,
that literature more often than not can neither assimilate
nor sublimate. He is the passive instead of the active agent
of the *Zeitgeist*, he lives off it rather than through it,
so that when his particular gifts happen to coincide with
the mood of the times he seems modern and contemporary, but once the mood has passed he is in danger of
being quickly discarded. Lacking the qualities of surprise and renewal, already Dreiser and Anderson, for
example, have a 'period' air about them that makes a rereading of their work something of a critical chore; and
one suspects that Hemingway, that perennial boy-man,
is more accurately understood as a descendant of Natty
Bumppo, the hero of Fenimore Cooper's Leather-

stocking tales, than as the portentously disillusioned character his legend makes him out to be.

As for the paleface, in compensation for backward cultural conditions and a lost religious ethic, he has developed a supreme talent for refinement, just as the Jew, in compensation for adverse social conditions and a lost national independence, has developed a supreme talent for cleverness. (In this connexion it is pertinent to recall T. S. Eliot's remark about Boston society, which he described as 'quite refined, but refined beyond the point of civilization'.) Now this peculiar excess of refinement is to be deplored in an imaginative writer, for it weakens his capacity to cope with experience and induces in him a fetishistic attitude toward tradition; nor is this species of refinement to be equated with the refinement of artists like Proust or Mann, as in them it is not an element contradicting an open and bold confrontation of reality. Yet the paleface, being above all a conscious individual, was frequently able to transcend or to deviate sharply from the norms of his group, and he is to be credited with most of the rigours and charms of the classic American books. While it is true, as John Jay Chapman put it, that his culture is 'secondary and tertiary' and that between him and the sky 'float the Constitution of the United States and the traditions and forms of English literature'—nevertheless, there exists the poetry of Emily Dickinson, there is *The Scarlet Letter*, there is *Moby Dick*, and there are not a few incomparable narratives by Henry James.

At this point there is no necessity to enter into a discussion of the historical and social causes that account for the disunity of the American creative mind. In various contexts a number of critics have disclosed and evaluated the forces that have worked on this mind and shaped it to their uses. The sole question that seems relevant is whether history will make whole again what it has rent asunder. Will James and Whitman ever be reconciled, will they finally discover and act upon each other? Only history can give a definite reply to this question. In the meantime, however, there are available the resources of effort and understanding, resources which even those who believe in the strict determination of the cultural object need not spurn.

HARRY LEVIN

1912–

OBSERVATIONS ON THE STYLE OF ERNEST HEMINGWAY

Contexts of Criticism, 1957

MR. HEMINGWAY would hardly be himself—which he is, of course, quite as consciously as any writer could be—if he did not take a dim view of criticism. This is understandable and, as he would say, right: since criticism, ever seeking perspective, moves in the very opposite direction from his object, which has been immediacy. His ardent quest for experience has involved him in a lifelong campaign against everything that tends to get in its way, including those more or less laboured efforts to interpret and communicate it which may be regarded—if not disregarded—as academic. Those of us who live in the shelter of the academy will not be put off by his disregard; for most of us have more occasion than he to be repelled by the incrustations of pedantry; and many of us are predisposed to sympathize with him, as well as with ourselves, when he tells us what is lacking in critics and scholars. That he continues to do so is a mark of attention which ought not to go unappreciated. Thus currently, in introducing a brilliant young Italian novelist to American readers, he departs from his subject to drive home a critical contrast:

The Italy that [Elio Vittorini] learned and the America that the American boys learned [writes Ernest Hemingway, making a skilful transition] has little to do with the Academic Italy or America that periodically attacks all writing like a dust storm and is always, until everything shall be completely dry, dispersed by rain.

Since Hemingway is sparing in his use of metaphors, the one he introduces here is significant. 'Dryasdust' has long been the layman's stock epithet for the results of scholarly inquiry; while drought, as evoked by T. S. Eliot, has become a basic symbol of modern anxiety. The country that seems to interest Hemingway most, Spain, is in some respects a literal wasteland; and his account of it—memorably his sound track for the Joris Ivens film, *The Spanish Earth*—emphasizes its dryness. Water, the contrasting element, for Hemingway as for his fellow men, symbolizes the purification and renewal of life. Rain beats out a cadence which runs through his work: through *A Farewell to Arms*, for example, where it lays the dust raised by soldiers' boots at the outset, accompanies the retreat from Caporetto, and stays with the hero when the heroine dies—even providing the very last word at the end. It is rain which, in a frequently quoted paragraph, shows up the unreality of 'the words sacred, glorious, and sacrifice and the expression in vain'. In the present instance, having reduced the contemporary situation to a handful of dust as it were, Hemingway comes back to that sense of reality which he is willing to share with Vittorini. In the course of a single sentence, utilizing a digressive

Ciceronian device, *paralipsis*, he has not only rounded up such writers as he considers academic; he has not only accused them of sterility, by means of that slippery logical shortcut which we professors term an enthymeme; but, like the veteran strategist he is, he has also managed to imply that they are the attackers and that he is fighting a strictly defensive action.

The conflict advances into the next paragraph, which opens on the high note that closed the previous one and then drops down again anticlimactically: 'Rain to an academician is probably, after the first fall has cleared the air, H_2O with, of course, traces of other things.' Even the ultimate source of nature's vitality is no more than a jejune scientific formula to us, if I may illustrate Hemingway's point by paraphrasing his sentence. Whereas—and for a moment it seems as if the theme of fertility would be sounded soon again—but no, the emphasis waxes increasingly negative:

To a good writer, needing something to bring the dry country alive so that it will not be a desert where only such cactus as New York literary reviews grow dry and sad, inexistent without the watering of their benefactors, feeding on the dried manure of schism and the dusty taste of disputed dialectics, their only flowering a desiccated criticism as alive as stuffed birds, and their steady mulch the dehydrated cuds of fellow critics; . . .

There is more to come, but we had better pause and ruminate upon this particular mouthful. Though we may or may not accept Hemingway's opinion, we must admit that he makes us taste his distaste. Characteristically, he does not counter-criticize or state the issue in intellectual terms. Instead he proceeds from agriculture to the dairy, through an atmosphere calculated to make New Yorkers uncomfortable, elaborating his earthy metaphor into a barnyard allegory which culminates in a scatological gesture. The gibe about benefactors is a curious one, since it appears to take commercial success as a literary criterion, and at the same time to identify financial support with spiritual nourishment. The hopeful adjective 'alive', repeated in this deadening context, is ironically illustrated by a musty ornithological specimen: so much for criticism! Such a phrase as 'disputed dialectics', which is unduly alliterative, slightly tautological, and—like 'cactus'—ambiguously singular or plural, touches a sphere where the author seems ill at ease. He seems more sure of his ground when, after this muttered parenthesis, he returns to his starting-point, turns the prepositional object into a subject, and sets out again toward his predicate, toward an affirmation of mellow fruitfulness:

. . . such a writer finds rain to be made of knowledge, experience, wine, bread, oil, salt, vinegar, bed, early mornings, nights, days, the sea, men, women, dogs, beloved motor cars, bicycles, hills and valleys, the appearance and disappearance of trains on straight and curved tracks, love, honor and disobey, music, chamber music and chamber pots, negative and positive Wassermanns, the arrival and non-arrival of expected munitions and/or reinforcements, replacements or your brother.

These are the 'other things' missed by the academician and discerned by the 'good writer'—whether he be Vittorini or Hemingway. It is by no means a casual inventory; each successive item, artfully chosen, has its meaningful place in the author's scheme of things. Knowledge is equated with experience, rendered concrete by the staple fare of existence, and wet down by essential liquids redolent of the Mediterranean; bed, with its double range of elementary associations, initiates a temporal cycle which revolves toward the timeless sea. Men, women, and dogs follow each other in unrelieved sequence; but the term of endearment, 'beloved', is reserved for motor cars; while wavering alternatives suggest the movement of other vehicles over the land. Then come the great abstractions, love and honour, which are undercut by a cynical negation of the marriage ceremony, 'disobey'. Since chamber music sounds highbrow, it must be balanced against the downright vulgarity of chamber pots. The pangs of sex are scientifically neutralized by the reference to Wassermann tests, and the agonies of war are deliberately stated in the cool and/or colourless jargon of military dispatches. The final choice, 'replacements or your brother', possibly echoes a twist of continental slang (*et ton frère!*); but, more than that, it suddenly replaces a strategic loss with a personal bereavement.

The sentence, though extended, is not periodic: instead of suspending its burden, it falls back on *anacoluthon*, the rhetoric of the gradual breakdown and the fresh start. Hence, the first half is an uncharacteristic and unsuccessful endeavour to complete an elaborate grammatical structure which soon gets out of control. The second half thereupon brings the subject as quickly and simply as possible to its object, which opens up at once into the familiar Hemingway catalogue, where effects can be gained *seriatim* by order rather than by construction. After the chain of words has reached its climactic phrase, 'your brother', it is rounded out by another transitional sentence: 'All these are a part of rain to a good writer along with your hated or beloved mother, may she rest in peace or in pieces, porcupine quills, cock grouse drumming on a bass-wood log, the smell of sweetgrass and fresh smoked leather and Sicily.' This time love dares to appear in its primary human connexion, but only in ambivalence with hatred, and the hazards of sentimentality are hysterically avoided by a trite pun. And though the final images resolve the paragraph by coming back to the Sicilian locale of Vittorini's novel, they savour more of the northern woods of Hemingway's Upper Peninsula. Meanwhile the digression has served its purpose for him and for ourselves; it has given us nothing less than his definition of knowledge—not book-knowledge, of course, but the real thing. Thus Robert Jordan decides to write a book about his adventures in Spain: 'But only about the things he knew, truly, and about what he knew.' Such a book is Hemingway's novel about him, *For Whom the Bell Tolls*; and what he knew, there put into words, is already one remove away from experience. And when Hemingway writes about Vittorini's novel, unaccustomed though he is to operating on the plane of criticism, he is two removes away from the objects he mentions in his analysis—or should I call it a hydroanalysis? Critics—and I have in mind Wyndham Lewis—have called his writing 'the prose of reality'. It seems to come closer to life than other prose, possibly too close for Mr. Lewis, yet for better or worse it happens to be literature. Its effectiveness lies in virtually persuading us that it is not writing at all. But though it may feel like walks in the rain or punches in the jaw, to be literal, it consists of words on the page. It is full of half-concealed art and self-revealing artifice. Since Hemingway is endlessly willing to explicate such artful and artificial pursuits as bullfighting and military tactics, he ought not to flinch under technical scrutiny.

Hemingway's hatred for the profession of letters stems quite obviously from a lover's quarrel. When Richard Gordon is reviled by his dissatisfied wife in *To Have and Have Not*, her most embittered epithet is 'you writer'. Yet Hemingway's writing abounds in salutes to various fellow writers, from the waitress's anecdote about Henry James in *The Torrents of Spring* to Colonel Cantwell's spiritual affinity with D'Annunzio. And from Nick Adams, who takes Meredith and Chesterton along on fishing trips, to Hemingway himself, who arranges to be interviewed on American literature in *Green Hills of Africa*, his heroes do not shy away from critical discussion. His titles, so often quoted from books by earlier writers, have been so apt that they have all but established a convention. He shows an almost academic fondness, as well as a remarkable flair, for epigraphs: the Colonel dies with a quotation on his lips. Like all of us, Hemingway has been influenced by T. S. Eliot's taste for Elizabethan drama and metaphysical poetry. Thus Hemingway's title, 'In Another Country', is borrowed from a passage he elsewhere cites, which he might have found in Marlowe's *Jew of Malta* or possibly in Eliot's 'Portrait of a Lady'. *A Farewell to Arms*, which echoes Lovelace's title, quotes in passing from Marvell's 'To His Coy Mistress', echoed more recently by Robert Penn Warren, which is parodied in *Death in the Afternoon*. Hemingway is no exception to the rule that makes parody the starting-point for realistic fiction. Just as Fielding took off from Richardson, so Hemingway takes off from Sherwood Anderson—indeed his first novel, *The Torrents of Spring*, which parodies Andersons' *Dark Laughter*, is explicit in its acknowledgements to *Joseph Andrews*. It has passages, however, which read today like a *pastiche* of the later Hemingway:

Yogi was worried. There was something on his mind. It was spring, there was no doubt of that now, and he did not want a woman. He had worried about it a lot lately. There was no question about it. He did not want a woman. He couldn't explain it to himself. He had gone to the Public Library and asked for a book the night before.

He looked at the librarian. He did not want her. Somehow she meant nothing to him.

A recoil from bookishness, after a preliminary immersion in it, provided Fielding's master, Cervantes, with the original impetus for the novel. In 'A Banal Story' Hemingway provides us with his own variation on the theme of *Don Quixote*, where a writer sits reading about romance in a magazine advertisement, while in far-off Madrid a bullfighter dies and is buried. The ironic contrast—romantic preconception exploded by contact with harsh reality—is basic with Hemingway, as it has been with all novelists who have written effectively about war. The realism of his generation reacted, not only against Wilsonian idealism, but against Wilsonian rhetoric. Hence the famous paragraph from the Caporetto episode describing Frederic Henry's embarrassment before such abstract words as 'glory' and 'honour', which seem to him obscene beside the concrete names of places and numbers of roads. For a Spaniard, Hemingway notes in *Death in the Afternoon*, the abstraction may still have concreteness: honour may be 'as real a thing as water, wine, or olive oil'. It is not so for us: 'All our words from loose using have lost their edge.' And 'The Gambler, the Nun, and the Radio' brings forward a clinching example: 'Liberty, what we believed in, now the name of a Macfadden publication.' That same story trails off in a litany which reduces a Marxist slogan to meaninglessness: 'the opium of the people' is everything and nothing. Even more desolating, in 'A Clean, Well-Lighted Place', is the reduction of the Lord's prayer to nothingness: 'Our nada who art in nada . . .' Since words have become inflated and devalued, Hemingway is willing to recognize no values save those which can be immediately felt and directly pointed out. It is his verbal scepticism which leads toward what some critics have called his moral nihilism. Anything serious had better be said with a smile, stranger. The classic echo, 'irony and pity', jingles through *The Sun Also Rises* like a singing commercial.

There is something in common between this attitude and the familiar British habit of understatement. 'No pleasure in anything if you mouth it too much', says Wilson, the guide in 'The Short, Happy Life of Francis Macomber'. Yet Jake, the narrator of *The Sun Also Rises*, protests—in the name of American garrulity—that the English use fewer words than the Eskimos. Spanish, the language of Hemingway's preference, is at once emotive and highly formal. His Spanish, to judge from *Death in the Afternoon*, is just as ungrammatical as his English. In 'The Undefeated' his Spanish bullfighters are made to speak the slang of American prizefighters. Americanisms and Hispanisms, archaic and polyglot elements are so intermingled in *For Whom the Bell Tolls* that it calls to mind what Ben Jonson said of *The Faerie Queene*: 'Spenser writ no language.' Hemingway offers a succinct example by translating '*Eras mucho caballo*' as 'Thou wert plenty of horse'. It is somewhat paradoxical that a writer, having severely cut down his English vocabulary, should augment it by continual importation from other languages, including the Swahili. But this is a facet of the larger paradox that a writer so essentially American should set the bulk of his work against foreign backgrounds. His characters, expatriates for the most part, wander through the ruins of Babel, smattering many tongues and speaking a demotic version of their own. Obscenity presents another linguistic problem, for which Hemingway is not responsible; but his coy ways of circumventing the taboos of censorship are more of a distraction than the conventional blanks. When he does permit himself an expression not usually considered printable, in *Death in the Afternoon*, the context is significant. His interlocutor, the Old Lady, requests a definition and he politely responds: 'Madam, we apply the term now to describe unsoundness in abstract conversation or, indeed, any overmetaphysical tendency in speech.'

For language, as for literature, his feeling is strongly ambivalent. Perhaps it could be summed up by Pascal's maxim: 'True eloquence makes fun of eloquence.' Like the notorious General Cambronne, Hemingway feels that one short spontaneous vulgarism is more honest than all those grandiloquent slogans which rhetoricians dream up long after the battle. The disparity between rhetoric and experience, which became so evident during the First World War, prompted the twenties to repudiate the genteel stylistic tradition and to accept the American vernacular as our norm of literary discourse. 'Literary' is a contradiction in terms, for the resultant style is basically oral; and when the semi-literate speaker takes pen in hand, as Hemingway demonstrates in 'One Reader Writes'—as H. L. Mencken demonstrated in 'A Short View of Gamalielese'—the result is even more artificial than if it had been written by a writer. A page is always flat, and we need perspective to make it convey the illusion of life in the round. Yet the very fact that words mean so much less to us than the things they represent in our lives is a stimulus to our imaginations. In 'Fathers and Sons' young Nick Adams reads that Caruso has been arrested for 'mashing', and asks his father the meaning of that expression.

'It is one of the most heinous of crimes', his father answered. Nick's imagination pictured the great tenor doing something strange, bizarre, and heinous with a potato masher to a beautiful lady who looked like the pictures of Anna Held on the inside of cigar boxes. He resolved, with considerable horror, that when he was old enough he would try mashing at least once.

The tone of this passage is not altogether typical of Hemingway. Rather, as the point of view detaches itself affectionately and ironically from the youth, it approximates the early Joyce. This may help to explain why it suggests a more optimistic approach to language than the presumption that, since phrases can be snares and delusions, their scope should be limited to straight denotation. The powers of connotation, the possibilities of oblique suggestion and semantic association, are actually grasped by Hemingway as well as any writer of our time. Thus he can retrospectively endow a cheap and faded term like 'mashing' with all the promise and poetry of awakening manhood. When Nick grows up, foreign terms will hold out the same allure to him; like Frederic Henry, he will seek the actuality that resides behind the names of places; and Robert Jordan will first be attracted to Spain as a professional philologist. But none of them will find an equivalence between the word and the thing; and Hemingway, at the end of *Death in the Afternoon*, laments that no book is big enough to do final justice to its living subject. 'There was so much to write', the dying writer realizes in 'The Snows of Kilimanjaro', and his last thoughts are moving and memorable recollections of some of the many things that will now go unwritten. Walt Whitman stated this challenge and this dilemma, for all good writers, when he spoke of expressing the inexpressible.

The inevitable compromise, for Hemingway, is best expressed by his account of Romero's bullfighting style: 'the holding of his purity of line through the maximum of exposure.' The maximum of exposure—this throws much light upon the restlessness of Hemingway's career, but here we are primarily concerned with the holding of his purity of line. It had to be the simplest and most flexible of lines in order to accommodate itself to his desperate pursuit of material. His purgation of language has aptly been compared, by Robert Penn Warren, to the revival of diction that Wordsworth accomplished with *Lyrical Ballads*. Indeed the question that Coleridge afterward raised might once again be asked: why should the speech of some men be more real than that of others? Today that question restates itself in ideological terms: whether respect for the common man necessitates the adoption of a commonplace standard. Everyone who writes faces the same old problems, and the original writers—like Wordsworth or Hemingway—are those who develop new ways of meeting them. The case of Wordsworth would show us, if that of Hemingway did not, that those who break down conventions tend to substitute conventions of their own. Hemingway's prose is not without precedents; it is interesting to recall that his maiden effort, published by *The Double Dealer* in 1922, parodied the King James Bible. He has his forerunners in American fiction, from Cooper to Jack London, whose conspicuous lack was a style as dynamic as their subject-matter. The ring-tailed roarers of the frontier, such as Davy Crockett, were Colonel Cantwell's brothers under the skin; but as contrasted with the latter's tragic conception of himself, they were mock-heroic and serio-comic figures, who recommend themselves to the reader's condescension. Mark Twain has been the most genuine influence, and Hemingway has acknowledged this by declaring—with sweeping generosity—that *Huckleberry Finn* is the source of all modern American literature.

But Mark Twain was conducting a monologue, a

virtual *tour de force* of impersonation, and he ordinarily kept a certain distance between his narrative role and his characters. And among Hemingway's elder contemporaries, Ring Lardner was a kind of ventriloquist, who made devastating use of the vernacular to satirize the vulgarity and stupidity of his dummies. It remained for Hemingway—along with Anderson—to identify himself wholly with the lives he wrote about, not so much entering into them as allowing them to take possession of him, and accepting—along with their sensibilities and perceptions—the limitations of their point of view and the limits of their range of expression. We need make no word-count to be sure that his literary vocabulary, with foreign and technical exceptions, consists of relatively few and short words. The corollary, of course, is that every word sees a good deal of hard use. Furthermore, his syntax is informal to the point of fluidity, simplifying as far as possible the already simple system of English inflections. Thus 'who' is normally substituted for 'whom', presumably to avoid schoolmarmish correctness; and 'that', doing duty for 'which', seems somehow less prophetic of complexity. Personal pronouns frequently get involved in what is stigmatized, by teachers of freshman composition, as faulty reference; there are sentences in which it is hard to tell the hunter from his quarry or the bullfighter from the bull. 'When his father died he was only a kid and his manager buried him perpetually.' So begins, rather confusingly, 'The Mother of a Queen'. Sometimes it seems as if Hemingway were taking pains to be ungrammatical, as do many educated people out of a twisted sense of *noblesse oblige*. Yet when he comes closest to pronouncing a moral, the last words of Harry Morgan—the analphabetic hero of *To Have and Have Not*—seem to be half-consciously fumbling toward some grammatical resolution: 'A man

. . . ain't got no hasn't got any can't really isn't any way out . . . ?'

The effectiveness of Hemingway's method depends very largely upon his keen ear for speech. His conversations are vivid, often dramatic, although he comes to depend too heavily upon them and to scant the other obligations of the novelist. Many of his wisecracks are quotable out of context, but as Gertrude Stein warned him: 'Remarks are not literature.' He can get his story told, and still be as conversational as he pleases, by telling it in the first person. 'Brother, that was some storm', says the narrator, and the reader hears the very tone of his voice. In one of Hemingway's critical digressions, he declares that he has always sought 'the real thing, the sequence of motion and fact which [*sic*] made the emotion . . .' This seems to imply the clear-cut mechanism of verbal stimulus and psychological response that Eliot formulates in his theory of the objective correlative. In practice, however, Hemingway is no more of a behaviourist than Eliot, and the sharp distinction between motion and emotion is soon blurred. Consider his restricted choice of adjectives, and the heavy load of subjective implication carried by such uncertain monosyllables as 'fine' and 'nice'. From examples on nearly every page, we are struck by one which helps to set the scene for *A Farewell to Arms*: 'The town was very nice and our house was very fine.' Such descriptions—if we may consider them descriptions—are obviously not designed for pictorial effect. When the Colonel is tempted to call some fishing-boats picturesque, he corrects himself: 'The hell with picturesque. They are just damned beautiful.' Where 'picturesque' might sound arty and hence artificial, 'beautiful'—with 'damned' to take off the curse—is permissible because Hemingway has packed it with his own emotional charge. He even uses it in *For Whom the Bell Tolls* to express his aesthetic appreciation of gunfire. Like 'fine' and 'nice', or 'good' and 'lovely', it does not describe; it evaluates. It is not a stimulus but a projected response, a projection of the narrator's euphoria in a given situation. Hemingway, in effect, is saying to the reader: *Having wonderful time. Wish you were here.*

In short, he is communicating excitement; and if this communication is received, it establishes a uniquely personal relationship; but when it goes astray, the diction goes flat and vague. Hemingway manages to sustain his reputation for concreteness by an exploring eye for the incidental detail. The one typescript of his that I have seen, his carbon copy of 'The Killers' now in the Harvard College Library, would indicate that the arc-light and the tipped-back derby hat were later observations than the rest. Precision at times becomes so arithmetical that, in 'The Light of the World', it lines up his characters like a drill-sergeant: 'Down at the station there were five whores waiting for the train to come in, and six white men and four Indians.' Numbers enlarge the irony that concludes the opening chapter of *A Farewell to Arms* when, after a far from epic invocation, a casual introduction to the landscape, and a dusty record of troops falling back through the autumn, rain brings the cholera which kills 'only seven thousand'. A trick of multiplication, which Hemingway may have picked up from Gertrude Stein, is to generalize the specific episode: 'They always picked the finest places to have the quarrels.' When he offers this general view of a restaurant—'It was full of smoke and drinking and singing'—he is an impressionist if not an abstractionist. Thence to expressionism is an easy step: '. . . the room whirled.' It happens that, under pressure from his first American publishers, the author was compelled to modify the phrasing of 'Mr. and Mrs. Elliott'. In the original version, subsequently restored, the title characters 'try to have a baby'. In the modified version they 'think of having a baby'. It could be argued that, in characterizing this rather tepid couple, the later verb is more expressive and no more euphemistic than the earlier one; that 'think', at any rate, is not less precise or effectual than 'try'. But, whereas the sense of effort came naturally, the cerebration was an afterthought.

If we regard the adjective as a luxury, decorative more often than functional, we can well understand why Hemingway doesn't cultivate it. But, assuming that the sentence derives its energy from the verb, we are in for a shock if we expect his verbs to be numerous or varied or emphatic. His usage supports C. K. Ogden's argument that verb-forms are disappearing from English grammar. Without much self-deprivation, Hemingway could get along on the so-called 'operators' of Basic English, the sixteen monosyllabic verbs that stem from movements of the body. The substantive verb *to be* is predominant, characteristically introduced by an expletive. Thus the first story of *In Our Time* begins, and the last one ends, with the story-teller's gambit: 'there was', 'there were'. In the first two pages of *A Farewell to Arms* nearly every other sentence is of this type, and the third page employs the awkward construction 'there being'. There is—I find the habit contagious—a tendency to immobilize verbs by transposing them into gerunds. Instead of writing *they fought* or *we did not feel*, Hemingway writes 'there was fighting' and 'there was not the feeling of a storm coming'. The subject does little more than point impersonally at its predicate: an object, a situation, an emotion. Yet the idiom, like the French *il y a*, is ambiguous; inversion can turn the gesture of pointing into a physical act; and the indefinite adverb

can indicate, if not specify, a definite place. Contrast,
with the opening of *A Farewell to Arms*, that of 'In
Another Country': 'In the fall the war was always there,
but we did not go to it any more.' The negative is even
more striking, when Frederic Henry has registered the
sensations of his wound, and dares to look at it for the
first time, and notes: 'My knee wasn't there.' The adverb
is *there* rather than *here*, the verb is *was* rather than *is*,
because we—the readers—are separated from the event
in space and time. But the narrator has lived through it,
like the Ancient Mariner, and now he chooses his words
to grip and transfix us. *Lo!* he says. *Look! I was there.*

Granted, then, that Hemingway's diction is thin; that,
in the technical sense, his syntax is weak; and that he
would rather be caught dead than seeking the *mot juste*
or the balanced phrase. Granted that his adjectives are
not colourful and his verbs not particularly energetic.
Granted that he commits as many literary offences as
Mark Twain brought to book with Fenimore Cooper.
What is behind his indubitable punch, the unexampled
dynamics of Hemingway's style? How does he manage,
as he does, to animate this characteristic sentence from
'After the Storm'?

I said 'Who killed him?' and he said 'I don't know who
killed him but he's dead all right', and it was dark and
there was water standing in the street and no lights and
windows broke and boats all up in the town and trees
blown down and everything all blown and I got a skiff
and went out and found my boat where I had her inside
of Mango Key and she was all right only she was full of
water.

Here is a good example of Hemingway's 'sequence of
motion and fact'. It starts from dialogue and leads into
first-person action; but the central description is a single

clause, where the expletive takes the place of the observer and his observations are registered one by one. Hence, for the reader, it lives up to Robert Jordan's intention: 'you ... feel that all that happened to you.' Hemingway puts his emphasis on nouns because, among parts of speech, they come closest to things. Stringing them along by means of conjunctions, he approximates the actual flow of experience. For him, as for Marion Tweedy Bloom, the key word is *and*, with its renewable promise of continuity, occasionally varied by *then* and *so*. The rhetorical scheme is *polysyndeton*—a large name for the childishly simple habit of linking sentences together. The subject when it is not taken for granted, merely puts us in touch with the predicate: the series of objects that Hemingway wants to point out. Even a preposition can turn this trick as 'with' does in this account of El Sordo waiting to see the whites of his enemy's eyes:

Come on, Comrade Voyager ... Keep on coming with your eyes forward ... Look. With a red face and blond hair and blue eyes. With no cap on and his moustache is yellow. With blue eyes. With pale blue eyes. With pale blue eyes with something wrong with them. With pale blue eyes that don't focus. Close enough. Too close. Yes, Comrade Voyager. Take it, Comrade Voyager.

Prose gets as near as it can to physical conflict here. The figure enlarges as it advances, the quickening impression grows clear and sharp and almost unbearable, whereupon it is blackened out by El Sordo's rifle. Each clipped sentence, each prepositional phrase, is like a new frame in a strip of film; indeed the whole passage, like so many others, might have been filmed by the camera and projected on the screen. The course of Harry Morgan's launch speeding through the Gulf Stream, or of Frederic Henry's fantasy ascending the elevator with Catherine Barkley, is given this cinematographic presentation. *Green Hills of Africa* voices the long-range ambition of obtaining a fourth and fifth dimension in prose. Yet if the subordinate clause and the complex sentence are the usual ways for writers to obtain a third dimension, Hemingway keeps his writing on a linear plane. He holds the purity of his line by moving in one direction, ignoring sidetracks and avoiding structural complications. By presenting a succession of images, each of which has its brief moment when it commands the reader's undivided attention, he achieves his special vividness and fluidity. For what he lacks in structure he makes up in sequence, carefully ordering visual impressions as he sets them down and ironically juxtaposing the various items on his lists and inventories. 'A Way You'll Never Be' opens with a close-up showing the debris on a battlefield, variously specifying munitions, medicaments, and left-overs from a field kitchen, then closing in on the scattered papers with this striking montage-effect: '. . . group postcards showing the machine-gun unit standing in ranked and ruddy cheerfulness as in a football picture for a college annual; now they were humped and swollen in the grass . . . .' It is not surprising that Hemingway's verse, published by *Poetry* in 1923, is recognizably imagistic in character—and perhaps his later heroics are foreshadowed by the subject of one of those poems, Theodore Roosevelt.

In her observant book, *L'Age du roman américain*, Claude-Edmonde Magny stresses Hemingway's 'exaltation of the instant'. We can note how this emphasis is reflected in his timing, which—after his placing has bridged the distance from *there* to *here*—strives to close the gap between *then* and *now*. Where Baudelaire's clock said 'remember' in many languages, Robert Jordan's memory says: 'Now, *ahora*, *maintenant*, *heute*.' When death interrupts a dream, in 'The Snows of Kilimanjaro', the ultimate reality is heralded by a rising insistence upon the word 'now'. It is not for nothing that Hemingway is the younger contemporary of Proust and Joyce. Though his time is neither *le temps perdu* nor the past nostalgically recaptured, he spends it gathering roses while he can, to the ever accelerating rhythm of head-lines and telegrams and loud-speakers. The act, no sooner done than said, becomes simultaneous with the word, no sooner said than felt. Hemingway goes so far, in 'Fathers and Sons', as to render a sexual embrace by an onomatopoetic sequence of adverbs. But unlike Damon Runyon and Dickens, he seldom narrates in the present tense, except in such sporting events as 'Fifty Grand'. Rather, his timeliness expresses itself in con-tinuous forms of the verb and in his fondness for all kinds of participial constructions. These, compounded and multiplied, create an ambiance of overwhelming activity, and the epithets shift from El Sordo's harassed feelings to the impact of the reiterated bullets, as Hemingway recounts 'the last lung-aching, leg-dead, mouth-dry, bullet-spatting, bullet-cracking, bullet-singing run up the final slope of the hill'. More often the meaning takes the opposite turn, and moves from the external plane into the range of a character's senses, proceeding serially from the visual to the tactile, as it does when the 'Wine of Wyoming' is sampled: 'It was very light and clear and good and still tasted of the grapes.'

When Nick Adams goes fishing, the temperature is very tangibly indicated: 'It was getting hot, the sun hot on the back of his neck.' The remark about the weather is thereby extended in two directions, toward the dis-tant source of the heat and toward its immediate percep-tion. Again in 'Big Two-Hearted River', Nick's fatigue is measured by the weight of his pack: '. . . it was heavy.

It was much too heavy.' As in the movies, the illusion
of movement is produced by repeating the same shot
with further modification every time. Whenever a new
clause takes more than one step ahead, a subsequent
clause repeats it in order to catch up. Repetition, as in
'Up in Michigan', brings the advancing narrative back
to an initial point of reference. 'Liz liked Jim very much.
She liked it the way he walked over from the shop and
often went to the kitchen door to watch him start down
the road. She liked it about his moustache. She liked it
about how white his teeth were when he smiled.' The
opaque verb 'like', made increasingly transparent, is
utilized five more times in this paragraph; and the
fumbling preposition 'about' may be an acknowledgement of Hemingway's early debt to Gertrude Stein.
The situation is located somewhere between a subjective
Liz and an objective Jim. The theme of love is always a
test of Hemingway's objectivity. When Frederic kisses
Catherine, her responses are not less moving because
they are presented through his reflexes; but it is her
sentimental conversation which leaves him free to ask
himself: 'What the hell?' At first glance, in a behaviour-
istic formula which elsewhere recurs, Colonel Cantwell
seems so hard-boiled that motions are his only emotions:
'He saw that his hand was trembling.' But his vision is
blurred by conventionally romantic tenderness when he
contemplates a heroine whose profile 'could break your
. . . or anyone else's heart'. Hemingway's heroines,
when they aren't bitches, are fantasies—or rather, the
masculine reader is invited to supply his own, as with
the weather in Mark Twain's *American Claimant*. They
are pin-up girls.

If beauty lies in the eye of the beholder, Hemingway's
purpose is to make his readers beholders. This is easily
done when the narration is conducted in the first person;

we can sit down and drink, with Jake Barnes, and watch Paris walk by. The interpolated chapters of *In Our Time*, most of them reminiscences from the army, employ the collective *we*; but, except for 'My Old Man', the stories themselves are told in the third person. Sometimes, to strengthen the sense of identification, they make direct appeal to the second person; the protagonist of 'Soldier's home' is 'you' as well as 'he'—and, more generally, 'a fellow'. With the exception of Jake's confessions, that is to say *The Sun Also Rises*, all of Hemingway's novels are written in the *style indirect libre*—indirect discourse which more or less closely follows the consciousness of a central character. An increasing tendency for the author to intrude, commenting in his own person, is one of the weaknesses of *Across the River*. He derives his strength from a power to visualize episodes through the eyes of those most directly involved; for a page, in 'The Short, Happy Life of Francis Macomber', the hunt is actually seen from the beast's point of view. Hemingway's use of interior monologue is effective when sensations from the outer world are entering the stream of a character's consciousness, as they do with such a rush at El Sordo's last stand. But introspection is not Hemingway's genre, and the night-thoughts of *To Have and Have Not* are among his least successful episodes. His best are events, which are never far to seek; things are constantly happening in his world; his leg-man, Nick Adams, happens to be the eye-witness of 'The Killers'. The state of mind that Hemingway communicates to us is the thrill that Nick got from skiing in 'Cross Country Snow', which 'plucked Nick's mind out and left him only the wonderful, flying, dropping sensation in his body'.

If psychological theories could be proved by works of

fiction, Hemingway would lend his authority to the long-contested formula of William James, which equates emotion with bodily sensation. Most other serious writers, however, would bear witness to deeper ranges of sensibility and more complex processes of motivation than those he sees fit to describe. Some of them have accused Hemingway of aggressive anti-intellectualism: I am thinking particularly of Aldous Huxley. But Huxley's own work is so pure an example of all that Hemingway has recoiled from, so intellectual in the airiest sense, and so unsupported by felt experience, that the argument has played into Hemingway's hands. We have seen enough of the latter to know that he doesn't really hate books—himself having written a dozen, several of which are, and will remain, the best of their kind. As for his refusal to behave like a man of letters, he reminds us of Hotspur, who professes to be a laconic philistine and turns out—with no little grandiloquence—to be the most poetic character in Shakespeare's play. Furthermore, it is not Hemingway but the slogan-mongers of our epoch who have debased the language; he has been attempting to restore some decent degree of correspondence between words and things; and the task of verification is a heavy one, which throws the individual back on his personal resources of awareness. That he has succeeded within limits and with considerable strain, is less important than that he has succeeded, that a few more aspects of life have been captured for literature. Meanwhile the word continues to dematerialize, and has to be made flesh all over again; the first-hand perception, once it gets written down, becomes the second-hand notation; and the writer, who attains his individuality by repudiating literary affectation, ends by finding that he has struck a new pose and founded another school.

It is understandable why no critique of Hemingway, including this one, can speak for long of the style without speaking of the man. Improving on Buffon, Mark Schorer recently wrote: '[Hemingway's] style is not only his subject, it is his view of life.' It could also be called his way of life, his *Lebenstil*. It has led him to live his books, to brave the maximum of exposure, to tour the world in an endless search for wars and their moral equivalents. It has cast him in the special role of our agent, our plenipotentiary, our roving correspondent on whom we depend for news from the fighting fronts of modern consciousness. Here he is, the man who was there. His writing seems so intent upon the actual, so impersonal in its surfaces, that it momentarily prompts us to overlook the personality behind them. That would be a serious mistake; for the point of view, though brilliantly intense, is narrowly focused and obliquely angled. We must ask: who is this guide to whom we have entrusted ourselves on intimate terms in dangerous places? Where are his limitations? What are his values? We may well discover that they differ from our assumptions, when he shows us a photograph of a bullfighter close to a bull, and comments: 'If there is no blood on his belly afterwards you ought to get your money back.' We may be ungrateful to question such curiosity, when we are indebted to it for many enlargements of our vicarious knowledge; and it may well spring from the callowness of the tourist rather than the morbidity of the *voyeur*, from the American zest of the fan who pays his money to reckon the carnage. When Spain's great poet, García Lorca, celebrated the very same theme, averting his gaze from the spilling of the blood, his refrain was '*Que no quiero verla!*' ('I do not want to see it!').

Yet Hemingway wants to see everything—or possibly he wants to be in a position to tell us that he has seen everything. While the boy Nick, his seeing eye, eagerly watches a Caesarian childbirth in 'Indian Camp', the far from impassive husband turns away; and it is later discovered that he has killed himself. 'He couldn't stand things . . .', so runs the diagnosis of Nick's father, the doctor. This, for Nick, is an initiation to suffering and death; but with the sunrise, shortly afterward, youth and well-being reassert themselves; and the end of the story reaffirms the generalization that Hazlitt once drew: 'No young man ever thinks he shall die.' It is easy enough for such a young man to stand things, for he is not yet painfully involved in them; he is not a sufferer but a wide-eyed onlooker, to whom the word 'mashing' holds out mysterious enticements. Hemingway's projection of this attitude has given his best work perennial youthfulness; it has also armed his critics with the accusation that, like his Robert Cohen, he is 'a case of arrested development'. If this be so, his plight is generalized by the Englishman Wilson, who observes that 'Americans stay little boys . . . all their lives'. And the object of Wilson's observation, Francis Macomber, would furnish a classic case-history for Adler, if not for Freud—the masculine sense of inferiority which seeks to overcome itself by acts of prowess, both sanguinary and sexual. Despite these two sources of excitement, the story is a plaintive modulation of two rather dissonant themes: *None but the brave deserves the fair* and *The female of the species is more deadly than the male*. After Francis Macomber has demonstrated his manhood, the next step is death. The world that remains most alive to Hemingway is that stretch between puberty and maturity which is strictly governed by the ephebic code: a world of mixed apprehension and bravado before the rite of passage, the baptism of fire, the introduction to sex.

Afterward comes the boasting, along with such surviv-

ing ideals as Hemingway subsumes in the word *cojones*—
the English equivalent sounds more sceptical. But for Jake
Barnes, all passion spent in the First World War, or for
Colonel Cantwell, tired and disgruntled by the Second,
the aftermath can only be elegiac. The weather-beaten
hero of *Across the River*, which appeared in 1950, is fifty
years old and uneasily conscious of that fact; whereas
'the childish, drunken heroics' of *The Sun Also Rises*
took place just about twenty-five years ago. From his
spectacular arrival in the twenties, Hemingway's course
has paralleled that of our century; and now, at its mid-
point, he balks like the rest of us before the responsibilities of middle age. When, if ever, does the *enfant du
siècle*, that *enfant terrible*, grow up? (Not necessarily
when he grows a beard and calls himself 'Mr. Papa'.)
Frederic Henry plunges into the Po much as Huck Finn
dived into the Mississippi, but emerges to remind us
even more pointedly of Fabrice del Dongo in Stendhal's
Chartreuse de Parme, and of our great contemporary shift
from transatlantic innocence to old-world experience.
Certain intimations of later years are present in Hemingway's earlier stories, typically Ad Francis, the slap-happy
ex-champ in 'The Battler'. Even in 'Fifty Grand', his
most contrived tale, the beat-up prizefighter suffers more
than he acts and wins by losing—a situation which has
its corollary in the title of Hemingway's third collection,
Winner Take Nothing. The ultimate article of his credo,
which he shares with Malraux and Sartre, is the good
fight for the lost cause. And the ultimate protagonist is
Jesus in 'Today is Friday', whose crucifixion is treated
like an athletic feat, and whose capacity for taking
punishment rouses a fellow-feeling in the Roman
soldiers. The stoic or masochistic determination to take it
brings us back from Hemingway to his medium, which
—although it eschews the passive voice—is essentially

a receiving instrument, especially sensitized for recording a series of violent shocks.

The paradox of toughness and sensitivity is resolved, and the qualities and defects of his writing are reconciled, if we merely remember that he was—and still is—a poet. That he is not a novelist by vocation, if it were not revealed by his books, could be inferred from his well-known retort to F. Scott Fitzgerald. For Fitzgerald the rich were different—not quantitatively, because they had more money, but qualitatively, because he had a novelistic interest in manners and morals. Again, when we read André Gide's reports from the Congo, we realize what *Green Hills of Africa* lacks in the way of social or psychological insight. As W. M. Frohock has perceived, Hemingway is less concerned with human relations than with his own relationship to the universe —a concern which might have spontaneously flowered into poetry. His talents come out most fully in the texture of his work, whereas the structure tends to be episodic and uncontrived to the point of formlessness. *For Whom the Bell Tolls*, the only one of his six novels that has been carefully constructed, is in some respects an over-expanded short story. Editors rejected his earliest stories on the grounds that they were nothing but sketches and anecdotes, thereby paying incidental tribute to his sense of reality. Fragments of truth, after all, are the best that a writer can offer; and, as Hemingway has said, '. . . Any part you make will represent the whole if it's made truly.' In periods as confusing as the present, when broader and maturer representations are likely to falsify, we are fortunate if we can find authenticity in the lyric cry, the adolescent mood, the tangible feeling, the trigger response. If we think of Hemingway's temperamental kinship with E. E. Cummings, and of Cummings's 'Buffalo Bill' or 'Olaf glad and big', it is easy to think of Hemingway as a poet. After the attractions and distractions of timeliness have been outdated, together with categorical distinctions between the rich and the poor, perhaps he will be remembered for a poetic vision which renews our interrupted contact with the timeless elements of man's existence: bread, wine, bed, music, and just a few more of the concrete universals. When El Sordo raises his glance from the battlefield, he looks up at the identical patch of the blue sky that Henry Fleming saw in *The Red Badge of Courage* and that looked down on Prince Andrey in *War and Peace*.

RICHARD CHASE

1914–1962

THE BROKEN CIRCUIT: ROMANCE AND THE AMERICAN NOVEL

Anchor Review, 1957

THE imagination that has produced much of the best and most characteristic American fiction—that of Charles Brockden Brown, Cooper, Hawthorne, Melville, Henry James, Mark Twain, Frank Norris, Faulkner, and Hemingway, among others—has been shaped by the contradictions and not by the unities and harmonies of our culture. In a sense this may be true of all literatures of whatever time and place. Nevertheless there are some literatures which take their form and tone from polarities, opposites, and irreconcilables, but are content to rest in and sustain them, or to resolve them into unities, if at all, only by special and limited means.

The American novel tends to rest in contradictions and among extreme ranges of experience. When it attempts to resolve contradictions, it does so in oblique, morally equivocal ways. As a general rule it does so either in melodramatic actions or in pastoral idyls, although intermixed with both one may find the stirring instabilities of 'American humour'. These qualities constitute the uniqueness of that branch of the novelistic tradition which has flourished in this country. They help to account for the strong element of 'romance' in the American 'novel'.

Briefly, and hence dogmatically, the contradictions which have vivified and excited the American imagination seem traceable to these historical facts. First, there is the dual allegiance of the American, who in his intellectual culture belongs both to the old world and the new.

Second, there is the solitary position man has been placed in in this country, *vis-à-vis* the state and mankind in general—a position enforced, as Tocqueville points out, by the very institutions of democracy as those evolved in the eighteenth and nineteenth centuries. In aristocratic societies there was a shared body of inherited habits, attitudes, and institutions that stood in a mediating position between the individual and the state. But when democratic man contemplates his situation, as Tocqueville says, he is conscious of the stark, unmediated opposition between himself and 'the immense form of society' and 'the still more imposing aspect of mankind'. The ingrained tendency to conceive reality as involving irreconcilable contradictions was enforced also by New England Puritanism, which starkly opposed the individual to his God, and perhaps by the frontier experience, which opposed the individual to the immense form, not of society, but of nature.

Third, there is the special character of New England

Puritanism, which not only harshly confronted man with his God but which took on a positively Manichean quality. It is this quality which affects writers like Hawthorne and Melville and enters deeply into the national consciousness, reappearing, for example, in the mythology of Populism. From the historical point of view, New England Puritanism was a backsliding in religion as momentous in shaping the imagination as the cultural reversion Cooper studied on the frontier (see especially Chapter VI of *The Prairie*). For, at least as apprehended by the literary imagination, New England Puritanism—with its grand metaphors of election and damnation, its opposition of the kingdom of light and the kingdom of darkness, its eternal and autonomous contraries of good and evil—seems to have recaptured the Manichean sensibility. The American imagination, like the New England Puritan mind itself, seems less interested in redemption than in the melodrama of the eternal struggle of good and evil, less interested in incarnation and reconciliation than in alienation and disorder. If we may suppose ourselves correct in tracing to this origin the prevalence in the American novel of the symbols of light and dark, we may doubtless suppose also that this sensibility has been enhanced by the racial composition of our people and by the Civil War that was fought, if more in legend than in fact, over the Negro.

In contrast to the American novel, the English novel has followed a middle way. It is notable for its great practical sanity, its powerful, engrossing composition of wide ranges of experience into a moral centrality and equability of judgement. Oddity, distortion of personality, dislocations of normal life, recklessness of behaviour, malignancy of motive—these the English novel has included. Yet the profound poetry of disorder we find in the American novel is missing, with rare exceptions, from the English. Radical maladjustments and contradictions are reported but are seldom of the essence of form in the English novel, and although it is no stranger to suffering and defeat or to triumphant joy either, it gives the impression of absorbing all extremes, all maladjustments and contradictions into a normative view of life. In doing so, it shows itself to derive from the two great influences that stand behind it—classic tragedy and Christianity. The English novel has not of course always been, strictly speaking, tragic or Christian. Often it has been comic, but often, too, in that superior form of comedy which approaches tragedy. Usually it has been realistic or, in the philosophical sense of the word, 'naturalistic'. Yet even its peculiar kind of gross poetic naturalism has preserved something of the two great traditions that formed English literature. The English novel, that is, follows the tendency of tragic art and Christian art, which characteristically move through contradictions to forms of harmony, reconciliation, catharsis, and transfiguration.

Judging by our greatest novels, the American imagination, even when it wishes to assuage and reconcile the contradictions of life, has not been stirred by the possibility of catharsis or incarnation, by the tragic or Christian possibility. It has been stirred, rather, by the aesthetic possibilities of radical forms of alienation, contradiction, and disorder.

The essential difference between the American novel and the English will be strongly pointed up to any reader of F. R. Leavis's *The Great Tradition*. Mr. Leavis's 'great tradition' of the novel is really Anglo-American, and it includes not only Jane Austen, George Eliot, Conrad, and Henry James but, apparently, in one of its branches Hawthorne and Melville. The American novel is obviously a development from the English tradition. At least it was, down to 1880 or 1890. For at that time our novelists began to turn to French and Russian models and the English influence has decreased steadily ever since. The more extreme imagination of the French and Russian novelists has clearly been more in accord with the purposes of modern American writers than has the English imagination. True, an American reader of Mr. Leavis's book will have little trouble in giving a very general assent to his very general proposition about the Anglo-American tradition. Nevertheless, he will also be forced constantly to protest that there is another tradition of which Mr. Leavis does not seem to be aware, a tradition which includes most of the best American novels.

Ultimately, it does not matter much whether one insists that there are really *two* traditions, the English and the American (leaving aside the question of what writers each might be said to comprise), or whether one insists merely that there is a radical divergence within one tradition. All I hold out for is a provisional recognition of the divergence as a necessary step towards understanding and appreciation of the American novel. The divergence is brought home to an American reader of Mr. Leavis's book when, for example, he comes across the brief note allotted to the Brontës. Here is Mr. Leavis's comment on Emily Brontë:

I have said nothing about *Wuthering Heights* because that astonishing work seems to me a kind of sport . . . she broke completely, and in the most challenging way, both with the Scott tradition that imposed on the novelist a romantic resolution of his themes, and with the tradition coming down from the eighteenth century that demanded a plane-mirror reflection of the surface of 'real' life. Out of her a minor tradition comes, to which belongs, most notably, *The House with the Green Shutters*.

Of course Mr. Leavis is right; in relation to the great tradition of the English novel, *Wuthering Heights* is indeed a sport. But suppose it were discovered that *Wuthering Heights* was written by an American of New England Calvinist or southern Presbyterian background. The novel would be astonishing and unique no matter who wrote it or where. But if it were an American novel it would not be a sport; it has too close an affinity with too many American novels, and among them some of the best. Like many American fictions *Wuthering Heights* proceeds from an imagination that is essentially melodramatic, that operates among radical contradictions and renders reality indirectly or poetically, thus breaking, as Mr. Leavis observes, with the traditions that require a surface rendering of real life and a resolution of themes, 'romantic' or otherwise.

Those readers who make a dogma out of Mr. Leavis's views are thus proprietors of an Anglo-American tradition in which many of the most interesting and original and several of the greatest American novels are sports. Charles Brockden Brown's *Wieland* is a sport, and so are *The Scarlet Letter* and *The Blithedale Romance, Moby Dick, Pierre,* and *The Confidence Man, Huckleberry Finn, The Red Badge of Courage, McTeague, As I Lay Dying, The Sun Also Rises*—all are eccentric, in their differing ways, to a tradition of which, let us say, *Middlemarch* is a standard representative. Not one of them has any close kinship with the massive, temperate, moralistic rendering of life and thought we associate with Mr. Leavis's 'great tradition'.

The English novel, one might say, has been a kind of imperial enterprise, an appropriation of reality with the high purpose of bringing order to disorder. By contrast, as Lawrence observed in his *Studies in Classic American Literature,* the American novel has usually

seemed content to explore, rather than to appropriate
and civilize, the remarkable and in some ways unexampled territories of life in the new world and to
reflect its anomalies and dilemmas. It has not wanted to
build an imperium but merely to discover a new place
and a new state of mind. Explorers see more deeply,
darkly, privately, and disinterestedly than imperialists,
who must perforce be circumspect and prudential. The
American novel is more profound and clairvoyant than
the English novel, but by the same token it is narrower
and more arbitrary, and it tends to carve out of experience brilliant, highly wrought fragments rather than
massive unities.

In the history of the American novel, the tradition of
romance is major, whereas in the history of the English
novel it is minor. True, nothing is to be gained by trying
to separate too sharply the romance from the novel.
One of their chief advantages is that, as literary forms go,
they are relatively loose and flexible. But especially in
discussing American literature, these terms have to be
defined closely enough to distinguish between them,
even though the distinction itself may sometimes be
meaningless as applied to a given book and even though,
following usage, one ordinarily uses the word 'novel' to
describe a book like Cooper's *The Prairie* which might
more accurately be called a 'romance' or a 'romance-
novel'.

Doubtless the main difference between the novel and
the romance is the way in which they view reality. The
novel renders reality closely and in comprehensive
detail. It takes a group of people and sets them going
about the business of life. We come to see these
people in their real complexity of temperament and
motive. They are in explicable relation to nature, to each
other, to their social class, to their own past. Character is

more important than action and plot, and probably the tragic or comic actions of the narrative will have the primary purpose of enhancing our knowledge of and feeling for an important character, a group of characters, or a way of life. The events that occur will usually be plausible, given the circumstances, and if the novelist includes a violent or sensational occurrence in his plot, he will introduce it only into such scenes as have been (in the words of Percy Lubbock) 'already prepared to vouch for it'. Historically, as it has often been said, the novel has served the interests and aspirations of an insurgent middle class.

By contrast the romance, following distantly the medieval example, feels free to render reality in less volume and detail. It tends to prefer action to character, and action will be freer in a romance than in a novel, encountering, as it were, less resistance from reality. (This is not always true, as we see in what might be called the static romances of Hawthorne, in which the author uses the allegorical, rather than the dramatic, possibilities of the form.) The romance can flourish without providing much intricacy of relation. The characters, probably rather two-dimensional types, will not be complexly related to each other or to society or to the past. Human beings will on the whole be shown in ideal relation—that is, they will share emotions only after these have become abstract or symbolic. To be sure, characters may become profoundly involved in some way, as in Hawthorne or Melville, but it will be a deep and narrow, an obsessive, involvement. In American romances it will not matter much what class people come from, and where the novelist would arouse our interest in a character by exploring his origin, the romancer will probably do so by enveloping it in mystery. Character itself becomes, then, somewhat abstract and ideal, so much so in some romances that it seems to be merely a function of plot. The plot we may expect to be highly coloured. Astonishing events may occur, and these are likely to have a symbolic or perhaps ideological, rather than a realistic, plausibility. Being less committed to the immediate rendition of reality than the novel, the romance will more freely veer toward mythic, allegorical, and symbolistic forms.

Although some of the best works of American fiction have to be called, for purposes of criticism, romances rather than novels, we would be pursuing a chimera if we tried, except provisionally, to isolate a literary form known as the American prose romance, as distinguished from the European or the American novel. In actuality the romances of our literature, like European prose romances, are literary hybrids, unique only in their peculiar but widely differing amalgamation of novelistic and romance elements. Obviously, our fiction is historically a branch of the European tradition of the novel. And it is the better part of valour in the critic to understand the American romances as adaptations of traditional novelistic procedures to new cultural conditions and new aesthetic aspirations. It will not damage our appreciation of the originality and value of *Moby-Dick* or *The Blithedale Romance* to say that they both seem to begin as novels but then veer off into the province of romance, in the one case making a supreme triumph, in the other, a somewhat dubious but interesting medley of genres and intentions. Speaking generally, one may say that when the American novelists depart from the novelistic tradition, they do so, with variations, by way of melodrama or pastoral idyll, often both.

Most of the American writers of fiction, from Brown and Cooper to Norris, have described themselves as romancers rather than novelists. In the Preface to *The*

Yemassee (1835), for example, William Gilmore Simms dwells at length on this distinction. Echoing Cooper and Scott, as well as Aristotle's *Poetics*, he describes 'modern Romance' as the new form of epic. Epic turned out to be an important source of romance in American fiction, but, outside of *Moby-Dick*, Cooper's *The Prairie*, and one or two other books, not a major source.

Hawthorne's brief prefaces to his longer works explain and defend for the first time the distinctively American art of romance. And it is in Hawthorne that some of the considerable psychological and intellectual possibilities of romance are first explored. As he sees the problem confronting the American author, it consists in the necessity of finding (in the words of the Introduction to *The Scarlet Letter*) 'a neutral territory, somewhere between the real world and fairy-land, where the Actual and the Imaginary may meet, and each imbue itself with the nature of the other'. Romance is, as we see, a kind of 'border' fiction, whether the field of action is in the neutral territory between civilization and the wilderness, as in the adventure tales of Cooper and Simms or whether, as in Hawthorne and later romancers, the field of action is conceived not so much as a place as a state of mind—the borderland of the human mind where the actual and the imaginary intermingle. Romance does not plant itself, like the novel, solidly in the midst of the actual. Nor, when it is memorable, does it escape into the purely imaginary.

In saying, as he does in the preface to *The House of the Seven Gables*, that no matter what its extravagances romance must not 'swerve aside from the truth of the human heart', Hawthorne was in effect announcing the definitive adaptation of romance to America. To keep fiction in touch with the human heart is to give it a universal human significance. But this cannot be done memorably in prose fiction, even in the relatively loose form of the romance, without giving it a local significance. The truth of the heart as pictured in romance may be more generic or archetypal than in the novel; it may be rendered less concretely; but it must still be made to belong to a time and a place. Surely Hawthorne's romances do. In his writings romance was made for the first time to respond to the particular demands of an American imagination and to mirror, in certain limited ways, the American mind.

Among others, Melville, James, Mark Twain, Norris, Faulkner, and Hemingway comprise the tradition of the romance-novel established by Cooper, Brown, Simms, and Hawthorne. But there is, it should be parenthetically noted, a second stream of romance. This is the stream, justly contemned by Mark Twain and James, which descends directly from Scott and includes John Esten Cooke's *Surry of Eagle's Nest* (1866), Lew Wallace's *Ben Hur* (1880), Charles Major's *When Knighthood Was in Flower* (1898), and later books like *Gone With the Wind* and the historical tales of Kenneth Roberts. Although these works may have their points, according to the taste of the reader, they are, historically considered, the tag end of a European tradition that begins in the Middle Ages and has come down into our own literature without responding to the forms of imagination which the actualities of American life have inspired.

In the preceding pages I have tried to formulate preliminary definitions of 'romance' and the 'novel' and then to look briefly at the matter from a historical point of view. In order to amplify the discussion, both in the abstract and the concrete, it will be of value at this point to return, with the aid of Henry James's prefaces, to the question of definition. In doing so, I shall risk repeating one or two observations which have already been made.

The first four prefaces James wrote for the New York edition of his works set forth, or at least allude to, the main items of his credo as a novelist, and although they are perhaps well known, there may be some advantage in looking them over again before noticing what James had to say directly about the relation of the romance to the novel. The four prefaces are those to *Roderick Hudson, The American, The Portrait of a Lady*, and *The Princess Casamassima*.

We might take as a motto this sentence from the preface to *The Princess*: 'Experience, as I see it, is our apprehension and our measure of what happens to us as social creatures.' Although James himself does not overtly contrast his procedure with that of romance until he comes to the preface to *The American*, we shall be justified in ourselves making the contrast, since James is obviously seeking to show, among other things, how the imperfections of romance may be avoided. And thus we reflect that, in a romance, 'experience' has less to do with human beings as 'social creatures' than as individuals. Heroes, villains, victims, legendary types confronting other individuals or confronting mysterious or otherwise dire forces—this is what we meet in romances.

When James tells us that the art of the novel is the 'art of representation', the practice of which spreads 'round us in a widening, not in a narrow circle', we reflect on the relative paucity of 'representation' in the older American romances and their tendency towards a concentrated and narrow profundity. Again we hear that 'development' is 'of the very essence of the novelist's process', and we recall how in romances characters appear really to be given quantities rather than emerging and changing organisms responding to their circumstances as these themselves develop one out of another. For if characters change in a romance, let's say as Captain Ahab in *Moby Dick* or the Reverend Dimmesdale in *The Scarlet Letter* changes, we are not shown a 'development'; we are left rather with an element of mystery, as with Ahab, or a simplified and conventionalized alteration of character, as with Dimmesdale. Similarly, the episodes of romance tend to follow each other without ostensible causation; here too there is likely to be an element either of mystery or convention. To 'treat' a subject, James says, is to 'exhibit... relations'; and the novelist 'is in the perpetual predicament that the continuity of things is the whole matter, for him, of comedy and tragedy'. But in a romance much may be made of unrelatedness, of alienation and discontinuity, for the romancer operates in a universe that is less coherent than that of the novelist.

As for the setting, James says that it is not enough merely to report what it seems to the author to be, in however minute detail. The great thing is to get into the novel not only the setting but somebody's *sense* of the setting. We recall that in *The Scarlet Letter* the setting, although sketchy, is pictorially very beautiful and symbolically apropos. But none of the characters has a *sense* of the setting; that is all in the author's mind and hence the setting is never dramatized but remains instead a handsomely tapestried backdrop. In *Moby-Dick* the setting is less inert; it becomes, in fact, a kind of 'enveloping action'. Still, only in some of the scenes do we have Ishmael's sense of the setting; during most of the book Ishmael himself is all but banished as a dramatic presence.

The whole question of the 'point of command' or 'point of view' or 'centre of intelligence' is too complicated to go into here. Suffice it to say that the allotment of awareness, the question of what character shall be specially conscious of the meaning of what happens to and around him so that we see events and people more or less through his eyes, thus gaining a sense of dramatic coherence—these questions are less and less pertinent as fiction approaches pure romance. Natty Bumppo need be conscious only of what the Indians are going to do next. Hawthorne's Chillingworth and Melville's Ahab are clairvoyantly conscious, but with a profoundly obsessive distortion of the truth. They are not placed in context in order to give concrete dramatic form to a large part of what the author sees, as is the 'point of command' in a James novel; all we learn from them is how *they* see. And in *The Blithedale Romance*, the dyed-in-the-wool romancer Hawthorne merely proves that you mustn't have a central observer in your story, because if you do you simply point up the faults of romance and admit your incapacity to follow out a fully developed novelistic procedure. In the romance too much depends on mystery and bewilderment to risk a generally receptive intelligence in the midst of things. Too often the effect you are after depends on a universe that is felt to be irrational, contradictory, and melodramatic—whereas the effect of a central intelligence is to produce a sense of verisimilitude and dramatic coherence.

One or two further items from the prefaces may point up the contrast. A character, especially 'the fictive hero', as James says, 'successfully appeals to us only as an eminent instance, as eminent as we like, of our own conscious kind'. He must not be 'a morbidly special case'—but in romance he may well be. Again, says James, when economy demands the suppression of parts of the possible story they must not be merely 'eliminated'; they must be foreshortened, summarized, compressed, but nevertheless brought to bear on the whole. But in the looser universe of the romance, we may think 'elimination' will be less criminal, and unexplained hiatuses and discontinuities may positively contribute to the effect. To take an obvious case, in *Moby-Dick* we are content to think the sudden elimination of Bulkington an interesting oddity rather than a novelistic blunder and we gladly draw on the poetic capital Melville makes of it.

As for the moral significance of the novel, James sees a 'perfect dependence of the "moral" sense of a work of art on the amount of felt life concerned in producing it'. We must ask, he says, 'is it valid, in a word, is it genuine, is it sincere, the result of some direct impression or perception of life'. These questions bear less on the romance, one of the assumptions of which is that it need not contain a full amount of felt life, that life may be felt indirectly through legend, symbol, or allegory. Nor does the romance need the sincerity of the novel; indeed, as Lawrence points out, American romances, especially, tend to make their effect by a deep 'duplicity' or ironic indirection.

To come finally to James's specific comments on the question we are considering. In the prefaces he follows his own advice as expressed twenty-odd years earlier in 'The Art of Fiction'—he sees no reason, that is, why the practising writer should distinguish between novel and romance. There are good novels and bad ones, novels that have life and those that haven't—and this, for the novelist, is the only relevant question. The implication is that the novelist will be also the romancer if the 'life' he is rendering extends into the realm of the 'romantic'. But if we are not, except as critics and readers, to distinguish between novel and romance, we still have to distinguish, within the novel that may be also a romance, the 'romantic' from the 'real'. And this James essays in his Preface to *The American*.

In rereading this early novel James found a large element of romance in the free-and-easy way in which he had made his semi-legendary hero Christopher Newman behave on his European travels. Particularly, James thought, the picture of the Bellegard family was 'romantic'. James had made them reject Newman as a vulgar manufacturer when actually common sense tells us that 'they would positively have jumped at him'. And James comments that 'the experience here represented is the disconnected and uncontrolled experience—uncontrolled by our general sense of "the way things happen" —which romance alone more or less successfully palms off on us'. At the same time James finds an unexpected pleasure in rereading *The American*, which somewhat compensates for the lapses of verisimilitude. And his description of this pleasure makes a fair definition of the pleasure of romance—'the free play of so much unchallenged instinct . . . the happiest season of surrender to the invoked muse and the projected fable'.[1]

'The disconnected and uncontrolled experience', then, is of the essence of romance, and any adequate definition must proceed from this postulate. First, however, one may clear out of the way certain conventional but inadequate descriptions of romance. It is not 'a matter indispensably of boats, or of caravans, or of tigers, or of 'historical characters'', or of ghosts, or of forgers, or of detectives, or of beautiful wicked women, or of pistols and knives'—although one might perhaps be a little

[1] Cf. Melville's plea to his reality-minded readers for latitude in the depiction of character and incident. The ideal reader, he says, will 'want nature . . . ; but nature unfettered, exhilarated, in effect transformed. . . . It is with fiction as with religion: it should present another world, and yet one to which we feel the tie' (*The Confidence Man*, chap. 33).

readier than James to think that these things might be of service. Yet one follows him assentingly when he decides that the common element in sensational tales is 'the facing of danger' and then goes on to say that for most of us the danger represented by caravans and forgers is certainly benign or impotent compared with the 'common and covert' dangers we face in our everyday existence, which may 'involve the sharpest hazards to life and honour and the highest instant decisions and intrepidities of action'.

The 'romantic' cannot be defined, either, as 'the far and the strange', since, as such, these things are merely 'unknown', whereas the 'romantic' is something we know, although we know it indirectly. Nor is a novel romantic because its hero or heroine is. 'It would be impossible to have a more romantic temper than Flaubert's Madame Bovary, yet nothing less resembles a romance than the record of her adventures.' Nor can we say the presence or absence of 'costume' is a crucial difference, for 'where . . . does costume begin or end?'

James then arrives at the following formulation:

The only *general* attribute of projected romance that I can see, the only one that fits all its cases, is the fact of the kind of experience with which it deals—experience liberated, so to speak; experience disengaged, disembroiled, disencumbered, exempt from the conditions that we usually know to attach to it and, if we wish so to put the matter, drag upon it, and operating in a medium which relieves it, in a particular interest, of the inconvenience of a *related*, a measurable state, a state subject to all our vulgar communities.

And James goes on in words that are particularly illustrative of his own art:

The greatest intensity may so be arrived at evidently— when the sacrifice of community, of the 'related' sides of situations, has not been too rash. It must to this end not flagrantly betray itself; we must even be kept if possible, for our illusion, from suspecting any sacrifice at all.

In a fully developed art of the novel there is, as James says, a 'latent extravagance'. In men of 'largest responding imagination before the human scene', we do not find only the romantic or only reality, but a 'current . . . extraordinarily rich and mixed'. The great novelist responds to the 'need of performing his whole possible revolution, by the law of some rich passion in him for extremes'.

To have a rich passion for extremes is to grasp both the real and the romantic. By the 'real', James explains, he means 'the things we cannot possibly *not* know, sooner or later, in one way or another'. By the 'romantic' he means 'the things that, with all the facilities in the world, all the wealth and all the courage and all the wit and all the adventure, we never *can* directly know; the things that can reach us only through the beautiful circuit and subterfuge of our thought and our desire'.

We hear much in these prefaces of the novelist's rich and mixed 'current', of the possible 'revolution' of his mind among extremes, of the 'circuit' of thought and desire. James speaks, too, of the 'conversion' that goes on in the mind of the novelist's characters between what happens to them and their *sense* of what happens to them, and of 'the link of connexion' between a character's 'doing' and his 'feeling'. In other words James thinks that the novel does not find its essential being until it discovers what we may call the circuit of life among extremes or opposites, the circuit of life that passes through the real and the ideal, through the directly known and the mysterious or the indirectly known, through doing and feeling.

Much of the best American fiction does not meet

James's specifications. It has not made the circuit James requires of the 'largest responding imagination'. And the closer it has stuck to the assumptions of romance the more capital it has made, when any capital has been made, exactly by leaving the Jamesian circuits broken. That very great capital can be made in this way James does not acknowledge or know, and hence his own hostility and that of many of his followers, to the more extreme forms of American fiction—those we associate, for example, with Brockden Brown, Melville, and Faulkner.

In this trans-Jamesian realm of fiction there are certain special virtues. Among them are the 'intellectual energy' that Brown prized, the profundity described by Melville as 'the blackness of darkness', a certain intrepid and penetrating dialectic of action and meaning, a radical scepticism about ultimate questions, a certain rapidity, irony, and abstraction. By their use of these qualities the American novelists have made of romance something far more valuable than the escapism, fantasy, and sentimentality often associated with this form.

Nevertheless James's theory of the novel, his idea of the circuit of life which allows him to incorporate in his own novels so many of the attributes of romance, is the most complete and admirable theory, as at their best James's are the most complete and admirable novels yet produced by an American. And it is against James's theory and often, though certainly not always, his practice that we have to test the achievements of his compatriots. The danger is that in doing so we should lapse into an easy disapproval of that 'rich passion . . . for extremes' which James praised on his own grounds but which may be seen operating to advantage on other grounds too.

ALFRED KAZIN

1915-

ISHMAEL AND AHAB

Introduction to Houghton Mifflin 'Riverside' edition of
Moby-Dick

Moby-Dick is not only a very big book; it is also a peculiarly full and rich one, and from the very opening it conveys a sense of abundance, of high creative power, that exhilarates and enlarges the imagination. This quality is felt immediately in the style, which is remarkably easy, natural and 'American', yet always literary, and which swells in power until it takes on some of the roaring and uncontainable rhythms with which Melville audibly describes the sea. The best description of this style is Melville's own, when he speaks of the 'bold and nervous lofty language' that Nantucket whaling captains learn straight from nature. We feel this abundance in heroic types like the Nantucketers themselves, many of whom are significantly named after Old Testament prophets and kings, for these, too, are mighty men, and the mightiest of them all, Captain Ahab, will challenge the very order of the creation itself. This is the very heart of the book—so much so that we come to feel that there is some shattering magnitude of theme before Melville as he writes, that as a writer he had been called to an heroic new destiny.

It is this constant sense of power that constitutes the book's appeal to us, that explains its hold on our attention. *Moby-Dick* is one of those books that try to bring in as much of life as a writer can get both hands on. Melville even tries to create an image of life itself as a ceaseless creation. The book is written with a personal force of style, a passionate learning, a steady insight into our forgotten connexions with the primitive. It sweeps everything before it; it gives us the happiness that only great vigour inspires.

If we start by opening ourselves to this abundance and force, by welcoming not merely the story itself, but the manner in which it speaks to us, we shall recognize in this restlessness, this richness, this persistent atmosphere of magnitude, the essential image on which the book is founded. For *Moby-Dick* is not so much a book *about* Captain Ahab's quest for the whale as it is an experience *of* that quest. This is only to say, what we say of any true poem, that we cannot reduce its essential substance to a subject, that we should not intellectualize and summarize it, but that we should recognize that its very force and beauty lie in the way it is conceived and written, in the qualities that flow from its being a unique entity.

In these terms, *Moby-Dick* seems to be far more of a poem than it is a novel, and since it is a narrative, to be an epic, a long poem on an heroic theme, rather than the kind of realistic fiction that we know today. Of course Melville did not deliberately set out to write a formal epic; but half-consciously, he drew upon many of the traditional characteristics of epic in order to realize the utterly original kind of novel *he* needed to write in his time—the spaciousness of theme and subject, the martial atmosphere, the association of these homely and savage materials with universal myths, the symbolic wanderings of the hero, the indispensable strength of such a hero in Captain Ahab. Yet beyond all this, what distinguishes *Moby-Dick* from modern prose fiction, what ties it up with the older, more formal kind of narrative that was once written in verse, is the fact that Melville is not interested in the meanness, the literal truthfulness, the representative slice of life, that we think of as the essence of modern realism. His book has the true poetic emphasis in that the whole story is constantly being meditated and unravelled through a single mind.

'Call me Ishmael', the book begins. This Ishmael is not only a character in the book; he is also the single voice, or rather the single mind, from whose endlessly turning spool of thought the whole story is unwound. It is Ishmael's contemplativeness, his *dreaming*, that articulates the wonder of the seas and the fabulousness of the whale and the terrors of the deep. All that can be meditated and summed up and hinted at, as the reflective essence of the story itself, is given us by Ishmael, who possesses nothing but man's specifically human gift, which is language. It is Ishmael who tries to sum up the whole creation in a single book and yet keeps at the centre of it one American whaling voyage. It is Ishmael's gift for speculation that explains the terror we come to feel before the whiteness of the whale; Ishmael's mind that ranges with mad exuberance through a description of all the seas; Ishmael who piles up image after image of 'the mightiest animated mass that has survived the flood'. It is Ishmael who, in the wonderful chapter on the masthead, embodies for us man as a thinker, whose reveries transcend space and time as he stands watch high above the seas. And of course it is Ishmael, both actually and as the symbol of man, who is the one survivor of the voyage. Yet utterly alone as he is at the end of the book, floating on the Pacific Ocean, he manages, buoyed up on a coffin that magically serves as his life-buoy, to give us the impression that life itself can be honestly confronted only in the loneliness of each human heart. Always it is this emphasis on Ishmael's personal vision, on the richness and ambiguity of all events as the sceptical, fervent, experience-scarred mind of Ishmael feels and thinks them, that gives us, from the beginning, the new kind of book that *Moby-Dick* is. It is a book which is neither a saga, though it deals in large natural forces, nor a *classical* epic, for we feel too strongly the individual who wrote it. It is a book that is at once primitive, fatalistic, and merciless, like the very oldest books, and yet peculiarly personal, like so many twentieth-century novels, in its significant emphasis on the subjective individual consciousness. The book grows out of a single word, 'I', and expands until the soul's voyage of this 'I' comes to include a great many things that are unseen and unsuspected by most of us. And this material is always tied to Ishmael, who is not merely a witness to the story—someone who happens to be on board the *Pequod*—but the living and germinating mind who grasps the world in the tentacles of his thought.

The power behind this 'I' is poetical in the sense that everything comes to us through a constant intervention of language instead of being presented flatly. Melville does not wish, as so many contemporary writers do, to reproduce ordinary life and conventional speech. He seeks the marvellous and the fabulous aspects that life wears in secret. He exuberantly sees the world through language—things exist as his words for them—and much of the exceptional beauty of the book lies in the unusual incidence of passages that, in the most surprising contexts, are so piercing in their poetic intensity. But the most remarkable feat of language in the book is Melville's ability to make us see that man is not a blank slate passively open to events, but a mind that constantly seeks meaning in everything it encounters. In Melville the Protestant habit of moralizing and the transcendental passion for symbolizing all things as examples of 'higher laws' combined to make a mind that instinctively brought an inner significance to each episode. Everything in *Moby-Dick* is saturated in a mental atmosphere. Nothing happens for its own sake in this book, and in the midst of the chase, Ishmael can be seen meditating it, pulling things apart, drawing out its significant point.

But Ishmael is not just an intellectual observer; he is also very much in the story. He suffers; he is there. As his name indicates, he is an estranged and solitary man; his only friend is Queequeg, a despised heathen from the South Seas. Queequeg, a fellow 'isolato' in the smug world of white middle-class Christians, is the only man who offers Ishmael friendship; thanks to Queequeg, 'no longer my splintered heart and maddened hand were turned against the wolfish world. This soothing savage had redeemed it'. Why does Ishmael feel so alone? There are background reasons, Melville's own: his father went bankrupt and then died in debt when Melville was still a boy. Melville-Ishmael went to sea— 'And at first', he tells us, 'this sort of thing is unpleasant enough. It touches one's sense of honour, particularly if you come of an old established family in the land.' But there is a deeper, a more universal reason for Ishmael's apartness, and it is one that will strangely make him kin to his daemonic captain, Ahab. For the burden of his thought, the essential cause of his estrangement, is that he cannot come to any conclusion about anything. He feels at home with ships and sailors because for him, too, one journey ends only to begin another; 'and a second ended, only begins a third and so on, for ever and for aye. Such is the endlessness, yea, the intolerableness of all earthly effort.'

Ishmael is not merely an orphan; he is an exile, searching alone in the wilderness, with a black man for his only friend. He suffers from doubt and uncertainty far more than he does from homelessness. Indeed, this agony of disbelief *is* his homelessness. For him nothing is ever finally settled and decided; he is man, or as we like to think, modern man, cut off from the certainty that was once his inner world. Ishmael no longer has any sure formal belief. All is in doubt, all is in eternal flux, like the sea. And so condemned, like 'all his race from Adam down', to wander the seas of thought, far from Paradise, he now searches endlessly to put the whole broken story together, to find a meaning, to ascertain—where but in the ceaselessness of human thought?—'the hidden cause we seek'. Ishmael does not perform any great actions, as Ahab does; he is the most insignificant member of the fo'c'sle and will get the smallest share of the take. But his inner world of thought is almost unbearably symbolic, for he must think, and think, and think, in order to prove to himself that there is a necessary connexion between man and the world. He pictures his dilemma in everything he does on board the ship, but never so clearly as when he is shown looking at the sea, searching a meaning to existence from the inscrutable waters.

What Melville did through Ishmael, then, was to put man's distinctly modern feeling of 'exile', of abandonment, directly at the centre of his stage. For Ishmael there are no satisfactory conclusions to anything; no final philosophy is ever possible. All that man owns in this world, Ishmael would say, is his insatiable mind. This is why the book opens on a picture of the dreaming contemplativeness of mind itself: men tearing themselves loose from their jobs to stand 'like silent sentinels all around the town . . . thousands of mortal men fixed in ocean reveries'. Narcissus was bemused by that image which 'we ourselves see in all rivers and oceans', and this, says Ishmael when he is most desperate, is all that man ever finds when he searches the waters—a reflection of himself. All is inconclusive, restless, an endless flow. And Melville's own style rises to its highest level not in the neo-Shakespearean speeches of Ahab, which are sometimes bombastic, but in those amazing prose flights on the whiteness of the whale and on the Pacific where Ishmael reproduces, in the rhythms of the prose itself, man's brooding interrogation of nature.

II

But Ishmael is a witness not only to his own thoughts, but also a witness to the actions of Captain Ahab. The book is not only a great skin of language stretched to fit the world of man's philosophic wandering; it is also a world of moral tyranny and violent action, in which the principal actor is Ahab. With the entry of Ahab a harsh new rhythm enters the book, and from now on two rhythms—one reflective, the other forceful—alternate to show us the world in which man's thinking and man's doing each follows its own law. Ishmael's thought consciously extends itself to get behind the world of appearances; he wants to see and to understand everything. Ahab's drive is to *prove*, not to discover; the world that tortures Ishmael by its horrid vacancy has tempted Ahab into thinking that he can make it over. He seeks to dominate nature, to impose and to inflict his will on the outside world—whether it be the crew that must jump to his orders or the great white whale that is essentially indifferent to him. As Ishmael is all rumination, so Ahab is all will. Both are thinkers, the difference being that Ishmael thinks as a bystander, has identified his own state with man's utter unimportance in nature. Ahab, by contrast, actively seeks the whale in order to assert man's supremacy over what swims before him as 'the monomaniac incarnation' of a superior power:

'If man will strike, strike through the mask! How can the prisoner reach outside except by thrusting through the wall? To me, the white whale is that wall, shoved near to me. Sometimes I think there's naught beyond. But 'tis enough. He tasks me; he heaps me; I see in him outrageous strength, with an inscrutable malice sinewing it. That inscrutable thing is chiefly what I hate; and be the white whale agent, or be the white whale principal, I will wreak that hate upon him. Talk not to me of blasphemy, man; I'd strike the sun if it insulted me. For could the sun do that, then could I do the other; since there is ever a sort of fair play herein, jealousy presiding over all creations. But not my master, man, is even that fair play. Who's over me? Truth hath no confines.'

This is Ahab's quest—and Ahab's magnificence. For in this speech Ahab expresses more forcibly than Ishmael ever could, something of the impenitent anger against the universe that all of us can feel. Ahab may be a mad sea captain, a tyrant of the quarter deck who disturbs the crew's sleep as he stomps along on his ivory leg. But this Ahab does indeed speak for all men who, as Ishmael confesses in the frightening meditation on the whiteness of the whale, suspect that 'though in many of its aspects this visible world seems formed in love, the invisible spheres were formed in fright'. So man, watching the sea heaving around him, sees it as a mad steed that has lost its rider, and looking at his own image in the water, is tortured by the thought that man himself may be an accident, of no more importance in this vast oceanic emptiness than one of Ahab's rare tears dropped into the Pacific.

To the degree that we feel this futility in the face of a blind impersonal nature that 'heeds us not', and storm madly, like Ahab, against the dread that there's 'naught beyond'—to this extent all men may recognize Ahab's bitterness, his unrelentingness, his inability to rest in that uncertainty which, Freud has told us, modern man must learn to endure. Ahab figures in a symbolic fable; he is acting out thoughts which we all share. But Ahab, even more, is a hero; we cannot insist enough on that. Melville believed in the heroic and he specifically wanted to cast his hero on American lines—someone noble by nature, not by birth, who would have 'not the dignity of kings and robes, but that abounding dignity which has no robed investiture'. Ahab sinned against man and God, and like his namesake in the Old Testament, becomes a 'wicked king'. But Ahab is not just a fanatic who leads the whole crew to their destruction; he is a hero of thought who is trying, by terrible force, to reassert man's place in nature. And it is the struggle that Ahab incarnates that makes him so magnificent a *voice*, thundering in Shakespearian rhetoric, storming at the gates of the inhuman, silent world. Ahab is trying to give man, in one awful, final assertion that his will *does* mean something, a feeling of relatedness with his world.

Ahab's effort, then, is to reclaim something that man knows he has lost. Significantly, Ahab proves by the bitter struggle he has to wage that man is fighting in an unequal contest; by the end of the book Ahab abandons all his human ties and becomes a complete fanatic. But Melville has no doubt—nor should we!—that Ahab's quest is *humanly* understandable. And the quest itself supplies the book with its technical *raison d'être*. For it leads us through all the seas and around the whole world; it brings us past ships of every nation. Always it is Ahab's drive that makes up the *passion* of *Moby-Dick*, a passion that is revealed in the descriptive chapters on the whale, whale-fighting, whale-burning, on the whole gory and fascinating industrial process aboard ship that reduces the once proud whale to oil-brimming barrels in the hold. And this passion may be defined as a passion of longing, of hope, of striving: a passion that starts from the deepest loneliness that man can know. It is the great cry of man who feels himself exiled from his 'birthright, the merry May-day gods of old', who looks for a new god 'to enthrone . . . again in the now egotistical sky; in the now unhaunted hill'. The cry is Ahab's—'Who's to doom, when the judge himself is dragged to the bar?'

Behind Ahab's cry is the fear that man's covenant with God has been broken, that there is no purpose to our existence. The *Pequod* is condemned by Ahab to sail up and down the world in search of—a symbol. But this search, mad as it seems to Starbuck the first mate, who is a Christian, nevertheless represents Ahab's real humanity. For the ancient covenant is never quite broken so long as man still thirsts for it. And because Ahab, as Melville intended him to, represents the aristocracy of intellect in our democracy, because he seeks to transcend the limitations that good conventional men like Starbuck, philistine materialists like Stubb, and unthinking fools like Flask want to impose on everybody else, Ahab speaks for the humanity that belongs to man's imaginative vision of himself.

Yet with all this, we must not forget that Ahab's quest takes place, unceasingly, in a very practical world of whaling, as part of the barbaric and yet highly necessary struggle by man to support himself physically in nature. It is this that gives the book its primitive vitality, its burning authenticity. For *Moby-Dick*, it must be emphasized, is not simply a symbolic fable; nor, as we have already seen, can it possibly be construed as simply a 'sea story'. It is the story of agonizing thought in the midst of brutal action, of thought that questions every action, that annuls it from within, as it were—but that cannot, in this harsh world, relieve man of the fighting, skinning, burning, the back-breaking row to the whale, the flying harpoons, the rope that can take you off 'voicelessly as Turkish mutes bowstring their victims'. *Moby-Dick* is a representation of the passionate mind speaking, for its metaphysical concerns, out of the very midst of life. So, after the first lowering, Queequeg is shown sitting all night in a submerged boat, holding up a lantern like an 'imbecile candle in the heart of that almighty forlornness . . . the sign and symbol of a man without hope, hopelessly holding up hope in the midst of despair'. Melville insists that our thinking is *not* swallowed up by practical concerns, that man constantly searches for a reality equal to his inner life of thought— and it is his ability to show this in the midst of a brutal, dirty whaling voyage that makes *Moby-Dick* such an astonishing book. Just as Ahab is a hero, so *Moby-Dick* itself is a heroic book. What concerns Melville is not merely the heroism that gets expressed in physical action, but the heroism of thought itself as it rises above its seeming insignificance and proclaims, in the very teeth of a seemingly hostile and malevolent creation, that man's voice *is* heard for something against the watery waste and the deep, that man's thought has an echo in the universe.

III

This is the quest. But what makes *Moby-Dick* so fascinating, and in a sense even uncanny, is that the issue is always in doubt, and remains so to the end. Melville was right when he wrote to Hawthorne: 'I have written a wicked book, and feel as spotless as the lamb.' And people who want to construe *Moby-Dick* into a condemnation of mad, bad Ahab will always miss what Melville meant when he wrote of his book: 'It is not a piece of fine feminine Spitalfields silk—but it is of the horrible texture of a fabric that should be woven of ships' cables & hawsers. A Polar wind blows through it, & birds of prey hover over it.' For in the struggle between man's effort to find meaning in nature, and the indifference of nature itself, which simply eludes him (nature here signifies the whole external show and force of animate life in a world suddenly emptied of God, one where an 'intangible malignity' has reigned from the beginning), Melville often portrays the struggle from the side of nature itself. He sees the whale's view of things far more than he does Ahab's: and Moby-Dick's milk-white head, the tail feathers of the sea birds streaming from his back like pennons, are described with a rapture that is like the adoration of a god. Even in the most terrible scenes of the shark massacre, where the sharks bend around like bows to bite at their own entrails, or in the ceaseless motion of 'my dear Pacific', the 'Potters' fields of all four continents', one feels that Melville is transported by the naked reality of things, the great unending flow of the creation itself, where the great shroud of the sea rolls over the doomed ship 'as it rolled five thousand years ago'. Indeed, one feels in the end that it is only the necessity to keep one person alive as a witness to the story that saves Ishmael from the general ruin and wreck. In Melville's final vision of the whole, it is not fair but it is entirely *just* that the whale should destroy the ship, that man should be caught up on the beast. It is just in a cosmic sense, not in the sense that the prophet (Father Mapple) predicts the punishment of man's disobedience in the telling of Jonah's story from the beginning, where the point made is the classic reprimand of God to man when He speaks out of the whirlwind. What Melville does is to speak for the whirlwind, for the watery waste, for the sharks.

It is this that gives *Moby-Dick* its awful and crushing power. It is a unique gift. Goethe said that he wanted, as a writer, to know what it is like to be a woman. But Melville sometimes makes you feel that he knows, as a writer, what it is like to be the eyes of the rock, the magnitude of the whale, the scalding sea, the dreams that lie buried in the Pacific. It is all, of course, seen through human eyes—yet there is in Melville a cold, final, ferocious hopelessness, a kind of ecstatic masochism, that delights in punishing man, in heaping coals on his head, in drowning him. You see it in the scene of the whale running through the herd with a cutting spade in his body, cutting down his own; in the sharks eating at their own entrails and voiding from them in the same convulsion; in the terrible picture of Pip the cabin boy jumping out of the boat in fright and left on the Pacific to go crazy; in Tashtego falling into the 'honey head' of the whale; in the ropes that suddenly whir up from the spindles and carry you off; in the final awesome picture of the whale butting its head against the *Pequod*. In all these scenes there is an ecstasy in horror, the horror of nature in itself, nature 'pure', without God or man: the void. It is symbolized by the whiteness of the whale, the whiteness that is not so much a colour as the absence of colour. 'Is it that by its indefiniteness it shadows forth the heartless voids and immensities of the universe, and thus stabs us from behind with the thought of annihilation, when beholding the white depths of the milky way?' And it is this picture of existence as one where man has only a peep-hole on the mystery itself, that constitutes the most remarkable achievement of Melville's genius. For as in the meditation on the whiteness of the whale, it becomes an uncanny attempt to come to grips with nature as it might be conceived with man entirely left out; or, what amounts to the same thing, with man losing his humanity and being exclusively responsive to primitive and racial memories, to the trackless fathomless nothing that has been from the beginning, to the very essence of a beginning that, in contradiction to all man's scriptures, had no divine history, no definite locus, but just *was*—with man slipped into the picture much later.

This view of reality, this ability to side with nature rather than with man, means an ability to love what has no animation, what is inhumanly still, what is not in search, as man himself is—a hero running against time and fighting against 'reality'. Here Melville puts, as it were, his ear to reality itself: to the rock rather than to the hero trying to get his sword out of the rock. He does it by constantly, and bitterly, and savagely in fact, comparing man with the great thing he is trying to understand. Ahab may be a hero by trying to force himself on what is too much for him, but Melville has no doubt that man is puny and presumptuous and easily overwhelmed—in short, drowned—in the great storm of reality he tries to encompass.

This sense of scale lies behind the chapters on the natural history of the whale, and behind the constant impressing on our minds of the contrast between man and the whale—man getting into a small boat, man being overwhelmed by his own weapons. The greatest single metaphor in the book is that of bigness, and even when Melville laughs at himself for trying to hook this Leviathan with a pen—'Bring me a condor's quill! Bring me Vesuvius' crater for an inkstand!'—we know that he not merely feels exhilaration at attempting this mighty subject, but that he is also abashed, he feels grave; mighty waters are rolling around him. This compelling sense of magnitude, however, gets him to organize the book brilliantly, in a great flood of chapters —some of them very small, one or two only a paragraph long, in the descriptive method which is the great homage that he pays to his subject, and which so provides him with an inexhaustible delight in devoting himself to every conceivable detail about the whale. And, to go back to a theme mentioned earlier, it is this sense of a limitless subject that gives the style its peculiarly loping quality, as if it were constantly looking for connectives, since on the subject of the whale no single word or statement is enough. But these details tend, too, to heap up in such a staggering array as to combine into the awesomeness of a power against which Ahab's challenge is utterly vain, and against which his struggle to show his superiority over the ordinary processes of nature becomes blasphemous. The only thing left to man, Melville seems to tell us, is to take the span of this magnitude—to feel and to record the power of this mighty torrent, this burning fire.

And it is this, this poetic power, rather than any specifically human one, this power of transcription rather than of any alteration of life that will admit human beings into its tremendous scale, that makes up the greatness of the book—by giving us the measure of Melville's own relation to the nature that his hero so futilely attempts to master or defy. For though Melville often takes a grim and almost cruel pleasure in showing man tumbling over before the magnitude of the universe, and though much of the book is concerned, as in the sections on fighting and 'cooking' the whale, with man's effort to get a grip on external nature, first through physical assault and then by scientific and industrial cunning, man finds his final relatedness to nature neither as a hero (Ahab) nor by heeding Father Mapple's old prophetic warning of man's proper subservience to God. Though all his attempted gains from nature fail him, and all goes down with the *Pequod*—all man's hopes of profit, of adjustment to orthodoxy (Starbuck), even of the wisdom that is in madness (Pip)—man, though forever alien to the world, an Ishmael, is somehow in tune with it, with its torrential rhythms, by dint of his art, by the directness with which his words grasp the world, by the splendour of his perceptions, by the lantern which he holds up 'like a candle in the midst of the almighty forlornness'. Man is not merely a waif in the world; he is an ear listening to the sea that almost drowns him; an imagination, a mind, that hears the sea in the shell, and darts behind all appearance to the beginning of things, and runs riot with the frightful force of the sea itself. There, in man's incredible and unresting mind, is the fantastic gift with which we enter into what is not our own, what is even against us—and for this, so amazingly, we can speak.

IRVING HOWE

1920–

THE BOOK OF THE GROTESQUE

Sherwood Anderson, 1951

BETWEEN Sherwood Anderson's apprentice novels and *Winesburg, Ohio* there stands no intermediary work indicating a gradual growth of talent. *Mid-American Chants* testifies to both an increasing interest in the possibilities of language and a conscious submission to literary influence, but it is hardly a qualitative advance over its predecessors. From Anderson's Elyria work to the achievement that is *Winesburg* there is so abrupt a creative ascent that one wonders what elements in his Chicago experience, whether in reading or personal relations, might have served to release his talents.

The list of writers to whom Anderson acknowledged a serious debt was small: George Borrow, Mark Twain, Ivan Turgeniev. In the early 1920's D. H. Lawrence was added to the small group of masters who had decisively impinged on him, but in 1915 and 1916, the years when he wrote *Winesburg*, Anderson had, of course, not yet read Lawrence.

While his attachment to Borrow antedates his public career as a writer, it also testifies to a wish, once that career had begun, to fondle a certain image of himself as a literary personality. To Anderson, the artist always seemed a peculiarly fortunate being who could evade much of the drabness of daily life. By ordering his experience through the canny artifice available only to himself, the artist could establish a margin for the half-forgotten life of flair and largesse, could find a way of surmounting the barren passage of the routine. Unlike those American writers who take great pains to insist that their occupation is as 'normal' as any other, Anderson liked to proclaim the uniqueness of the artist's life.

To a writer enamoured of such a notion, the figure of George Borrow would naturally seem attractive. Borrow's picturesque narratives of gipsy life, virtually unclassifiable among the traditional genres, seemed significant to Anderson because they flowed from a conscious rejection of conventionality and charming because they did not flinch from the romantic, the garrulous, and the merely odd. Borrow provided Anderson with an image of a potential self: the sympathetic auditor of his people's inner history; and for the

Borrovian hero who wanders among 'backward peoples' he had a considerable admiration, particularly during those burdened years in Elyria when he thought the literary career an avenue to a liberated and adventurous life. Yet there are no significant traces of Borrow in any of Anderson's books; neither in subject-matter nor in structure is there an observable line of descent from, say, *Lavengro* to *Winesburg*. The relation is one of personal identification rather than literary influence; Borrow, it seemed to Anderson, was above all a guide to how a writer might live.

If Borrow suggested an attractive style of life, Turgeniev's *Memoirs of a Sportsman*, 'like low fine music', set the very tone Anderson wished to strike in his prose. In Turgeniev's masterpiece he admired most that purity of feeling which comes from creative tact, from the author's strict refusal to violate or impose himself on his characters. Between *Memoirs of a Sportsman*, which Anderson called 'the sweetest thing in all literature', and *Winesburg* there are obvious similarities: both are episodic novels containing loosely bound but closely related sketches, both depend for impact less on dramatic action than on a climactic lyrical insight, and in both the individual sketches frequently end with bland understatements that form an ironic coda to the body of the writing. These similarities could certainly be taken as tokens of influence—if only we were certain that Anderson had actually read Turgeniev before writing *Winesburg*.

When critics in the 1920's discovered that Anderson was indebted to Chekhov and Dostoevski (which he was not), he gleefully denied having known the Russian novelists until after the publication of *Winesburg*. This denial, however, is controverted by two statements in his correspondence, a remark in his *Memoirs*, and a recollection in an autobiographical fragment. His credibility as a witness of his own past is further damaged by the fact that in the early 1920's his publisher, probably at his instigation and certainly with his consent, issued a public statement denying that Anderson had read *Spoon River* before writing *Winesburg* and insisting that Masters's book appeared after the *Winesburg* sketches came out in magazines. Though the publisher was wrong on both counts, Anderson did not trouble to correct him. Like many untrained writers, he may have feared that an acknowledgement of a literary debt would cast doubt on the value or at least the originality of his work.

But if Turgeniev's influence on *Winesburg* is not quite certain, there can be no doubt about Mark Twain's. Between the America of Anderson's boyhood, which is the setting of his best work, and the America of Huck Finn there are only a few intervening decades, and the nostalgia for a lost moment of American pastoral which saturates *Huckleberry Finn* is also present in *Winesburg*. Twain's influence on Anderson is most obvious in the early portions of *Poor White* and some of the stories in *The Triumph of the Egg*, but it can also be seen in *Winesburg*, particularly in Anderson's attempt to use American speech as the base of a tensed rhythmic style. His identification with Borrow was to some extent a romantic whimsy, but his identification with Twain had a strong basis in reality. As he wrote to Van Wyck Brooks, Twain had also been an untrained man of natural talent 'caught up by the dreadful cheap smartness, the shrillness that was a part of the life of the country'; Twain had also been bedeviled by the problem of success and the need to conciliate the pressures of East and West.

These were pervasive influences; none of them could have provided the immediate shock, the specific impetus that turned Anderson to the style and matter of

Winesburg. Such an impetus, if one can be singled out at all, came not from any individual writer but from Anderson's dramatic exposure in 1913–15 to the Chicago literary world. When Max Wald, one of 'the little children of the arts', lent him a copy of *Spoon River*, Anderson raced through it in a night. This, he excitedly told his friends, is the real thing—by which he meant that Masters, in his imaginary Mid-western village, had bared the hidden lesions of the American psyche. Had Anderson stopped to notice the appalling frustration that motivated Masters's book he might have been somewhat less enthusiastic, but for the moment *Spoon River* suggested that in a prose equivalent Anderson might find a form allowing more freedom than the conventional novel and yet resulting in greater complexity of meaning than could be had in any individual sketch. Masters hardly influenced the vision behind *Winesburg*, but he did provide intimations of how it might be organized.

At about the same time Anderson was introduced by his brother Karl to the early writings of Gertrude Stein. Anderson has recalled that he 'had come to Gertrude Stein's book about which everyone laughed but about which I did not laugh. It excited me as one might grow excited in going into a new and wonderful country where everything is strange. . . .' The truth, however, was somewhat more complex than Anderson's memory. His first reactions to Stein were antagonistic: at a Chicago party in 1915 he told Edna Kenton that he thought it merely funny that anyone should take *Tender Buttons* seriously, and shortly afterwards he even composed a parody of Stein for his advertising cronies.

But his inaccurate recollection had, as usual, a point of genuine relevance. For though he laughed at Stein when he first read her, she seems to have stimulated him in a way few other writers could. Nearly always one parodies, for good or bad, those writers who deeply matter. To Anderson Stein suggested that, at least in the actual process of composition, words could have an independent value: they could be fresh or stale, firm or gruelly, coloured or drab. After reading the fanatically monosyllabic *Three Lives* Anderson would hardly try again, as he had in his first two novels, to write 'literary' English. But despite such surface similarities as repetition of key words and an insistently simple syntax, their styles had little in common. Stein's language was opaque, leading back into itself and thereby tending to replace the matter of fiction, while the language of *Winesburg* was translucent, leading quickly to the centre of the book's action. Stein was the best kind of influence: she did not bend Anderson to her style, she liberated him for his own.

And that, essentially, was what the Chicago literary milieu did. It persuaded Anderson that American writers needed an indigenous style which, if only they were bold enough, they could then and there construct; it taught him that before language could be used creatively it might have to be crumbled into particles; and it made him conscious of the need for literary consciousness. For the time being that was enough.

Anderson has recalled that during the years immediately preceding *Winesburg* he would often take with him on advertising trips pages torn from Gideon Bibles, which he read over and over again. This recollection tells us most of what needs to be known about the making of *Winesburg*. Its author had not the slightest interest in religion, but his first involvement in a literary environment had made him aware of writing as writing and had taught him where to find its greatest English source. He had begun to work as a conscious craftsman:

the resulting ferment was *Mid-American Chants*, the substance *Winesburg*.

The history of *Winesburg* is a curious instance of the way criticism, with its passion for 'placing', can reduce a writer to harmless irrelevance. At various times the book has been banished to such categories as the revolt against the village, the rejection of middle-class morality, the proclamation of sexual freedom, and the rise of cultural primitivism. Whatever the justification for such tags may once have been, it is now quite obvious that Anderson's revolt was directed against something far more fundamental than the restrictions of the American village and was, for that matter, equally relevant to the American city; that *Winesburg* is not primarily concerned with morality, middle-class or otherwise, if only because most of its characters are not in a position to engage in moral choice; that while its subject is frequently tangential to sex it expresses no opinions about and offers no proposals for sexual conduct, free or restricted; and that its style is only dimly related to anything that might be called primitive. If read as social fiction *Winesburg* is somewhat absurd, for no such town could possibly exist. If read as a venture into abnormal psychology the book seems almost lurid, for within its total structure the behaviour of its hysterics and paranoids is quite purposeless and, in the absence of any norms to which their deviations might be compared, even incomprehensible. In fact, if read according to the usual expectations of twentieth-century naturalistic or conventionally realistic fiction, *Winesburg* seems incoherent and the charge of emotion it can still raise inexplicable.

In its fundamental quality *Winesburg* is non-realistic; it does not seek to gratify the eye with a verisimilitude to social forms in the way a Dreiser or a Lewis novel

does. In rather shy lyrical outbursts the book conveys a
vision of American life as a depressed landscape cluttered
with dead stumps, twisted oddities, grotesque and pitiful wrecks; a landscape in which ghosts fumble erratic-
ally and romance is reduced to mere fugitive brushings
at night; a landscape eerie with the cracked echoes of
village queers rambling in their lonely eccentricity.
Again and again *Winesburg* suggests that beneath the
exteriors of our life the deformed exert dominion,
that the seeming health of our state derives from a deep
malignancy. And *Winesburg* echoes with American
loneliness, that loneliness which could once evoke
Nigger Jim's chant of praise to the Mississippi pastoral
but which has here become fearful and sour.

Winesburg is a book largely set in twilight and darkness, its backgrounds heavily shaded with gloomy
blacks and marshy greys—as is proper for a world of
withered men who, sheltered by night, reach out for
that sentient life they dimly recall as the racial inheritance that has been squandered away. Like most fiction,
Winesburg is a variation on the theme of reality and
appearance, in which the deformations caused by day
(public life) are intensified at night and, in their very
extremity, become an entry to reality. From Anderson's
instinctively right placement of the book's central actions
at twilight and night comes some of its frequently
noticed aura of 'lostness'—as if the most sustaining and
fruitful human activities can no longer be performed in
public communion but must be grasped in secret.

The two dozen central figures in *Winesburg* are hardly
characters in the usual novelistic sense. They are not
shown in depth or breadth, complexity or ambiguity;
they are allowed no variations of action or opinion; they
do not, with the exception of George Willard, the
book's 'hero', grow or decline. For Anderson is not

trying to represent through sensuous images the immediate surface of human experience; he is rather drawing the abstract and deliberately distorted paradigm of an extreme situation, and for that purpose fully rounded characterizations could only be a complicating blemish.

The figures of *Winesburg* usually personify to fantastic excess a condition of psychic deformity which is the consequence of some crucial failure in their lives, some aborted effort to extend their personalities or proffer their love. Misogyny, inarticulateness, frigidity, God-in-fatuation, homosexuality, drunkenness—these are symptoms of their recoil from the regularities of human intercourse and sometimes of their substitute gratifications in inanimate objects, as with the unloved Alice Hindman who 'because it was her own, could not bear to have anyone touch the furniture of her room'. In their compulsive traits these figures find a kind of dulling peace, but as a consequence they are subject to rigid monomanias and are deprived of one of the great blessings of human health: the capacity for a variety of experience. That is why, in a sense, 'nothing happens' in *Winesburg*. For most of its figures it is too late for anything to happen, they can only muse over the traumas which have so harshly limited their spontaneity. Stripped of their animate wholeness and twisted into frozen postures of defence, they are indeed what Anderson has called them: grotesques.

The world of *Winesburg*, populated largely by these back-street grotesques, soon begins to seem like a buried ruin of a once vigorous society, an atrophied remnant of the egalitarian moment of nineteenth-century America. Though many of the book's sketches are placed in the out-of-doors, its atmosphere is as stifling as a tomb. And the reiteration of the term 'grotesque' is felicitous in a way Anderson could hardly have been aware of; for it was first used by Renaissance artists to describe arabesques painted in the underground ruins, *grotte*, of Nero's 'Golden House'.

The conception of the grotesque, as actually developed in the stories, is not merely that it is an unwilled affliction but also that it is a mark of a once sentient striving. In his introductory fantasy, 'The Book of the Grotesque', Anderson writes: 'It was the truths that made the people grotesques . . . the moment one of the people took one of the truths to himself, called it his truth, and tried to live his life by it, he became a grotesque and the truth he embraced a falsehood.' There is a sense, as will be seen later, in which these sentences are at variance with the book's meaning, but they do suggest the significant notion that the grotesques are those who *have* sought 'the truths' that disfigure them. By contrast the banal creatures who dominate the town's official life, such as Will Henderson, publisher of the paper for which George Willard works, are not even grotesques: they are simply clods. The grotesques are those whose humanity has been outraged and who to survive in Winesburg have had to suppress their wish to love. Wash Williams becomes a misogynist because his mother-in-law, hoping to reconcile him to his faithless wife, thrusts her into his presence naked; Wing Biddlebaum becomes a recluse because his wish to blend learning with affection is fatally misunderstood. Grotesqueness, then, is not merely the shield of deformity; it is also a remnant of misshapen feeling, what Dr. Reefy in 'Paper Pills' calls 'the sweetness of the twisted apples'.

Winesburg may thus be read as a fable of American estrangement, its theme the loss of love. The book's major characters are alienated from the basic sources of emotional sustenance—from the nature in which they live but to which they can no longer have an active relationship; from the fertility of the farms that flank them but no longer fulfil their need for creativity; from the community which, at least by the claim of the American mythos, once bound men together in fraternity but is now merely an institution external to their lives; from the work which once evoked and fulfilled their sense of craft but is now a mere burden; and, most catastrophic of all, from each other, the very extremity of their need for love having itself become a barrier to its realization.

The grotesques rot because they are unused, their energies deprived of outlet, and their instincts curdled in isolation. As Waldo Frank has noticed in his fine study of *Winesburg*, the first three stories in the book suggest this view in a complete theme-statement. The story, 'Hands', through several symbolic referents, depicts the loss of creativity in the use of the human body. The second story, 'Paper Pills', directly pictures the progressive ineffectuality of human thought, pocketed in paper pellets that no one reads. And the third story, 'Mother', relates these two themes to a larger variant: the inability of Elizabeth Willard, *Winesburg's* mother-figure, to communicate her love to her son. 'The form of the mother, frustrate, lonely, at last desperate', Frank writes, 'pervades the variations that make the rest of the book: a continuity of variation swelling, swirling into the corners and crannies of the village life; and at last closing in the mother's death, in the loss forever of the $800 which Elizabeth Willard had kept for twenty years to give her son his start away from Winesburg, and in the son's wistful departure.' In the rupture of family love and the consequent loss of George Willard's heritage, the theme-statement of the book is completed.

The book's central strand of action, discernible in about half the stories, is the effort of the grotesques to establish intimate relations with George Willard, the young reporter. At night, when they need not fear the mockery of public detection, they hesitantly approach him, almost in supplication, to tell him of their afflictions and perhaps find health in his voice. Instinctively, they sense his moral freshness, finding hope in the fact that he has not yet been calloused by knowledge and time. To some of the grotesques, such as Dr. Reefy and Dr. Parcival, George Willard is the lost son returned, the Daedalus whose apparent innocence and capacity for feeling will redeem Winesburg. To others among the grotesques, such as Tom Foster and Elmer Cowley, he is a reporter-messenger, a small-town Hermes, bringing news of a dispensation which will allow them to re-enter the world of men. But perhaps most fundamentally and subsuming these two visions, he seems to the grotesques a young priest who will renew the forgotten communal rites by which they may again be bound together. To Louise Trunnion he will bring a love that is more than a filching of flesh; to Dr. Parcival the promise to 'write the book that I may never get written' in which he will tell all men that 'everyone in the world is Christ and they are all crucified'; to the Reverend Curtis Hartman the willingness to understand a vision of God as revealed in the flesh of a naked woman; to Wash Williams the peace that will ease his sense of violation; and to Enoch Robinson the 'youthful sadness, young man's sadness, the sadness of a growing boy in a village at the year's end [which can open] the lips of the old man'.

As they approach George Willard, the grotesques seek not merely the individual release of a sudden expressive outburst, but also a relation with each other that may restore them to collective harmony. They are distraught communicants in search of a ceremony, a social value, a manner of living, a lost ritual that may, by some means, re-establish a flow and exchange of emotion. Their estrangement is so extreme that they cannot turn to each other though it is each other they really need and secretly want; they turn instead to George Willard who will soon be out of the orbit of their life. The miracle that the Reverend Curtis Hartman sees and the message over which Kate Swift broods could bind one to the other, yet they both turn to George Willard who, receptive though he may wish to be, cannot understand them.

In only one story, 'Death', do the grotesques seem to meet. Elizabeth Willard and Dr. Reefy embrace in a moment of confession, but their approach to love is interrupted by a stray noise. Elizabeth leaves: 'The thing that had come to life in her as she talked to her one friend died suddenly.' A few months later, at her death-bed, Dr. Reefy meets George Willard and puts out 'his hand as though to greet the young man and then awkwardly [draws] it back again'. Bloom does not find his Daedalus; the hoped-for epiphany comes at the verge of death and, as in all the stories, is aborted; the ritual of communal love remains unrealized.

The burden which the grotesques would impose on George Willard is beyond his strength. He is not yet himself a grotesque mainly because he has not yet experienced very deeply, but for the role to which they would assign him he is too absorbed in his own ambition and restlessness. The grotesques see in his difference from them the possibility of saving themselves, but actually it is the barrier to an ultimate companionship. George Willard's adolescent receptivity to the grotesques can only give him the momentary emotional illumination described in that lovely story, 'Sophistication'. On the eve of his departure from Winesburg, George Willard reaches the point 'when he for the first time takes the backward view of life. . . . With a little gasp he sees himself as merely a leaf blown by the wind through the streets of his village. He knows that in spite of all the stout talk of his fellows he must live and die in uncertainty, a thing blown by the winds, a thing destined like corn to wilt in the sun. . . . Already he hears death calling. With all his heart he wants to come close to some other human, touch someone with all his hands. . . .' For George this illumination is enough, but it is not for the grotesques. They are a moment in his education, he a confirmation of their doom. 'I have missed something. I have missed something Kate Swift was trying to tell me', he says to himself one night as he falls asleep. He has missed the meaning of Kate Swift's life; it is not his fault; her salvation, like the salvation of the other grotesques, is beyond his capacities.

In the story 'Queer' these meanings receive their most generalized expression, for its grotesque, Elmer Cowley, has no specific deformity; he is the grotesque as such. 'He was, he felt, one condemned to go through life without friends and he hated the thought.' Wishing to talk to George Willard, he loses courage and instead rants to a half-wit: 'I had to tell some one and you were the only one I could tell. I hunted out another queer one, you see. I ran away, that's what I did.' When Elmer Cowley does call George Willard out of the newspaper office, he again becomes tongue-tied in his presence. Desparing over 'his failure to declare his determination not to be queer', Elmer Cowley decides to leave Winesburg, but in a last effort at communication he asks George Willard to meet him at the midnight local. Again he cannot speak. 'Elmer Cowley danced with fury beside the groaning train in the darkness on the station platform. . . . Like one struggling for release from hands that held him he struck, hitting George Willard blow after blow on the breast, the neck, the mouth.' Unable to give Elmer Cowley the love that might dissolve his queerness, George Willard suffers the fate of the rejected priest.

From the story 'Queer', it is possible to abstract the choreography of *Winesburg*. Its typical action is a series of dance manœuvres by figures whose sole distinctive characteristic is an extreme deformity of movement or posture. Each of these grotesques dances, with angular indirection and muted pathos, toward a central figure who seems to them young, fresh, and radiant. For a moment they seem to draw close to him and thereby to abandon their stoops and limps, but this moment quickly dissolves in the play of the dance and perhaps it never even existed: the central figure cannot be reached. Slowly and painfully, the grotesques withdraw while the young man leaves the stage entirely. None of the grotesques is seen full-face for more than a moment, and none of them is individually important to the scheme of the dance. For this is a dance primarily of spatial relationships rather than solo virtuosity; the distances established between the dancers, rather than their personalities, form the essence of the dance. And in the end, its meaning is revealed in the fact that all but the one untouched youth return to precisely their original places and postures.

When Anderson first sent his *Winesburg* stories to the *Masses*, *Seven Arts*, and the *Little Review*, he intended each of them to be a self-contained unit, as in fact they may still be regarded. But there was clearly a unifying conception behind all the stories: they were set in the same locale, many of the characters appeared in several stories, and there was a remarkable consistency of mood that carried over from story to story. Consequently, when Anderson prepared them for book publication in 1919, he had only to make a few minor changes, mostly insertions of place and character names as connectives, in order to have a unified book.

Particularly if approached along the lines that have been suggested here, *Winesburg* seems remarkably of a piece. The only stories that do not fit into its pattern are the four-part narrative of Jesse Bentley, a failure in any case, and possibly 'The Untold Lie', a beautiful story measuring the distance between middle age and youth. Of the others only 'Tandy' is so bad that its omission would help the book. On the other hand, few of the stories read as well in isolation as in the book's context. Except for 'Hands', 'The Strength of God', 'Paper Pills', and 'The Untold Lie', they individually lack the dramatic power which the book has as a whole.

Winesburg is an excellently formed piece of fiction, each of its stories following a parabola of movement which abstractly graphs the book's meaning. From a state of feeling rather than a dramatic conflict there develops in one of the grotesques a rising lyrical excitement, usually stimulated to intensity by the presence of George Willard. At the moment before reaching a climax, this excitement is frustrated by a fatal inability at communication and then it rapidly dissolves into its original diffuse base. This structural pattern is sometimes varied by an ironic turn, as in 'Nobody Knows' and 'A Man of Ideas', but in only one story, 'Sophistication', is the emotional ascent allowed to move forward without interruption.

But the unity of the book depends on more than the congruous design of its parts. The first three stories of

Winesburg develop its major theme, which, after several variations, reaches its most abstract version in 'Queer'. The stories following 'Queer' seem somewhat of a thematic afterthought, though they are necessary for a full disposal of the characters. The one conspicuous disharmony in the book is that the introductory 'Book of the Grotesque' suggests that the grotesques are victims of their wilful fanaticism, while in the stories themselves grotesqueness is the result of an essentially valid resistance to forces external to its victims.

Through a few simple but extremely effective symbols, the stories are both related to the book's larger meaning and defined in their uniqueness. For the former of these purposes, the most important symbol is that of the room, frequently used to suggest isolation and confinement. Kate Swift is alone in her bedroom, Dr. Reefy in his office, the Reverend Curtis Hartman in his church tower, Enoch Robinson in his fantasy-crowded room. Enoch Robinson's story 'is in fact the story of a room almost more than it is the story of a man'. The tactful use of this symbol lends *Winesburg* a claustrophobic aura appropriate to its theme.

Most of the stories are further defined by symbols related to their particular meanings. The story of the misogynist Wash Williams begins by rapidly thrusting before the reader an image of 'a huge, grotesque kind of monkey, a creature with ugly sagging, hairless skin', which dominates its subsequent action. And more valid than any abstract statement of theme is the symbolic power of that moment in 'The Strength of God' when the Reverend Curtis Hartman, in order to peek into Kate Swift's bedroom, breaks his church window at precisely the place where the figure of a boy stands 'motionless and looking with rapt eyes into the face of Christ'.

Though *Winesburg* is written in the bland accents of

the American story-teller, it has an economy impossible to oral narration because Anderson varies the beat of its accents by occasionally whipping them into quite formal rhetorical patterns. In the book's best stretches there is a tension between its underlying loose oral cadences and the stiffened superimposed beat of a prose almost Biblical in its regularity. Anderson's prose is neither 'natural' nor primitive; it is rather a hushed bardic chant, low-toned and elegiacally awkward, deeply related to native speech rhythms yet very much the result of literary cultivation.

But the final effectiveness of the prose is in its prevalent tone of tender inclusiveness. Between writer and materials there is an admirable equity of relationship. None of the characters is violated, none of the stories, even the failures, leaves the reader with the bitter sense of having been tricked by cleverness or cheapness or toughness. The ultimate unity of the book is a unity of feeling, a sureness of warmth, and a readiness to accept Winesburg's lost grotesques with the embrace of humility. Many American writers have taken as their theme the loss of love in the modern world, but few, if any at all, have so thoroughly realized it in the accents of love.

REPRINTED LITHOGRAPHICALLY IN GREAT BRITAIN
AT THE UNIVERSITY PRESS, OXFORD
BY VIVIAN RIDLER
PRINTER TO THE UNIVERSITY